QUESTIONS & ANSWERS:
Civil Procedure

LexisNexis
Law School Publishing
Advisory Board

QUESTIONS & ANSWERS:
Civil Procedure

SECOND EDITION

*Multiple Choice and Short Answer
Questions and Answers*

By

WILLIAM V. DORSANEO, III

Professor of Law and
Chief Justice John and Lena Hickman
Distinguished Faculty Fellow
SMU Dedman School of Law

ELIZABETH G. THORNBURG

Professor of Law
SMU Dedman School of Law

ISBN#: 9781422411728

NOTE TO USERS
To ensure that you are using the latest materials available in this area, please be sure to periodically check the LexisNexis Law School web site for downloadable updates and supplements at www.lexisnexis.com /lawschool

---

Editorial Offices
744 Broad Street, Newark, NJ 07102 (973) 820-2000
201 Mission St., San Francisco, CA 94105-1831 (415) 908-3200
701 East Water Street, Charlottesville, VA 22902-7587 (434) 972-7600
www.lexis.com

(Pub.3173)

ABOUT THE AUTHORS

William V. Dorsaneo, III is Professor of Law and Chief Justice John and Lena Hickman Distinguished Faculty Fellow at Dedman School of Law, Southern Methodist University. Professor Dorsaneo was a litigation specialist in Dallas after graduation from law school. He is the principal author of the twenty-six volume TEXAS LITIGATION GUIDE and the co-author of the five-volume TEXAS CIVIL TRIAL GUIDE, as well as three casebooks entitled CASES AND MATERIALS ON CIVIL PROCEDURE, TEXAS PRE-TRIAL LITIGATION, and TEXAS TRIAL & APPELLATE PRACTICE, and several other volumes on Texas litigation. He has written numerous articles on civil procedure. He is Board certified by the Texas Board of Legal Specialization in Civil Appellate Law and maintians an active appellate practice. He is also a board member of the Appellate Judges' Education Institute and a member of the Institute's Education Committee, a member of the Advisory Committee to the Texas Supreme Court, and Chairman of the Committee's Appellate Rules Subcommittee and a member of the American Law Institute.

Elizabeth G. Thornburg is Professor of Law at Dedman School of Law, Southern Methodist University. After clerking for a federal judge, Professor Thornburg was a commercial litigator before she began teaching at SMU. She is a member of the American Law Institute, the American Bar Association, and the State Bar of Texas. She has served on the Executive Committee and the Complex Litigation Committee of the Civil Procedure section of the Association of American Law Schools, as well as on Texas Supreme Court task forces on procedure issues. Professor Thornburg specializes in the areas of civil procedure, alternative dispute resolution, conflict of laws, and comparative civil procedure. Her publications include numerous articles on civil procedure issues, as well as co-authorship of TEXAS PRE-TRIAL LITIGATION and TEXAS TRIAL & APPELLATE PRACTICE.

Together, Professors Dorsaneo and Thornburg have taught procedure for more than 50 years.

PREFACE TO THE SECOND EDITION

The Second Edition of *Questions and Answers: Civil Procedure* is designed to be a supplementary text for use by first-year Civil Procedure students who want to attain a basic mastery of the materials typically covered in a sophisticated first-year course. Building on the solid foundation established in the original text, the Second Edition contains the following major revisions and additions:

- Comprehensive coverage of supplemental jurisdiction including the incorporation of *Exxon Mobil Corp. v. Allapattah.*

- Expanded coverage of federal question jurisdiction covering *Grable & Sons Metal Products, Inc. v. Darue Engineering & Manufacturing.*

- The Supreme Court's revision of pleading requirements and the test that should be used to determine whether a complaint states a claim on which relief can be granted, incorporating *Bell Atlantic Corp. v. Twombly* and other recent decisions.

- Expanded coverage of federal procedural rules concerning the joinder of claims and parties.

- Coverage of the Class Action Fairness Act of 2005.

- Detailed coverage of e-discovery rules and e-discovery practice.

- Coverage of postjudgment motion practice and appellate complaint preservation requirements, incorporating *Unitherm Food Systems, Inc. v. Swift-Eckrich, Inc.*

- The addition of two new topics covering Appellate Jurisdiction and Appellate Practice.

Amendments made to the Federal Rules of Civil Procedure and the Federal Rules of Appellate Procedure that became effective after the publication of the First Edition and the proposed "restyling" amendments expected to become effective in December of 2007 also have been incorporated in the Second Edition.

There are several ways in which the Second Edition can be used. Professors can easily incorporate the topics covered in the Second Edition in a course syllabus to assist the students' learning process, whether or not the questions and answers are actually covered in class.

Alternatively, students can make independent use of the text to clarify, reinforce, and extend their comprehension of first-year course material.

We hope and expect that this Second Edition will ease the path to a solid professional comprehension of Civil Procedure topics. As with the First Edition, we would like to thank our students, upon whom these questions have been tested for many years. Special thanks must also be given to Ms. Corinna Chandler, Juris Doctor Candidate (2009) of Dedman School of Law at SMU for her dedicated and very capable assistance in the production of this Second Edition.

PROFESSOR WILLIAM V. DORSANEO, III
PROFESSOR ELIZABETH THORNBURG
Dallas, Texas
September, 2007

PREFACE TO THE FIRST EDITION

Understanding Civil Procedure can unravel the mysteries of both the Civil Procedure course itself and the procedural context that shapes the cases you read in your other first-year courses. At its most basic, Civil Procedure covers a set of quite technical rules that litigators must master in order to guide their clients and their cases through the court system. Mastery at this technical level is important, but the fun of Civil Procedure comes when you begin to understand how the rules interact, and how they can be used to achieve legitimate goals. At a deeper level, a sophisticated knowledge of Civil Procedure is the key to thoughtful analysis of the policy issues involved: who do the rules benefit, and why? Who should they benefit? Should changes be made in order to better serve the interests of justice?

This book is designed to help you understand the nature and operation of the rules that govern procedure in the federal courts in the United States. The questions range from simple identification of the rules themselves to applying the rules to complex hypothetical fact patterns. Some questions invite you to begin to think about the strategic use of the rules, and about the policy implications of the choices the rules make. The individual topics address issues one at a time, while the Final Examination allows you to test your skill at recognizing the interplay of a number of issues in simulated cases.

The book begins by walking you through the steps of a typical lawsuit: the parties' pleadings, the proper joinder of claims and parties, the discovery process, summary judgment, trial, post-trial motions, and the binding effect of judgments. It also covers questions about where suits can be brought. Finally, the book examines a specialized question of law application: when must the federal courts apply state rather than federal law (a topic often called the *Erie* doctrine). Civil Procedure teachers and texts introduce these topics in different orders. The topics are therefore treated independently, so you can use this book in the order in which you study procedure.

Questions & Answers: Civil Procedure is designed so that you can use the questions either to reinforce and clarify material as you move through the first-year course, or to test yourself in preparation for your final examination. As you read each question, try to identify the rule or rules involved, and then apply them to the facts presented. Think about the issues raised by both the correct and incorrect answers. This should help you to answer multiple choice format questions such as those found in this book. It should also help you to understand the rules in operation, and to recognize patterns of issues that will help you in answering questions on essay exams.

We hope that this book will help you enjoy Civil Procedure. Once the initial unfamiliarity begins to fade, it will in fact start to hang together. We would also like to thank our students over the years, who have given us ideas for both right and wrong answers.

Professor William V. Dorsaneo, III
Professor Elizabeth Thornburg
Dallas, Texas
September, 2003

TABLE OF CONTENTS

TABLE OF CONTENTS

QUESTIONS

Crockett was driving north on Hillcrest Road in Dallas when his car collided with Boone's car, driving west on Mockingbird Lane. Both Crockett and Boone suffered serious personal injuries, and both cars were damaged. Crockett wants to sue Boone in federal court in Dallas.

1. To meet the requirements of the Federal Rules of Civil Procedure, Crockett's complaint:

    (A) must state facts sufficient to form a cause of action.

    (B) must state a claim in ordinary and concise language without repetition.

    (C) must plead facts but not evidence.

    (D) must be a short and plain statement of the claim showing that Crockett is entitled to relief.

2. What are the functions of pleadings in the federal court system?

ANSWER:

After the heading and the jurisdictional allegations, Crockett's complaint describes his claim as follows:

> "On June 1, 2007, in the 2700 block of Mockingbird Lane, Boone negligently drove his car into Crockett's car. As a result, Crockett suffered a broken pelvis and other physical injuries, suffered severe physical and mental pain and suffering and in all reasonable probability will continue to suffer physical and mental pain and suffering for a long time into the future, a loss of earnings in the past and in reasonable probability a loss of future earning capacity, and has also incurred medical and hospital expenses in the sum of twenty five thousand dollars.

> "Wherefore, plaintiff demands judgment against defendant in the sum of $90,000."

3. Is this complaint sufficient to meet the requirements of Rule 8?

ANSWER:

4. Crockett's complaint alleges various types of injuries and damages. Which of them constitute special damages required to be alleged specifically within the meaning of Rule 9(g)?

   (A) All of them, including the allegation about Crockett's pelvis, are special damages allegations.

   (B) Allegations of past and future pain and suffering concern general damages, not special damages; the remainder are special damage allegations.

   (C) Allegations of pain and suffering in the past are general damage allegations; the remainder are special damage allegations.

   (D) Allegations about medical and hospital expenses are allegations claiming special damages; the rest are general damage allegations.

5. Boone's vehicle actually held two persons at the time of the crash: Boone and Travis. Both were thrown from the car by the collision. Crockett believes that Boone was the driver, but he is not certain. He therefore wants to sue both Travis and Boone as the driver. May Crockett do so?

   (A) No. These allegations are inconsistent and so they both cannot be filed in good faith.

   (B) No. The rules allow a party to plead in the alternative, but they do not allow factually inconsistent claims.

   (C) Yes, but Crockett will have to elect whether to proceed against Boone or Travis before the case goes to the jury.

   (D) Yes, under these circumstances the pleading is proper.

6. Crockett noticed after the accident that Boone's car had a bumper sticker proclaiming "Lawyers Do It In Their Briefs." Crockett has always loathed bad puns, and he would like to add a cause of action for "annoyance." He can describe at length the bumper sticker and his reaction to it. The annoyance claim, if filed:

   (A) is improper. The complaint must show that the pleader is entitled to relief.

   (B) is proper. If a pleader has one good claim against an opposing party, claims of other types may be added.

   (C) is improper. A plaintiff may not combine claims for negligent and intentional torts.

   (D) is proper. Crockett will be able to provide sufficient detail to meet the requirements of Rule 8.

Crockett was driving north on Hillcrest Road in Dallas when his car collided with Boone's car, driving west on Mockingbird Lane. Both Crockett and Boone suffered serious personal injuries, and both cars were damaged.

7. Assume that Crockett sues only Boone, and that the complaint includes both negligence claims arising out of the car wreck and the claim for annoyance. Boone wants to get rid of the annoyance claim. The best procedural vehicle for Boone is:

   (A) a motion to dismiss for failure to state a claim upon which relief can be granted.

   (B) a motion for summary judgment.

   (C) a motion for more definite statement.

   (D) a general demurrer.

8. Boone is annoyed about Crockett's bogus annoyance claim. He believes that Crockett personally is sincere but is nonetheless deluded about the claim; he spends a lot of time stuck in traffic jams around Dallas and is really tired of other people's irritating bumper stickers. Boone has heard that Crockett's lawyer is a nice guy and tries to do the right thing but got a D in Legal Research and prefers to avoid the library whenever possible. Boone has a lot of friends who are lawyers (one of whom gave him the offending bumper sticker), and they have told him to investigate something called Rule 11. Does the annoyance claim violate Rule 11?

   (A) Yes, it violates Rule 11(b)(1).

   (B) Yes, it violates Rule 11(b)(2).

   (C) Yes, it violates Rule 11(b)(3).

   (D) No, Crockett may get evidentiary support for the annoyance claim after a reasonable opportunity for further investigation or discovery.

9. Boone has talked to his lawyer, who agrees that the annoyance claim may violate Rule 11. Boone is pretty mad about this, and he wants to go to the court immediately. Is this a good idea?

ANSWER:

10. Some time has gone by, and the more Boone thinks about this annoyance claim and what it is costing him, the madder he gets. He wants to know if there is any way to

make Crockett compensate him for the attorney's fees he will have to pay defending the annoyance claim, including filing the motion to get rid of that claim and including filing the motion asking for the fees. His lawyer sent Crockett a demand to withdraw the annoyance claim a month ago, hoping that Crockett would voluntarily withdraw it, but he got no response. Boone's lawyer has therefore filed the Rule 11 motion with the court. Could the judge use Rule 11 to force Crockett to pay Boone?

(A) Because the annoyance claim is not warranted by existing law or a nonfrivolous argument for the modification of existing law, Boone can recover all of his attorney's fees.

(B) Although the annoyance claim is not warranted by existing law or a nonfrivolous argument for the modification of existing law, all monetary penalties must be paid to the court and not to Boone.

(C) Because the annoyance claim is not warranted by existing law or a nonfrivolous argument for the modification of existing law, Crockett could be ordered to pay Boone all or part of his attorney's fees if warranted for effective deterrence.

(D) Because the annoyance claim is not warranted by existing law or a nonfrivolous argument for the modification of existing law, Crockett's lawyer could be ordered to pay Boone all or part of his attorney's fees if warranted for effective deterrence.

11. Boone has been served with Crockett's lawsuit and must respond. Boone is from Kentucky and had never been to Texas prior to the day he ran into Crockett. He would like to claim that he cannot be sued in Texas. His lawyer also informs him that the lawsuit papers were delivered to him incorrectly. Boone files a motion to dismiss for insufficiency of service of process. The court denies the motion. Boone then files an answer, complaining that Texas cannot properly assert personal jurisdiction over him, denying Crockett's negligence allegations, and stating that he is without knowledge or information sufficient to form a belief as to the truth of the damages allegations. Under these circumstances:

(A) The court should dismiss the case for want of jurisdiction.

(B) The court should let Crockett's case go forward.

(C) The court should retain the negligence claim and order Boone to respond by admitting or denying the damages allegations.

(D) The court should dismiss Crockett's claim because Boone has denied negligence.

12. Assume that Crockett filed his lawsuit on July 1, and that Boone did not file a pre-answer motion but did file and serve his answer on July 30. A week later, Boone realized to his horror that he had failed to include a claim that the case should be dismissed for lack of personal jurisdiction; therefore Boone quickly amended his answer to include this defense. Boone has:

(A) waived the personal jurisdiction defense by failing to file a pre-answer motion.

(B)   waived the personal jurisdiction defense by failing to include it in his answer.

(C)   preserved the personal jurisdiction defense by including it in his answer. Complaints about jurisdiction can be raised at any time.

(D)   preserved the personal jurisdiction defense because the amended answer was one allowed as a matter of course.

13.   Boone has another issue he wants to raise. He maintains that even if he might have been driving slightly negligently, the accident was not his fault, or at least not all his fault. Crockett was not driving safely either and that contributed to the cause of the accident, and so Boone does not think he should have to pay for all of the damages. If Boone wants to raise this at trial, does he have to include anything other than his denials?

ANSWER:

14.   Boone was himself injured in the accident, and his car required expensive repairs. Because Boone believes the accident was Crockett's fault, he thinks Crockett should pay for these damages. What vehicle should Boone use to make this claim?

ANSWER:

15.   Boone has another claim against Crockett for damages arising out of Crockett's breach of contract. Prior to the Hillcrest Road accident, Boone agreed to sell Crockett three antique flintlock long rifles for $80,000. Boone promised that these rifles had been used at the failed defense of the Alamo. Crockett and Boone memorialized this agreement by reducing it to writing, which both parties signed. Crockett refused to take delivery of the rifles because he determined that they were not used at the Alamo. If Boone adds this claim in a separate part of his answer headed "Counterclaim," what, if anything, does Crockett need to file in response?

(A)   Crockett does not need to file anything, the allegations in the answer, including the counterclaim, are taken as denied or avoided.

(B)   Crockett needs to file a reply to Boone's counterclaim, including denial defenses, but not affirmative defenses.

(C)   Crockett needs to file a reply to Boone's counterclaim, including denial defenses and affirmative defenses.

(D)   Crockett needs to file a reply to Boone's entire answer, including the counterclaim, including denial and affirmative defenses.

16.   What avoidance defenses should be made by Crockett based on his determination that the long rifles are not authentic Alamo rifles?

ANSWER:

17. In his answer, Boone also pleads the affirmative defense of release, alleging that Crockett
     has signed a release settling the matter between them. Crockett wants to claim that the
     release was procured by fraud. Does Crockett need any additional pleading to be allowed
     to raise the fraud issue?

     (A) Yes. Fraud is an affirmative defense that must be pleaded according to Rule 8(c).

     (B) No. Rule 8(d) [8(b)(6) of restyled rules] provides that "averments in a pleading to
              which no responsive pleading is required or permitted shall be taken as denied or
              avoided." The fraud claim avoids the affirmative defense of release.

     (C) Yes. Responsive pleadings to answers are required under Rule 7, and so Rule 8(d)
              does not apply here.

     (D) No. The pleading of issues in avoidance is always optional.

18. The judge to whom *Crockett v. Boone* has been assigned thinks there is too much litigation clogging the federal courts. He is especially unenthusiastic about personal injury litigation and has adopted a practice of requiring that plaintiffs plead their claims with particularity. He therefore orders Crockett to plead in detail his factual theories of negligence (e.g. speeding, running a red light, etc.). This order:

    (A) is improper. Judges may not create heightened pleading requirements not found in Rule 9.

    (B) is proper. Pleading specificity requirements may be adjusted according to the needs of particular cases.

    (C) is improper, but the judge could order Crockett to file a "Reply" under Rule 7, setting forth this information.

    (D) is proper. *Leatherman v. Tarrant County Narcotics & Intelligence Coordination Unit*, 507 U.S. 163 (1993), left an opening for judges to impose heightened pleading requirements.

19. Prime, Inc. entered into a construction contract with Hotels, Inc. to build a hospital facility in Houston, Texas. Prime, Inc. contracted with Planners Co., an architectural firm, and Dirt, Inc., an engineering firm hired to do soil testing. Because the completed facility has been sinking into the ground, Hotels, Inc. has sued Prime, Inc. for breach of contract and, in addition to alleging the facts contained in this question, has asserted the following fraud allegations in an amended complaint: "Prime, Inc. defrauded Hotels, Inc. by intentionally inflating the costs of the project and taking kickbacks from one or more of Prime, Inc.'s subcontractors." If Prime, Inc. moves to dismiss, what result?

    (A) The motion should be denied because the complaint contains enough factual detail for Prime, Inc. to fashion an answer and raise defenses.

    (B) The motion should be granted because the complaint does not aver knowledge specifically.

    (C) The motion should be granted because the complaint contains insufficient details of fraud.

    (D) The motion should be denied because it does not appear beyond doubt that Hotels, Inc. can prove no state of facts entitling it to recover for fraud.

20. Imagine that the Advisory Committee on the Rules of Civil Procedure changes Rule 8 to require plaintiffs to plead "with particularity facts constituting a cause of action." In your opinion, would such a change tend to favor plaintiffs, defendants, or neither?

ANSWER:

In January of 1998, Bitsy Boxer began a dog breeding operation with two small dogs; the business quickly grew to include over three hundred dogs. Initially, Boxer fed her dogs a dog food called K-9 and used a technique allowing them to eat their fill. Beginning in January of 2000, Boxer began feeding the dogs Broken Bone Dog Food. Boxer noticed no problems at first. On January 22, 2001, however, Boxer discontinued using the product because the dogs were not eating it.

On November 19, 2002, Boxer filed suit against BBD, Inc. in federal district court, serving process on its President, Martin Mastiff, and claiming that BBD manufactured Broken Bone Dog Food and that the food was low in calcium and therefore caused certain defects and abnormalities in the dogs. Asserting a claim for breach of warranty, Boxer asked for damages in the amount of $100,000. BBD filed and served its answer on December 1, 2002.

21. In the defendant's initial answer, it admitted that the dog food had a low calcium level. The defendant planned to rely on the testimony of its expert witness, Dr. Hund, who was expected to opine that the calcium could not have caused the symptoms of Boxer's dogs. When Dr. Hund's opinion turned out to be more equivocal, the defendant asked the court on January 15, 2003, for permission to amend its answer to deny that the dog food was low in calcium. Under these circumstances:

    (A) The judge should allow the amendment. This early in the litigation, the amendment could not prejudice Boxer.

    (B) The judge should allow the amendment because it could have been done as a matter of course.

    (C) The judge should deny the amendment because parties are not allowed to change their factual contentions.

    (D) The judge should allow the amendment because prejudice is unlikely, but the defendant should be sure it has a factual basis for its denial.

22. Boxer also needs a pleading amendment. The original complaint identified "BBD, Inc." as the defendant. Shortly after filing, however, Boxer's lawyer discovered that the business had never been properly incorporated and no such corporation existed. Therefore, on February 1, 2003, Boxer filed a motion for leave to amend her complaint, changing the identity of the defendant to "Martin Mastiff, doing business as BBD Products." The proposed amended complaint also added a new claim for the recovery of consequential damages, which Boxer's lawyer had inadvertently omitted from the original complaint. Assume for purposes of this question only that there is no problem with the statute of limitations. Should the court allow the requested amendments?

ANSWER:

23. Assume that the court is favorably disposed toward allowing Boxer's proposed amendments. Boxer has an additional problem. The statute of limitations on any claim against Mastiff ran out on January 21, 2003. Therefore, Boxer's claims would be barred by the statute of limitations unless the amendment relates back to the filing of the original complaint. Should the amendment, if allowed, relate back?

    (A) No. The consequential damages claim does not arise out of the same conduct, transaction, or occurrence as Boxer's original claim for damages.

    (B) Yes, it arises out of the same transaction, Mastiff got timely notice, and he should have known that, but for a mistake, the suit would have been brought against him.

    (C) No, the change to the defendant's name was not based on a mistake concerning the identity of the proper party.

    (D) Yes, there would not likely be any prejudice to the defendant.

24. Boxer believes the flaw in the dog food is due to a chemical additive that Mastiff purchases from another company and adds to the mix. She has been unable to discover the name of the company that manufactured and sold it to Mastiff. Because the statute of limitations was about to bar her claim, Boxer sued "ABC Corporation." (Boxer knew this was not the correct name and was using ABC the way one would use "John Doe" for an unknown human party.) She later (but after limitations ran) learned through discovery that the manufacturer of the chemical was in fact PoroCal Company. Boxer filed a motion to amend her complaint to sue "PoroCal Company," and she asked that the change relate back to the filing of her original complaint. PoroCal argued that relation back should not be allowed because the misnomer was not based on a mistake. How should the court rule?

ANSWER:

25. Why do the rules allow pleadings to be amended? Given this purpose, why do the rules put limits on amendments?

ANSWER:

26. Paris and Hector, who live on adjacent farms, got into a boundary dispute that ultimately involved who was responsible for fence maintenance and crop damage caused by trespassing livestock. When Paris impounded Bessie, one of Hector's cows, Hector filed a criminal complaint for cattle theft against Paris. After the criminal case was dismissed, Paris confronted Hector who retaliated by breaking Paris' nose and blackening both of his eyes. Paris has brought suit against Hector for malicious prosecution and battery. Claiming misjoinder of claims, Hector has filed a motion for dismissal and an alternative motion for severance of the claims. How should the court rule?

(A) The motion must be denied because in a case involving only one plaintiff and one defendant, there can be no misjoinder of claims. Neither dismissal nor severance is permitted in the absence of misjoinder.

(B) The motion should be denied because the claims arise from the same transaction or occurrence or series of transactions or occurrences and, hence, are properly joined.

(C) The motion must be granted because the claims are unrelated and misjoinder is a basis for severance of unrelated claims.

(D) The trial judge has discretion to sever the claims or to dispose of them in the same proceeding.

27. Hector's father, Priam, has counseled Hector about avoiding satisfaction of Paris' tort claims in the event judgment is entered against Hector. As a result of Priam's advice, Hector has transferred his farm to Priam ostensibly in payment of a debt Hector owed Priam. Can Paris add the fraudulent transfer claim to his malicious prosecution and battery claims *before* obtaining such a judgment?

(A) No, applicable state law controls the joinder issue under the *Erie* doctrine.

(B) No, claims need to be mature under substantive principles before they can be filed in court.

(C) Yes, Rule 18(b) allows such a claim to be stated in a complaint as long as no relief is granted until after the claim is matured by a judgment establishing the claim for money.

(D) Yes, the trial judge has discretion to permit or to deny joinder of related claims.

28. Morris has a claim for malicious prosecution against Boris resulting from Boris' complaint to the police. Morris also has a separate and unrelated claim against Doris for assault and battery. Morris wants to sue them in the same case to save time. May he?

    (A) Morris' attempt to sue Boris and Doris in the same case should not survive a motion to dismiss for misjoinder of parties.

    (B) Morris' attempt to sue Boris and Doris in the same case should not survive a motion for severance or for a separate trial.

    (C) Morris can join both claims in the same action to avoid a multiplicity of suits.

    (D) The trial judge has discretion to allow or to disallow joinder of the claims against Doris and Boris.

29. Martin wants to bring a lawsuit against Mantle and Maris for breach of a contract that both Mantle and Maris signed. In addition, he wants to sue Maris for libel because one year ago Maris called Martin "an unscrupulous con artist with no morals." In this situation, if Mantle filed a motion for dismissal or, in the alternative, severance of the libel claim based on misjoinder, how should the court rule on the motion?

    (A) The motion to dismiss should be granted because Mantle is not concerned with the libel claim against Maris and joinder is improper for this reason.

    (B) The motion to dismiss should be denied because Mantle and Maris are properly joined on the contract claim and Rule 18 does not require the libel claim to be related to the contract claim against them.

    (C) Although Mantle's motion for dismissal based on misjoinder should be denied to avoid any prejudice resulting from the joinder of the libel claim, Mantle may be granted a severance and may move for a separate trial, which the trial court also has discretion to grant.

    (D) (B) and (C) are both correct.

30. Albert, Barbara, Clarence, and David each have a claim against Edward for labor and material separately supplied by each of them to Edward in connection with the construction of Edward's summer home in the country. Foxworth has a deed of trust to the house and lot executed by Edward to finance the construction of the summer house. Assuming no subject matter jurisdiction problems exist, may Albert, Barbara, Clarence, and David join together as plaintiffs in the same action to foreclose their respective mechanics' and materialmen's liens on Edward's property, without joining Foxworth as a party?

(A) No, the joinder of the claims of Albert, Barbara, Clarence, and David is improper because each one separately furnished labor and material.

(B) Yes, the joinder of Albert, Barbara, Clarence, and David as coplaintiffs is proper and Foxworth is not a person needed for just adjudication.

(C) No, although the claims of Albert, Barbara, Clarence, and David satisfy Rule 20, Foxworth is a person to be joined if feasible under Rule 19, assuming that Edward files a Rule 12(b)(7) motion complaining about Foxworth's nonjoinder.

(D) No, although the claims of Albert, Barbara, Clarence, and David satisfy Rule 20, Foxworth is jurisdictionally indispensable to the adjudication of any claim concerning Edward's summer house.

31. If Foxworth is not joined as a party and his absence is not raised in the trial court by Edward or by any of the other parties, and if Edward loses in the trial court because judgment is rendered judicially foreclosing the plaintiffs' mechanics' and materialmen's liens, can Edward challenge the judgment on appeal because of Foxworth's nonjoinder?

(A) Yes, Foxworth's deed of trust lien represents a substantive right that makes him indispensable to the trial court's exercise of jurisdiction.

(B) Yes, Foxworth must be "regarded as indispensable" given the nature of his lien interest in the summer home.

(C) No, insofar as the judgment affects Edward, Edward's failure to raise Foxworth's nonjoinder in the trial court forecloses Edward's ability to attack the judgment foreclosing the mechanics' and materialmen's liens on Edward's property.

(D) No, Edward cannot challenge the judgment because of Foxworth's nonjoinder because Foxworth's deed of trust lien is inferior to the plaintiffs' liens.

32. If Foxworth is not joined as a party, can Foxworth judicially foreclose his deed of trust lien on the property described in his deed of trust? Who may or must be added as parties in such an action?

ANSWER:

Albert Riggs of Odessa, Texas, had a full life that came to a peaceful end when he did not awaken on a cold November morning in 2005. For the last 15 years of his life, Albert worked as a petroleum engineer for Rough Rider Exploration Co. Part of his compensation included coverage under a Group Life Insurance Policy purchased by Rough Rider Exploration Co. for the benefit of certain highly paid employees. The policy was issued by Confederation Life, a Connecticut corporation having its principal office in Hartford, Connecticut. The policy provided a death benefit in the sum of $125,000 to Albert's spouse or another designated beneficiary. When Albert began work for the company, he designated his wife, Cookie Riggs, as his beneficiary. Some few years later Cookie and Albert divorced and Albert remarried Dorothy Riggs, but without changing beneficiaries. This was the status-quo when Albert died. Both Cookie and Dorothy are Texas domiciliaries and both have made conflicting claims to the policy proceeds. Dorothy is aided by a Texas statute that dedesignates ex-spouses as beneficiaries unless a dedesignation would be contrary to the insured's intent.

33. In view of the conflicting claims, can Confederation Life bring suit against Cookie and Dorothy in federal court in a judicial district in Texas to determine who is entitled to the policy proceeds?

   (A) No, Confederation Life cannot interplead Cookie and Dorothy because there is no diversity of citizenship between Dorothy and Cookie.

   (B) Yes, Rule 22 allows the interpleader of conflicting claimants, who do not need to be of diverse citizenship as between themselves.

   (C) Yes, Rule 22 has liberalized the requirements for interpleading conflicting claimants and Confederation Life may use interpleader to avoid double vexation and double liability.

   (D) (B) and (C) are both correct.

34. If the death benefit does not exceed $75,000 and if Cookie is actually domiciled in New Mexico when suit is filed, must Confederation Life restrict its efforts to interplead Cookie and Dorothy to state court?

   (A) No, statutory interpleader is available under 28 U.S.C. § 1335 if the value of the group policy amounts to $500 or more.

   (B) No, statutory interpleader under 28 U.S.C. § 1335 is available because Dorothy and Cookie do not reside in the same state.

   (C) No, 28 U.S.C. §§ 1397 and 2361 solve potential problems of personal jurisdiction and venue.

(D) (A), (B), and (C) are correct.

35. If Cookie sues Confederation Life in Connecticut before Confederation Life brings suit in Texas or New Mexico, what, if anything, can Confederation Life do to protect itself?

ANSWER:

Albert places a deed in Ben's hands with instructions to Ben to deliver the deed to Clarence on payment by Clarence of $5,000. Ben notifies Clarence of this escrow arrangement, but before Clarence acts, Albert instructs Ben to hold the deed in escrow pending further instructions. At the same time, Clarence tenders $5,000 to Ben and demands the deed. Ben seeks further instructions from Albert, who instructs Ben to deliver the deed to Albert's legal counsel.

36. If Clarence does bring an action against Ben for delivery of the deed and Ben does not attempt to interplead Albert, may Albert intervene in the action to protect his interest?

  (A) Albert may not intervene in the action, unless a statute confers the right to intervene.

  (B) Albert may have the permissive right to intervene because his claim and the main action have common questions of law or fact.

  (C) Albert probably must be permitted to intervene because he claims an interest in the property or transaction and the disposition of the action in his absence may impair or impede Albert's ability to protect his interest.

  (D) The trial judge has broad discretion to grant or to deny Albert's motion to intervene.

Duds Laundry Co.'s driver Juan Rios had an intersectional collision in San Antonio, Texas, with Hubert Nelson. Duds is a Nevada corporation, with its principal place of business in San Antonio, Texas. Rios is also a citizen of Texas. Nelson lives and works in Chicago, Illinois, but is considering a move to Texas. As a result of the accident, Duds' truck was totaled and both Rios and Nelson suffered severe personal injuries.

At the time of the accident, Nelson was driving a passenger car manufactured by Big Motors, a Delaware corporation, having its principal place of business in Detroit, Michigan.

Under Texas substantive law, negligence claims are available against parties whose negligence proximately caused personal injuries or property damage. Texas law also provides for strict tort liability claims against sellers of defective products that cause injuries and damages. In addition, contribution statutes authorize jointly and severally liable defendants to sue other tortfeasors for contribution to the extent of any "overpayment of the defendants' contribution shares."

37. After settlement negotiations failed, Duds brought a property damage claim in a Texas district court in San Antonio, Texas, against Nelson for damages to its laundry truck, which did not exceed $75,000. Nelson brought a third party action impleading Rios to recover for Nelson's personal injury damages, which do exceed $75,000. Assuming that the Texas Rules of Civil Procedure are identical in all material respects to Federal Rules 13 and 14, was the third party action an appropriate method for joining Rios in the action?

    (A) Yes, Rios' potential liability to Nelson for personal injury damages could be the basis for a third party action.

    (B) No, third party actions are available for contribution and indemnity claims, not as a basis for the defendant's individual tort claims against nonparties.

    (C) Yes, impleader must be permitted to avoid a multiplicity of suits.

    (D) (A) and (C) are correct.

38. Assuming that Nelson made a claim for contribution against Rios in Nelson's third-party complaint, can Nelson also assert his personal injury claims against Rios in the same complaint?

    (A) Yes, because Rios is properly joined in the contribution claim, Nelson can assert any claims of his against Rios.

    (B) No, although the tort damages claims can probably be added later after Rios is impleaded for contribution, they cannot be included in the third party complaint.

(C)   No, third party practice is not a basis for direct damage claims.

(D)   (B) and (C) are correct.

Duds Laundry Co.'s driver Juan Rios had an intersectional collision in San Antonio, Texas, with Hubert Nelson. Duds is a Nevada corporation, with its principal place of business in San Antonio, Texas. Rios is also a citizen of Texas. Nelson lives and works in Chicago, Illinois, but is considering a move to Texas. As a result of the accident, Duds' truck was totaled and both Rios and Nelson suffered severe personal injuries.

At the time of the accident, Nelson was driving a passenger car manufactured by Big Motors, a Delaware corporation, having its principal place of business in Detroit, Michigan.

Under Texas substantive law, negligence claims are available against parties whose negligence proximately caused personal injuries or property damage. Texas law also provides for strict tort liability claims against sellers of defective products that cause injuries and damages. In addition, contribution statutes authorize jointly and severally liable defendants to sue other tortfeasors for contribution to the extent of any "overpayment of the defendants' contribution shares."

39. After settlement negotiations failed, Nelson brought a diversity action against Duds and Rios, seeking personal injury damages in excess of $75,000. Duds and Rios would prefer to wait and see what happens in the federal case and file suit in Texas state court against Nelson for damages. Are there any problems presented by such a choice?

   (A) Yes, because Duds' and Rios' damages claims arise from the same occurrence as the claim made by Nelson, their counterclaims are compulsory, which could ultimately preclude prosecution of the claims in state court.

   (B) Yes, because Nelson is an "opposing party" as provided in Rule 13(a).

   (C) Yes, Duds' and Rios' counterclaims are within the federal court's supplemental jurisdiction, even if one or both of the claims are below $75,000.

   (D) (A), (B), and (C) are all correct.

40. Assume further that Nelson files an amended complaint in federal court and joins Big Motors as a co-defendant with Duds and Rios, claiming that the car was defectively designed and that the defect was a proximate cause of the intersectional collision and Nelson's injuries. Must Duds and Rios file their negligence and contribution claims against Big Motors in the same action?

   (A) No, cross-claims between co-parties are permissive, not compulsory.

   (B) Yes, Duds' and Rios' claims are compulsory because they arise from the same occurrence as Nelson's claims against them.

   (C) No, the claims are not within the court's supplemental jurisdiction.

(D) (A) and (C) are both correct.

41. If Duds and Rios do cross-claim against Big Motors for damage to Duds' truck and for Rios' personal injury damages, may Big Motors assert a claim against Duds and Rios for contribution?

   (A) No, because Big Motors' contribution claim is not mature under Texas law until Big Motors pays Nelson more than Big Motors' contribution share, a cross-claim is also not available to Big Motors for contribution under Rule 13(g).

   (B) No, any contribution claim by Big Motors against Duds and Rios would be a compulsory counterclaim, which would be premature until Nelson obtains payment from Big Motors.

   (C) Yes, because Big Motors' contribution claim is premature, Big Motors is not required or permitted to make a counterclaim for contribution in the federal action, but Big Motors is expressly permitted to file a cross-claim under Rule 13(g).

   (D) No, premature contribution claims must be made the subject of a separate action under federal joinder rules.

42. Andie, a purchaser of a sewing machine manufactured by Panos, Ltd., has filed an antitrust class action in federal district court on behalf of a nationwide class of approximately 1,000 sewing machine purchasers, each of whom is alleged to have suffered an economic loss based on alleged price fixing by Panos and its supposed business competitors. Andie purchased her sewing machine directly from Panos, but all other purchasers bought them from the regional distributors (wholesalers) used by Panos to market its products. Assume that Andie's claim is much easier to prove because she dealt directly with Panos, but that the class claimants could prevail in an action for money damages on proof that a direct pass-through of prices from the wholesalers to them had occurred. Andie is prepared to aggressively litigate all claims through well-qualified and well-heeled class action counsel. Panos has filed an answer denying liability and an objection to class certification on multiple grounds. What threshold requirement(s) of Rule 23 will be the most difficult to prove at the certification hearing?

(A) The claims or defenses of the representative parties are typical of the claims or defenses of the class.

(B) The class is so numerous that joinder of all members is impracticable.

(C) The representative parties will fairly and adequately protect the interests of the class.

(D) There are questions of law or fact common to the class.

43. If Andie satisfied all requirements under Rule 23(a), under which provision of Rule 23(b) would her class claim most likely be certified?

(A) Individual actions by class members would lead to inconsistent adjudications that would prejudice the party opposing the class.

(B) The questions of law or fact that are common to class members predominate over individual questions and a class action is a superior method to resolve the dispute.

(C) The party opposing the class has acted on grounds generally applicable to the class, thereby making injunctive relief appropriate for the class.

(D) Individual actions by class members would prejudice the interests of members who are not parties to those individual actions.

44. If notice to the class is required, the costs of sending required notices to class members must be paid by:

(A) Defendant Panos because it is more able to bear the costs and it is likely to lose on the merits because it lost to the government on a similar claim.

(B) Andie, the named representative, because she has brought the action and is responsible for prosecution of the class action.

(C) The members of the class who will substantially benefit if Andie wins the case and they recover damages, and who will be responsible for costs of suit if the class loses on the merits.

(D) Andie and Panos, with costs divided based on an allocation determined by the court in a probable merit hearing prior to certification.

After an unpleasant dispute with local authorities gave her an interest in the law, Hester Prynne went to law school. While in school she married Holgrave, a fellow student, who also adopted Hester's daughter Pearl. After graduation, both began practice in Massachusetts. Both parents doted on Pearl, and both reduced their billable hours in order to spend more time with her. Concerned about quality child care, Prynne contacted Nanny Nation, a respected national agency that trains and recruits child care providers from throughout the United States and the world, with its main office in New York. Through Nanny Nation, Prynne and Holgrave hired Hibbins, a twenty-two-year-old British citizen, to live in their home, do light housework and cooking, and care for Pearl while they were at work.

About a month later, tragedy struck. Hibbins picked up Pearl from piano lessons and was driving her home. Unfortunately, Hibbins had succumbed to homesickness for the local pub and had three beers before getting Pearl. On the way home they were involved in a serious traffic accident. Hibbins suffered only superficial injuries, but Pearl received significant head and neck injuries. Prynne fired Hibbins, and she returned home to England.

Pearl has recovered from most of her injuries, although the doctors continue to watch for signs of permanent brain damage. Prynne and Holgrave have paid substantial medical bills for her treatment and have lost income while tending to her psychological and medical needs. They have suffered mental anguish from watching Pearl struggle with her injuries. Prynne and Holgrave no longer feel comfortable leaving Pearl with anyone other than a family member, and so Holgrave has retired from practice and takes care of Pearl full time.

Prynne and Holgrave sued Nanny Nation for damages in federal district court in Massachusetts. Their theories of recovery are negligence (in hiring and training Hibbins), gross negligence (for a pattern of ignoring serious psychological and behavioral problems of potential nannies), and fraud (for representing that their nannies are highly responsible and well qualified to care for young children), and they seek both actual and punitive damages.

45. Which of the following types of information does Nanny Nation need to disclose to the plaintiffs even without a formal discovery request?

   (A) The names of disgruntled former clients.

   (B) The e-mail addresses of persons likely to have discoverable information that Nanny Nation may use to support its defense.

   (C) A copy or a description by category and location, of Nanny Nation's entire file on Hibbins, including a troublesome evaluation from Hibbins' former employer mentioning a possible drinking problem.

(D)   The names and contact information for persons that Nanny Nation may use as supportive witnesses at trial.

46.   Prynne and Holgrave have claimed $5 million in damages. What further information do they have to provide to Nanny Nation at the outset of the litigation?

(A)   A computation only of economic damages such as medical bills and lost income.

(B)   A computation of each type of damages, including the underlying documents showing the nature and extent of their injuries.

(C)   Correspondence with their attorney concerning the best way to compute their damages.

(D)   A computation of any out-of-pocket expenses that they will claim as damages.

47.   The Rule 16(b) scheduling order in this case is due on August 30. Assuming that each required conference takes place on the last possible day, and that the court has not entered an order changing the deadlines, when are the parties' automatic initial disclosures due?

ANSWER:

48.   Both Prynne/Holgrave and Nanny Nation will be hiring expert witnesses to testify in support of their claims and defenses. In the absence of a court order to the contrary, the following disclosures will be required regarding these experts:

(A)   Prynne/Holgrave must identify their expert witnesses. For each expert they must provide a report describing the expert's opinions and the basis for the opinions, the information considered by the expert in forming the opinions, any exhibits to be used while testifying, the expert's qualifications, the compensation to be paid the expert, and a list of other cases in which the witness has testified as an expert at trial or by deposition within the preceding four years. This must be done at least 90 days before the trial date. Nanny Nation must do the same within 30 days after Prynne/Holgrave's disclosure.

(B)   Prynne/Holgrave must identify their expert witnesses. For each expert they must provide a report describing the expert's opinions and the basis for the opinions, the information considered by the expert in forming the opinions, any exhibits to be used while testifying, the expert's qualifications, the compensation to be paid the expert, and a list of other cases in which the witness has testified as an expert at trial or by deposition within the preceding four years. This must be done at least 90 days before the trial date. Nanny Nation must do the same thing simultaneously with Prynne/Holgrave's disclosure.

(C)   The parties only need to make these disclosures about expert witnesses if specifically so ordered by the court.

(D) The parties need to make the disclosures described in Rule 26(a)(2) only with respect to one expert each.

49. Nanny Nation has disclosed that it will use Mary Bobbins, an employee from its Human Resources department, to testify and give an opinion on industry standards for nanny recruitment and training. Bobbins is a bit nervous about this, as she has never testified before. Does she have to prepare a report prior to being deposed?

(A) Yes. Rule 26(a)(2) requires reports for all testifying experts, and the need for the report to make the deposition efficient is the same for employees as for retained experts.

(B) Yes. Rule 26(a)(2) requires reports of testifying experts over whom the litigant has control, whether by regular employment or by specially retaining them to testify in the case.

(C) No. Bobbins' duties do not regularly involve giving expert testimony.

(D) No. As an employee, Bobbins is a fact witness, not an expert.

50. Rule 26(f) says that in the initial discovery conference you should discuss "any issues relating to claims of privilege or of protection as trial-preparation material, including — if the parties agree on a procedure to assert such claims after production — whether to ask the court to include their agreement in an order." What kind of agreement might the parties want to make?

(A) That production of a privileged document automatically waives the privilege.

(B) That if the producing party inadvertently produces a privileged document, production does not waive the privilege and it may claim privilege and request the return of the document after it has been produced.

(C) That a judge will personally supervise all document production as it occurs in order to rule on any privilege claims.

(D) That production of privileged documents may or may not waive privilege, depending on a number of factors such as the efforts made to screen for privilege, the volume of documents produced, and the centrality of the documents to the subject matter of the litigation.

51. If Nanny Nation's counsel shares privileged information with Mary Bobbins to prepare her for giving testimony as an expert witness, can Prynne/Holgrave obtain discovery of the information?

ANSWER:

52. The discovery rules provide that parties may obtain discovery regarding

   (A) any matter, not privileged, that is relevant to the subject matter of the litigation.

   (B) any matter, not privileged, that is relevant to the claim or defense of any party and is admissible in evidence.

   (C) any matter, not privileged, that is relevant to the claim or defense of any party, including relevant information that would be inadmissible but that appears reasonably calculated to lead to the discovery of admissible evidence.

   (D) any matter, not privileged, that is relevant to the claim or defense of any party and for which the discovering party can show good cause.

After an unpleasant dispute with local authorities gave her an interest in the law, Hester Prynne went to law school. While in school she married Holgrave, a fellow student, who also adopted Hester's daughter Pearl. After graduation, both began practice in Massachusetts. Both parents doted on Pearl, and both reduced their billable hours in order to spend more time with her. Concerned about quality child care, Prynne contacted Nanny Nation, a respected national agency that trains and recruits child care providers from throughout the United States and the world, with its main office in New York. Through Nanny Nation, Prynne and Holgrave hired Hibbins, a twenty-two-year-old British citizen, to live in their home, do light housework and cooking, and care for Pearl while they were at work.

About a month later, tragedy struck. Hibbins picked up Pearl from piano lessons and was driving her home. Unfortunately, Hibbins had succumbed to homesickness for the local pub and had three beers before getting Pearl. On the way home they were involved in a serious traffic accident. Hibbins suffered only superficial injuries, but Pearl received significant head and neck injuries. Prynne fired Hibbins, and she returned home to England.

Pearl has recovered from most of her injuries, although the doctors continue to watch for signs of permanent brain damage. Prynne and Holgrave have paid substantial medical bills for her treatment and have lost income while tending to her psychological and medical needs. They have suffered mental anguish from watching Pearl struggle with her injuries. Prynne and Holgrave no longer feel comfortable leaving Pearl with anyone other than a family member, and so Holgrave has retired from practice and takes care of Pearl full time.

Prynne and Holgrave sued Nanny Nation for damages in federal district court in Massachusetts. Their theories of recovery are negligence (in hiring and training Hibbins), gross negligence (for a pattern of ignoring serious psychological and behavioral problems of potential nannies), and fraud (for representing that their nannies are highly responsible and well qualified to care for young children), and they seek both actual and punitive damages.

53.   Nanny Nation has heard rumors about Prynne's pre-law school exploits. They have asked her to describe in detail her sexual history. Is this discoverable?

    (A)   Yes. Prynne's sexual conduct gives insight into her character and is therefore relevant.

    (B)   Yes. Prynne has waived any privacy rights she might have by bringing this lawsuit.

    (C)   No. Prynne's sex life is not relevant to the claims against Nanny Nation.

    (D)   Yes. The truthfulness or falsity of Prynne's answer to this question will help to show whether she is a truthful person, and that might be admissible to impeach her testimony generally.

54.   Nanny Nation will defend itself, in part, by asserting that Hibbins' driving did not cause the accident in which Pearl was injured. It, therefore, sends an interrogatory asking for the names, addresses, and phone numbers of all persons who witnessed the accident. Is this information relevant?

    (A)   No. The relevant issue is Hibbins' intoxication, and these people will not have knowledge of that.

    (B)   No. These names will not be admissible in evidence.

    (C)   Yes. These people have knowledge of the circumstances surrounding the accident, which may, in turn, be relevant to the issue of causation.

    (D)   Yes. Nanny Nation may discover the identity of anyone to whom Prynne's lawyers talked while investigating the case.

55.   Why would Nanny Nation want to send the interrogatory discussed above when it will already have learned, through automatic initial disclosures, the identity of people who Prynne knows have information about the case?

ANSWER:

56.   Nanny Nation is skeptical of the lost income amounts claimed by Holgrave. They doubt that his practice was ever as successful as he claims, and they therefore doubt that Holgrave's lost future income is as great as he claims. Nanny Nation has sent a request for production of documents to Holgrave, asking for all documents relevant to his income from law practice. The request asks for every piece of paper related to Holgrave's practice. Are these documents relevant?

    (A)   Yes, they are relevant to the amount of Holgrave's claim for damages and must be produced.

(B) While some of the documents will be relevant, Holgrave should object to the request as drafted because many of the documents clearly will not be relevant.

(C) No. Information relevant only to damages is not discoverable beyond that required in the automatic initial disclosure rules.

(D) All of them are relevant, but some should be withheld because they will be protected by the attorney-client privilege.

57. Discuss how the definition of discovery relevance interacts with the rules on pleadings, including how the pleading/discovery process fits into the overall philosophy of the FRCP.

ANSWER:

TOPIC 15:
DISCOVERY: WORK PRODUCT

58. When is material protected from discovery by work product protection?

(A) When it is confidential material prepared by a party's representative.

(B) When it is prepared in anticipation of litigation or for trial by a party or by or for that party's representative.

(C) When it is a confidential communication between a party and that party's attorney.

(D) When it is prepared in anticipation of litigation or for trial by any person.

After an unpleasant dispute with local authorities gave her an interest in the law, Hester Prynne went to law school. While in school she married Holgrave, a fellow student, who also adopted Hester's daughter Pearl. After graduation, both began practice in Massachusetts. Both parents doted on Pearl, and both reduced their billable hours in order to spend more time with her. Concerned about quality child care, Prynne contacted Nanny Nation, a respected national agency that trains and recruits child care providers from throughout the United States and the world, with its main office in New York. Through Nanny Nation, Prynne and Holgrave hired Hibbins, a twenty-two-year-old British citizen, to live in their home, do light housework and cooking, and care for Pearl while they were at work.

About a month later, tragedy struck. Hibbins picked up Pearl from piano lessons and was driving her home. Unfortunately, Hibbins had succumbed to homesickness for the local pub and had three beers before getting Pearl. On the way home they were involved in a serious traffic accident. Hibbins suffered only superficial injuries, but Pearl received significant head and neck injuries. Prynne fired Hibbins, and she returned home to England.

Pearl has recovered from most of her injuries, although the doctors continue to watch for signs of permanent brain damage. Prynne and Holgrave have paid substantial medical bills for her treatment and have lost income while tending to her psychological and medical needs. They have suffered from mental anguish from watching Pearl struggle with her injuries. Prynne and Holgrave no longer feel comfortable leaving Pearl with anyone other than a family member, and so Holgrave has retired from practice and takes care of Pearl full time.

Prynne and Holgrave sued Nanny Nation for damages in federal district court in Massachusetts. Their theories of recovery are negligence (in hiring and training Hibbins), gross negligence (for a pattern of ignoring serious psychological and behavioral problems of potential nannies), and fraud (for representing that their nannies are highly responsible and well-qualified to care for young children), and they seek both actual and punitive damages.

59. Prynne's lawyer hired a private investigator to look into Hibbins' background. This investigator interviewed Prynne's neighbors about Hibbins' habits and took notes on those interviews. Nanny Nation wants to discover those notes. Are they discoverable?

(A) Yes. Only notes created by the lawyer are work product.

(B) No. They are opinion work product.

(C) No. They are ordinary work product and Nanny Nation could easily discover the substantial equivalent of this information.

(D) Yes. The information in the notes concerns pre-lawsuit behavior and so they are not made in anticipation of litigation.

60. Prynne sends Nanny Nation an interrogatory asking about Hibbins' behavior during the nanny training program. Nanny Nation's CEO knows some of this information only because she learned it from the investigations brought on by the lawsuit. Does she have to disclose this part of the information to Prynne?

ANSWER:

61. A year before Prynne came to Nanny Nation, the company did an internal review of its recruiting policies. The reviewer looked at two years' worth of files and wrote a report to the CEO that suggested improvements that could be made to the recruiting practices in order to weed out undesirable potential nannies. Prynne has sent Nanny Nation a request for production of documents that covers this report. Must Nanny Nation produce it?

(A) Yes. It is relevant to Prynne's claim of a pattern of misconduct and it is not protected by work product.

(B) No. It is relevant to Prynne's claim of a pattern of misconduct and it is protected by work product.

(C) Yes. It is relevant to Prynne's claim of a pattern of misconduct and it is protected by work product, but Prynne could show substantial need of the report and undue hardship if the report is not produced.

(D) No. Searching for this report would be too burdensome.

62. Nanny Nation has hired a private investigator to help with this lawsuit. The investigator has gone to Hibbins' village in England to learn more about her background. The investigator interviewed Phoebe Pyncheon, a childhood friend of Hibbins, and taped the interview. The tape concerns Hibbins' habits as a teenager, including her drinking habits and her proficiency at driving. Pyncheon has since left England for an extended stay in Afghanistan, where she is helping to set up schools for women. Prynne would like to hear the tape, but Nanny Nation does not want to produce it. Is the tape discoverable?

    (A)   No. It is protected as ordinary work product.

    (B)   No. It is protected as opinion work product.

    (C)   Yes. It is protected as ordinary work product, but Prynne can show substantial need of the report and that she is unable without undue hardship to obtain the substantial equivalent of this information by other means.

    (D)   Yes. Relevant information is always discoverable.

63.   Nanny Nation's lawyer has interviewed Holgrave's former boss in order to help get information about Holgrave's lost income claim. The lawyer took notes on the interview, including evaluative comments about the kind of witness the boss would make and the impact that information might have on Nanny Nation's case. Prynne wants to discover the lawyer's notes. Are they discoverable?

    (A)   No. They are protected as ordinary work product.

    (B)   No. They are protected as opinion work product.

    (C)   Yes. They are protected as ordinary work product but Prynne could meet the substantial need/undue hardship requirement.

    (D)   Yes. They are not protected because Holgrave's boss is not the client of the lawyer who did the interview.

64.   Why do the rules protect work product from discovery? What is being protected? What are its costs?

ANSWER:

65. Which of the following is NOT required for a communication to be protected by the attorney-client privilege?

(A) The communication was made in confidence.

(B) The communication was for the purpose of securing legal advice.

(C) The communication was made in anticipation of litigation or for trial.

(D) The communication was not voluntarily revealed.

After an unpleasant dispute with local authorities gave her an interest in the law, Hester Prynne went to law school. While in school she married Holgrave, a fellow student, who also adopted Hester's daughter Pearl. After graduation, both began practice in Massachusetts. Both parents doted on Pearl, and both reduced their billable hours in order to spend more time with her. Concerned about quality child care, Prynne contacted Nanny Nation, a respected national agency that trains and recruits child care providers from throughout the United States and the world, with its main office in New York. Through Nanny Nation, Prynne and Holgrave hired Hibbins, a twenty-two-year-old British citizen, to live in their home, do light housework and cooking, and care for Pearl while they were at work.

About a month later, tragedy struck. Hibbins picked up Pearl from piano lessons and was driving her home. Unfortunately, Hibbins had succumbed to homesickness for the local pub and had three beers before getting Pearl. On the way home they were involved in a serious traffic accident. Hibbins suffered only superficial injuries, but Pearl received significant head and neck injuries. Prynne fired Hibbins, and she returned home to England.

Pearl has recovered from most of her injuries, although the doctors continue to watch for signs of permanent brain damage. Prynne and Holgrave have paid substantial medical bills for her treatment and have lost income while tending to her psychological and medical needs. They have suffered mental anguish from watching Pearl struggle with her injuries. Prynne and Holgrave no longer feel comfortable leaving Pearl with anyone other than a family member, and so Holgrave has retired from practice and takes care of Pearl full time.

Prynne and Holgrave sued Nanny Nation for damages in federal district court in Massachusetts. Their theories of recovery are negligence (in hiring and training Hibbins), gross negligence (for a pattern of ignoring serious psychological and behavioral problems of potential nannies), and fraud (for representing that their nannies are highly responsible and well-qualified to care for young children), and they seek both actual and punitive damages.

66. Nanny Nation's lawyer has organized an internal investigation into the hiring of Hibbins. He sent a questionnaire to all of the employees who might have been part of that process, and he has now received the employees' responses. One completed questionnaire comes from Matthew Maule, Vice President for Human Resources. This questionnaire is:

(A)   protected by attorney-client privilege only in a "subject matter test" jurisdiction.

(B)   protected by attorney-client privilege only in a "control group test" jurisdiction.

(C)   protected by attorney-client privilege in either type of jurisdiction.

(D)   not protected by the attorney-client privilege.

67.   Another completed questionnaire comes from Roger Chillingworth, a disgruntled former vice president with a reputation for finding fault. This questionnaire is:

(A)   protected by attorney-client privilege only in a "subject matter test" jurisdiction.

(B)   protected by attorney-client privilege only in a "control group test" jurisdiction.

(C)   protected by attorney-client privilege in either type of jurisdiction.

(D)   not protected by the attorney-client privilege.

68.   Prynne has sent an interrogatory to Nanny Nation that reads, "What did Nanny Nation's CEO tell the company's attorney about the circumstances surrounding the hiring of Hibbins?" Nanny Nation has objected to this interrogatory on the basis of work product and attorney-client privilege. The judge has sustained the objection. What alternative method(s) might Prynne use to get information about Nanny Nation's hiring of Hibbins?

ANSWER:

After an unpleasant dispute with local authorities gave her an interest in the law, Hester Prynne went to law school. While in school she married Holgrave, a fellow student, who also adopted Hester's daughter Pearl. After graduation, both began practice in Massachusetts. Both parents doted on Pearl, and both reduced their billable hours in order to spend more time with her. Concerned about quality child care, Prynne contacted Nanny Nation, a respected national agency that trains and recruits child care providers from throughout the United States and the world, with its main office in New York. Through Nanny Nation, Prynne and Holgrave hired Hibbins, a twenty-two-year-old British citizen, to live in their home, do light housework and cooking, and care for Pearl while they were at work.

About a month later, tragedy struck. Hibbins picked up Pearl from piano lessons and was driving her home. Unfortunately, Hibbins had succumbed to homesickness for the local pub and had three beers before getting Pearl. On the way home they were involved in a serious traffic accident. Hibbins suffered only superficial injuries, but Pearl received significant head and neck injuries. Prynne fired Hibbins, and she returned home to England.

Pearl has recovered from most of her injuries, although the doctors continue to watch for signs of permanent brain damage. Prynne and Holgrave have paid substantial medical bills for her treatment and have lost income while tending to her psychological and medical needs. They have suffered mental anguish from watching Pearl struggle with her injuries. Prynne and Holgrave no longer feel comfortable leaving Pearl with anyone other than a family member, and so Holgrave has retired from practice and takes care of Pearl full time.

Prynne and Holgrave sued Nanny Nation for damages in federal district court in Massachusetts. Their theories of recovery are negligence (in hiring and training Hibbins), gross negligence (for a pattern of ignoring serious psychological and behavioral problems of potential nannies), and fraud (for representing that their nannies are highly responsible and well-qualified to care for young children), and they seek both actual and punitive damages.

69. Prynne has hired a child care expert, Nate Hawthorne, to consult in the preparation of her case against Nanny Nation. Hawthorne will not be testifying when the case goes to trial. Nanny Nation wants to learn Hawthorne's identity and take his deposition. Will this be allowed?

ANSWER:

70. Nanny Nation employs Bellingham, who has a Ph.D. in early childhood education, to design and evaluate its training program. She has worked for Nanny Nation for the last

ten years. Prynne would like to take Bellingham's deposition and ask about Nanny Nation's program, but Nanny Nation says she is a protected consulting expert witness. Under these circumstances:

(A)   Bellingham may be deposed. She was not retained as an expert in anticipation of litigation, so the consulting expert privilege does not apply to her.

(B)   Bellingham may be deposed. She is not an expert.

(C)   Bellingham may not be deposed. She is a non-testifying expert, and so she is protected by Rule 26(b)(4).

(D)   Bellingham may not be deposed. Employees may always be designated as protected consulting experts.

71.   Discuss the reasons expert witnesses are used by parties to litigation and how those reasons are reflected in the discovery rules concerning experts.

ANSWER:

After an unpleasant dispute with local authorities gave her an interest in the law, Hester Prynne went to law school. While in school she married Holgrave, a fellow student, who also adopted Hester's daughter Pearl. After graduation, both began practice in Massachusetts. Both parents doted on Pearl, and both reduced their billable hours in order to spend more time with her. Concerned about quality child care, Prynne contacted Nanny Nation, a respected national agency that trains and recruits child care providers from throughout the United States and the world, with its main office in New York. Through Nanny Nation, Prynne and Holgrave hired Hibbins, a twenty-two-year-old British citizen, to live in their home, do light housework and cooking, and care for Pearl while they were at work.

About a month later, tragedy struck. Hibbins picked up Pearl from piano lessons and was driving her home. Unfortunately, Hibbins had succumbed to homesickness for the local pub and had three beers before getting Pearl. On the way home they were involved in a serious traffic accident. Hibbins suffered only superficial injuries, but Pearl received significant head and neck injuries. Prynne fired Hibbins, and she returned home to England.

Pearl has recovered from most of her injuries, although the doctors continue to watch for signs of permanent brain damage. Prynne and Holgrave have paid substantial medical bills for her treatment and have lost income while tending to her psychological and medical needs. They have suffered mental anguish from watching Pearl struggle with her injuries. Prynne and Holgrave no longer feel comfortable leaving Pearl with anyone other than a family member, and so Holgrave has retired from practice and takes care of Pearl full time.

Prynne and Holgrave sued Nanny Nation for damages in federal district court in Massachusetts. Their theories of recovery are negligence (in hiring and training Hibbins), gross negligence (for a pattern of ignoring serious psychological and behavioral problems of potential nannies), and fraud (for representing that their nannies are highly responsible and well-qualified to care for young children), and they seek both actual and punitive damages.

72. Prynne wants to make sure her lawsuit has correctly identified Nanny Nation and its corporate structure. She would also like to know precisely who is in charge of what. What would be the best discovery device to use to get this information?

    (A) Request for admissions confirming Prynne's beliefs about these facts.

    (B) Request for production of articles of incorporation and corporate organizational charts.

    (C) Interrogatories asking for this information.

    (D) Deposition of Nanny Nation's Director of Human Resources (DHR) asking these questions.

73. Nanny Nation wants reliable information about Pearl's current medical condition. They think her treating physician is exaggerating the possibilities of future complications. What would be the best discovery device to use to get this information?

(A) Request for admissions admitting that Pearl has recovered fully.

(B) Request for production of Pearl's medical records.

(C) Interrogatories asking for this information.

(D) Motion for physical examination of Pearl.

74. Nanny Nation is skeptical of Holgrave's lost income claims. They have requested copies of his financial records from two years prior to Pearl's accident to the present. Holgrave has refused to produce them, saying he does not keep copies of such records and so Nanny Nation will have to get them from his accountant. Is Holgrave correct?

ANSWER:

75. Prynne wants to know everything about the circumstances that led to Hibbins' hiring, and everything about Hibbins' training, but she does not know who within the Nanny Nation hierarchy would have this information. What can she do to depose the knowledgeable employees?

(A) She can notice the deposition, by name, of all Nanny Nation employees she knows about who might possibly have information about Hibbins.

(B) She can notice the deposition of Nanny Nation and describe with reasonable particularity the matters on which she wants to examine the company.

(C) She can notice the deposition of Nanny Nation's DHR and force him to find out the answers to her questions.

(D) She can depose Hibbins and ask her who knows about her hiring and training.

76. Prynne has learned that Nanny Nation subcontracts some of its headhunting activities to Poppins, Ltd. and that Poppins may have been the first to recruit Hibbins. Prynne wants to depose Poppins' DHR and see any documents relating to Hibbins. What discovery device should Prynne use?

(A) Prynne can notice the deposition of Poppins' DHR and send Poppins a request for production of documents.

(B) Prynne can subpoena Poppins' DHR for deposition and include in the subpoena a command to produce designated documents.

(C) Prynne can force Nanny Nation to produce Poppins' DHR for deposition.

(D) Prynne will have to wait until trial of the case to compel answers from Poppins. There is no pre-trial device to get information from non-parties.

77. Nanny Nation wants to take Prynne's deposition. It believes she has a lot of information relevant to its defense on both liability and damage claims. Absent agreement or court order, for how long can Nanny Nation depose Prynne?

ANSWER:

78. Prynne is trying to minimize litigation costs, and she has heard that interrogatories are the least expensive way to get information. How many interrogatories may Prynne use in this case without needing permission from the court?

ANSWER:

79. How might Prynne combine the various discovery devices into a coherent discovery plan for this case?

ANSWER:

Thomas Eliot is a serious cat lover. He was devoted to his favorite tabby cat, Jennyanydots. Jenny (her nickname) was a lovely, loving feline, but a picky eater. Eliot, therefore, carefully bought her only Special Kitty Select Cuts, sold by Kliban Foods. Kliban sells only on the internet, through its website www.lovetoeatthemmousies.com. Its customers go to the company website, place an order, provide a credit card number, and the food is delivered to their homes. Kliban's elite clientele spread the news of the wonders of its cat food by word of mouth — the company has never advertised except by paying Google for sponsored links that appear when anyone searches for "gourmet cat food."

Kliban, in December, decided it could increase its profits by purchasing inexpensive wheat gluten from China to use in its cat food. Unfortunately, it turned out that the gluten contained an industrial chemical called melamine, used to falsely increase the apparent protein content of the wheat gluten. Melamine is helpful in making fertilizer, but can be toxic when ingested in large quantities.

Eliot, as was his habit, bought Special Kitty Select Cuts for Jenny throughout the early spring. In late March, Jenny became very lethargic and suffered from a loss of appetite and vomiting, and so Eliot took her to a veterinarian. The vet diagnosed Jenny as suffering from kidney failure, and eventually Jenny had to be euthanized to relieve her suffering.

Eliot is beside himself with grief. He has filed suit against Kliban in federal district court, seeking damages in excess of $100,000. (The courts in his state allow pet owners to recover damages for emotional distress arising from the loss of a pet.) The complaint alleges that Kliban is liable for breach of warranty, for negligently inspecting the cat food, and for delaying its recall of tainted food until early April even though it knew of the problems much sooner. He believes that Kliban may have known about the problem as early as January, and the press has reported that its Chief Financial Officer sold half of his shares in the company in late February. Consider the following issues that may arise concerning discovery in *Eliot v. Kliban*.

80. Defendant Kliban has been served with process and answered. It is time for counsel to confer regarding discovery. Under Rule 26(f), they will have to discuss "any issues relating to disclosure or discovery of electronically stored information ("ESI"), including the form or forms in which it should be produced." If you represented Eliot, what would you need to know before going into this conference? What would you want to find out at the conference? What would you want Kliban to agree to with regard to format?

ANSWER:

81. A dispute has arisen about the proper format for the production of ESI. Kliban maintains that when it is the producing party, it gets to designate the format and that it has an absolute right to choose to produce the information in .pdf format or to print it out in hard copy. Is Kliban correct?

    (A) Yes. Rule 34 provides that the responding party may indicate the form it intends to use for production.

    (B) No. Absent agreement or court order, Kliban must produce ESI in the form in which it is normally maintained or which is reasonably usable.

    (C) No. Rule 34 allows the requesting party to specify the format in which ESI should be produced.

    (D) Yes and No. Kliban has a right to convert data to .pdf files as it can be searched, but hard copy is not searchable and therefore not reasonably usable.

82. Eliot sent a discovery request to Kliban seeking "all documents concerning Pound's sale of his Kliban stock on February 28, 2007." Kliban had agreed at the discovery conference to put a "litigation hold" on the destruction of documents relevant to the litigation. Its tech support people interpreted this to include only desktop computers kept on company property. Kliban, however, supplies all of its management-level employees with laptops and with Blackberries that allow the employees to bring work home and on the road. So while work done on the desktop computers was retained, many employees continued to routinely delete documents from their mobile devices, including documents relevant to claims about cats with kidney failure. In particular, in early May of 2007, Ezra Pound (Kliban's CFO) deleted all e-mail files from his mobile devices for the period January–April 2007, in what he called a "routine spring cleaning." In many instances, therefore, there is no easy way to get at relevant e-mails and text messages. Kliban has produced only a few pieces of paper in response to the request for information about Pound's stock sale. Eliot believes the missing data is relevant, but can't afford to employ computer forensic experts to try to reconstruct the lost data. Should the court order Kliban to pay for it?

    (A) No. Rule 37 provides that there should be no sanctions for the routine, good faith deletion of data.

    (B) Yes. The producing party is responsible for paying the costs of production.

    (C) No. Kliban will point out that the deleted communications are not reasonably accessible because of undue burden or cost.

    (D) Yes. The information requested is relevant to Kliban's knowledge of the tainted cat food, Eliot's request is sufficiently specific, and the deletion of the data was not routine or in good faith.

After an unpleasant dispute with local authorities gave her an interest in the law, Hester Prynne went to law school. While in school she married Holgrave, a fellow student, who also adopted Hester's daughter Pearl. After graduation, both began practice in Massachusetts. Both parents doted on Pearl, and both reduced their billable hours in order to spend more time with her. Concerned about quality child care, Prynne contacted Nanny Nation, a respected national agency that trains and recruits child care providers from throughout the United States and the world, with its main office in New York. Through Nanny Nation, Prynne and Holgrave hired Hibbins, a twenty-two-year-old British citizen, to live in their home, do light housework and cooking, and care for Pearl while they were at work.

About a month later, tragedy struck. Hibbins picked up Pearl from piano lessons and was driving her home. Unfortunately, Hibbins had succumbed to homesickness for the local pub and had three beers before getting Pearl. On the way home they were involved in a serious traffic accident. Hibbins suffered only superficial injuries, but Pearl received significant head and neck injuries. Prynne fired Hibbins, and she returned home to England.

Pearl has recovered from most of her injuries, although the doctors continue to watch for signs of permanent brain damage. Prynne and Holgrave have paid substantial medical bills for her treatment and have lost income while tending to her psychological and medical needs. They have suffered from mental anguish, watching Pearl struggle with her injuries. Prynne and Holgrave no longer feel comfortable leaving Pearl with anyone other than a family member, and so Holgrave has retired from practice and takes care of Pearl full time.

Prynne and Holgrave sued Nanny Nation for damages in federal district court in Massachusetts. Their theories of recovery are negligence (in hiring and training Hibbins), gross negligence (for a pattern of ignoring serious psychological and behavioral problems of potential nannies), and fraud (for representing that their nannies are highly responsible and well-qualified to care for young children), and they seek both actual and punitive damages.

83.   Prynne sent a request for production of documents to Nanny Nation. Nanny Nation produced a handful of documents, objecting that the remaining requests called for material that was not relevant to the claims and defenses in the lawsuit. Prynne disagrees. She believes that the requested documents are discoverable. What should she do next?

    (A)   Confer or attempt to confer in good faith with Nanny Nation in an effort to secure the material. Absent agreement, move for an order compelling production of the documents and reimbursement of Prynne's expenses incurred in making the motion, including attorney's fees.

    (B)   Move for an order compelling production of the documents and reimbursement of Prynne's expenses incurred in making the motion, including attorney's fees.

(C)   Confer or attempt to confer in good faith with Nanny Nation in an effort to secure the material. Absent agreement, move for an order striking Nanny Nation's answer as a sanction for its noncompliance with a proper discovery request.

(D)   Move for an order striking Nanny Nation's answer as a sanction for its noncompliance with a proper discovery request.

84.   Imagine that *Prynne & Holgrave v. Nanny Nation* is in trial. Nanny Nation is attempting to call a very important witness on its behalf, and this witness was not disclosed in the initial disclosures or any amendment thereof, and the witness also has not been disclosed in response to any discovery device. What are the most severe sanctions available?

ANSWER:

85. The primary difference between a motion for summary judgment and a motion for judgment as a matter of law at the close of all the evidence is:

(A) The standard the movant must meet.

(B) The non-movant's burden to avoid summary judgment.

(C) The record on which the court will base its decision.

(D) The nature of the court's review of the record.

86. Prior to the U.S. Supreme Court's decision in *Celotex Corp. v. Catrett*, 477 U.S. 317 (1986), a defendant moving for summary judgment based on the weakness in the plaintiff's case had to meet which of the following burdens before the plaintiff was required to respond?

(A) Demonstrate the existence of a fact issue regarding all elements of the plaintiff's cause of action.

(B) Negate some element of the plaintiff's cause of action.

(C) Negate each element of the plaintiff's cause of action.

(D) Claim that some element of the plaintiff's cause of action would lack evidentiary support.

87. In the Supreme Court's 1970 decision, *Adickes v. S.H. Kress & Co.*, 398 U.S. 144 (1970), the plaintiff Sandra Adickes needed to prove the existence of a conspiracy between defendant Kress and the police. The trial court granted summary judgment, and the court of appeals affirmed, finding that the record contained no evidence from which a reasonably minded person could draw an inference of conspiracy. The Supreme Court reversed. Justice Harlan's opinion explained that Kress had failed to meet its burden as a summary judgment movant because:

(A) Kress failed to foreclose the possibility that there was a policeman in the Kress store while Adickes was awaiting service, and that this policeman reached an understanding with some Kress employee that Adickes was not to be served.

(B) Kress was not specific enough in pointing out to the trial court the weaknesses in Adickes' claim.

(C) Adickes had not been given sufficient time for discovery in order to acquire evidence to use in opposing summary judgment.

(D) Adickes could defeat summary judgment by referring to the allegations of her complaint.

88. In *Celotex*, Justice Rehnquist's plurality opinion requires the summary judgment movant to:

   (A) negate some element of the non-moving party's claim.

   (B) point out the absence of evidence to support some element of the non-moving party's case.

   (C) produce some evidence to show there is a fact issue regarding the non-moving party's case.

   (D) wait until the end of the discovery period before filing a motion for summary judgment.

89. Justice White's concurring opinion in *Celotex* provides the crucial fifth vote. His opinion requires:

   (A) more than a conclusory allegation that the plaintiff has no evidence to prove her case.

   (B) the movant to disprove the claimed basis for the suit.

   (C) the plaintiff to depose the witnesses whose testimony she wants to use in opposition to summary judgment.

   (D) simply that the defendant move for summary judgment; this obligates the plaintiff to reveal enough evidence to support her claim.

90. Once a defendant has met its initial burden of moving for summary judgment, the plaintiff must:

   (A) produce evidence in admissible form showing the existence of a genuine issue of material fact.

   (B) point to the parts of the plaintiff's pleadings that allege the matters in issue.

   (C) point out to the court supporting evidence already in the record that would support a reasonable inference in the plaintiff's favor.

   (D) point out to the court evidence already in the record, or provided in response to the motion for summary judgment, reducible to admissible evidence, that would support a reasonable inference in the plaintiff's favor.

91. In considering the summary judgment record, what attitude should the court adopt in evaluating the materials offered?

   (A) The court should draw all reasonable inferences in favor of the party moving for summary judgment.

   (B) The court should draw all reasonable inferences in favor of the non-movant.

(C) The court should weigh the evidence and decide whether there is a genuine issue of material fact.

(D) The court should deny summary judgment if there is any doubt as to the facts.

92. What are the consequences of the shifts in the Supreme Court's attitude toward summary judgment?

ANSWER:

Newlyweds Pip and Estella agreed to have their bedroom redone as part of a new reality TV show, "While You Were Trading Spaces" (WYWTS). Their friends, the Havishams, redid the room in Victorian style with the help of the show's professional designer and carpenter. One of the changes in the room involved the installation of the show's trademark ceiling fan. Unfortunately, two weeks after the TV people left the fan crashed onto the bed in the middle of the night, breaking Pip's leg and disfiguring Estella's pretty face.

Pip and Estella have sued the company that produces the show, alleging negligence in the selection and installation of the ceiling fan. WYWTS has denied their claims, alleging that the ceiling fan fell because of hidden flaws in the ceiling. WYWTS also relies on a contract that Pip and Estella signed, absolving the show of liability for any damages caused by the redecoration.

93. About two months after being sued, WYWTS took Estella's deposition. They asked her, "What makes you think it was the show's fault that the ceiling fan fell?" She answered, "Well I don't really know yet, but it's certainly not my fault." Based on this answer, WYWTS filed a motion for summary judgment. The motion, which is extremely brief, states that the plaintiffs have no evidence to support the necessary elements of breach of duty and causation. It points to Estella's deposition testimony in support of its motion. The plaintiffs, in fact, have no evidence right now, but they know that ceiling fans are not supposed to fall on you. How should the plaintiffs respond?

    (A)   The plaintiffs can ignore the motion. They have not had enough time for discovery.

    (B)   In the interest of caution, the plaintiffs should respond to the motion. While it is not clear whether this motion meets the movant's burden, it would be safer to formally ask the court for more time to respond under Rule 56(f).

    (C)   They should assemble evidence, including drafting affidavits, all of which must be in admissible form, and file them with the court in opposition to the motion.

    (D)   The plaintiffs can ignore the motion. WYWTS has not disproved either breach or causation.

94. Assume that the court denies the original WYWTS motion for the time being, with leave to refile it after more time for discovery. WYWTS files a second motion for summary judgment, this one based on the release. They include an affidavit proving that Pip and Estella signed the release. Under applicable substantive law, however, such releases are not enforceable when they purport to release a party from its own negligence. The plaintiffs respond to the motion, briefing this legal issue, but they do not come forward with any evidence in opposition to summary judgment. Under these circumstances:

(A) The court should grant the motion because the plaintiffs have not demonstrated the existence of a genuine issue of material fact as to whether they signed the release.

(B) The court should deny the motion because successive motions for summary judgment are improper.

(C) The court should deny the motion because, as a matter of law, this release is not enforceable. The issue of the genuineness of the signatures is not material.

(D) The court should grant the motion because the plaintiffs did not produce evidence of the cases about releases.

95. After about a year, WYWTS renews its original motion for summary judgment. It supports its motion with an affidavit from an expert structural engineer. The engineer opines, based on his examination of the post-accident fan and the plaintiffs' bedroom, that the ceiling fan was correctly designed and correctly installed. He further swears that the ceiling material was weakened by invisible wood rot that caused the fan to fall. The plaintiffs do not respond. How should the court rule?

(A) The court should deny the motion for summary judgment. WYWTS has not canvassed the discovery record and pointed out the weakness in the plaintiffs' case.

(B) The court should deny the motion for summary judgment. Such motions cannot be based on expert testimony.

(C) The court should grant the motion. The motion was adequately supported and the plaintiffs failed to respond in a way that demonstrates that a fact issue exists.

(D) The court should grant the motion and must do so whenever the non-movant fails to respond.

 96. Assume that WYWTS files the same motion as in the previous question, but this time the plaintiffs respond with an affidavit from their own expert and their own motion for summary judgment. The plaintiffs' expert swears that he has examined the wood of the ceiling and there is no wood rot. He further notes that if there were wood rot any competent carpenter would have seen it, and so it would have been negligent to proceed with the plan to install a ceiling fan. The plaintiffs' expert opines that the fifty-pound ceiling fan was negligently attached only to sheet rock rather than to a sturdier ceiling joist, and that the weight of the fan plus its inadequate anchoring caused it to fall. How should the court rule?

(A) The court should grant the plaintiffs' motion. Their expert is more believable.

(B) The court should grant the defendant's motion. Its expert is more believable.

(C) The court should deny both motions. Neither one was adequately supported.

(D) The court should deny both motions. The conflicting expert affidavits demonstrate that there is a genuine issue of material fact.

97. Imagine a different motion this time. WYWTS files a motion for summary judgment. The motion argues that the plaintiffs have had a year to do discovery and still lack

evidence of breach and causation. It supports its motion by pointing to the plaintiffs' automatic initial disclosures, which contain no evidence of negligence, and their answer to Defendant's Interrogatory No. 3. The interrogatory stated, "Please identify all evidence that you intend to use to prove that the negligence of defendant caused the occurrence in question." The plaintiffs' answer was: "Unknown at this time. Will supplement after further discovery."

The plaintiffs respond to the motion with the following: 1) a letter from their insurance adjuster stating that the fan had been improperly installed; and 2) the deposition of Mrs. Havisham (who has since died) from a separate lawsuit brought against her by the designer, claiming intentional infliction of emotional distress, in which Mrs. Havisham blames the carpenter for poor work. The plaintiffs also claim that they intend to call the carpenter as a witness at trial, but they have so far been unable to locate him to depose or subpoena him.

How should the court rule on the defendant's motion, and why?

ANSWER: (Two Paragraphs)

98. Martha and Fred own adjoining tracts of land in Starr County, Texas. Fred claims that Martha has interfered with Fred's use and enjoyment of the property. Fred brings suit on this claim in federal district court in the Southern District of Texas, the requirements of diversity jurisdiction being satisfied. Which of the following propositions is most accurate?

   (A) If Fred seeks an injunction, Martha will be entitled to a jury trial of all fact issues.

   (B) If Fred seeks a money judgment, Martha will not be entitled to a jury trial of all fact issues.

   (C) If Fred seeks both an injunction and incidental money damages, Fred will not be entitled to a jury trial of all fact issues.

   (D) If Fred seeks both money damages and an injunction, he will be entitled to a jury trial of all fact issues.

99. Down-South Corporation filed suit in federal district court in New Orleans, Louisiana, seeking damages and an award of declaratory and injunctive relief against Peppy Cola Corporation and four of its officers. Shortly thereafter, Cotton Corporation intervened in the case. Down-South and Cotton Corporation alleged that the defendants had violated Sections 1 and 2 of the Sherman Act and Section 2 of the Robinson Patman Act. If Down-South made a jury demand by endorsing it on the Complaint filed and served on Peppy Cola Corporation, is Down-South entitled to a jury trial?

   (A) Down-South is not entitled to a jury trial of any fact questions because the gist of the action is equitable.

   (B) Down-South is not entitled to a jury trial because there were no antitrust statutes in 1791.

   (C) Down-South is entitled to a jury trial of all fact issues under the Seventh Amendment.

   (D) Down-South is entitled to a jury trial on the claims for declaratory and injunctive relief.

100. After extensive pretrial discovery it is apparent that the factual issues in the case are very complex and arguably beyond the practical abilities of the jurors to resolve. As a result, Peppy Cola Corporation has filed a motion to strike the jury demand made by Down-South Corporation on the basis that the complexity of the case has made it necessary to regard the antitrust claims as equitable rather than legal or call for the application of a complexity exception to the 7th Amendment. How should the trial judge rule on the motion?

ANSWER:

101. Bunker engaged Dr. Kildare to remove his appendix. After Dr. Kildare performed the operation, Bunker experienced pain in his abdomen and reported his problems to Dr. Kildare who told Bunker that an infection had developed and that a second operation would be necessary. Both before and after the second operation, performed by Dr. Kildare, Bunker experienced severe abdominal pain and could not work or engage in normal physical activities for several months. Ultimately, after being billed more than $2,000 for the second operation, Bunker sued Dr. Kildare for medical negligence. At trial, which was before a six person jury in the federal district court in Montana, Bunker testified to the foregoing matters and also testified that, in his opinion, Dr. Kildare was extremely sloppy and negligent in not preventing the infection. After presenting other evidence concerning his injuries and loss of income due to his inability to work, Bunker rested his case. Dr. Kildare has moved for judgment as a matter of law. How should the federal judge rule on Bunker's Rule 50 motion?

ANSWER:

Kate sues Dave, alleging that his negligence caused her personal injuries. Dave denied these allegations and also raised the affirmative defense of contributory negligence. Assume that in this jurisdiction contributory negligence must be proved by the defendant and is a complete bar to any recovery by the plaintiff.

102. At a trial of *Kate v. Dave,* as to the elements of Kate's claim,

(A) Kate would have the burden of production and the burden of persuasion on all elements of her cause of action.

(B) Kate would have the burden of production initially, but it shifts to Dave after Kate puts on legally sufficient evidence of each element of her claim. The burden of persuasion remains on Kate.

(C) Kate would have the burdens of production and persuasion initially, but both shift to Dave after Kate puts on her case in chief.

(D) Because he has raised the affirmative defense of contributory negligence, Dave has the burdens of production and persuasion throughout the case to show that Kate was negligent and that he was not.

103. At a trial of *Kate v. Dave*,

(A) Kate's failure to prove the elements of her claim by a preponderance of the evidence could result in the judge entering judgment as a matter of law for Dave before the case goes to the jury.

(B) Kate's failure to produce evidence on which a reasonable jury could find for Kate could result in the judge entering judgment as a matter of law for Dave before the case goes to the jury.

(C) Kate's right to jury trial under the Seventh Amendment means that her case must be permitted to go to the jury even if she fails to meet her burden of production.

(D) If Kate produces evidence in her case in chief demonstrating that no reasonable jury could fail to find for Kate, it is irrelevant what evidence Dave might have; the judge could grant judgment as a matter of law for Kate before the case goes to the jury.

104. At a trial of *Kate v. Dave*,

(A) Dave would have the burden of production and the burden of persuasion on all elements of his affirmative defense.

(B) Dave would have the burden of persuasion but not the burden of production on all elements of his affirmative defense.

(C) Dave would have the burden of persuasion and the burden of production on at least one element of his affirmative defense.

(D) Dave would have the burden of production but not the burden of persuasion on all elements of his affirmative defense.

105. Maurice, who is clearly not a public figure, brought a libel suit against News Ltd. alleging that News Ltd.'s publication of a news story defamed Maurice by casting him as a *de facto* member of Creedlove, a phony charity actually involved in the distribution of illegal drugs for private gain. After removing the action to federal court, and asserting the defense of truth, News Ltd. defended the case at a jury trial by obtaining admissions from Maurice that Maurice had regularly attended Creedlove's public meetings and made cash contributions for the last ten years. At trial, Maurice testified that his reputation had been ruined by News Ltd., causing him humiliation and economic harm. With respect to the issue of his *de facto* membership in Creedlove, Maurice testified that, although he had attended some meetings and made annual contributions, Creedlove's membership rolls did not include his name and that over the same period he had published several magazine articles showing opposition to Creedlove's practices. After Maurice rested, News Ltd. moved for judgment as a matter of law based on its affirmative defense of truth on the issue of Maurice's *de facto* membership in Creedlove. How should the trial judge rule on the motion?

(A) The trial judge should grant the motion because Maurice's testimony is unbelievable.

(B) The trial judge should overrule the motion because there is a factual controversy about the pivotal fact of Maurice's membership based on the totality of the direct and circumstantial evidence.

(C) The trial court should deny the motion because Maurice's direct evidence negates any reasonable inference that could be drawn from the circumstantial evidence about meetings and contributions.

(D) The trial court should grant the motion if the trial judge concludes that Maurice's testimony is unconvincing.

106. Assume the same facts as in question 105, but assume further that the case is tried to the court in a bench trial rather than to a jury. How may the court rule?

ANSWER:

107. Rule 50(b) provides that a motion for judgment as a matter of law made before submission of the case to the jury may be renewed after verdict by filing a motion no later than 10 days after entry of judgment, with an alternative motion for new trial under Rule 59. But if no motion is made before submission of the case to the jury, a Rule 50(b) motion cannot properly be sustained after entry of judgment. What is the reason for this approach?

ANSWER:

108. In *Maurice v. News Ltd.*, what if News Ltd.'s pre-verdict motion is denied and News Ltd. does not renew the motion after judgment?

(A) Unless the 50(b) renewal motion is made and ruled on by the trial judge, News Ltd. cannot complain about the overruling of the 50(a) motion on appeal.

(B) News Ltd. is not required to renew the 50(a) motion after judgment to complain about the overruling of the 50(a) motion on appeal.

(C) News Ltd. can probably complain about the legal insufficiency of the evidence on appeal, if News Ltd. made a post-verdict motion for new trial complaining about the legal insufficiency of the evidence; appellate relief will be limited to a remand under these circumstances.

(D) (A) and (C) are both correct.

109. In *Maurice v. News Ltd.*, if News Ltd. moved for summary judgment contending that it was entitled to judgment as a matter of law on the issue of Maurice's *de facto* membership in Creedlove, can the denial of this motion for judgment as a matter of law be a basis for appellate complaint after full trial on the merits?

ANSWER:

110.   Clark brings an action against Sunderland for copyright infringement concerning a book
        about Civil Procedure. The case is tried to a jury. Assume that Clark offered and the
        trial court admitted evidence, over Sunderland's objection, that Sunderland had
        committed other copyright violations involving stories about lawyers. Assume further
        that the trial judge instructed the jury erroneously that Clark had to prove that Sunderland
        knowingly violated the copyright laws by clear and convincing evidence. Nonetheless,
        the jury returned a verdict for Clark.

Which of the following statements is most accurate?

   (A)   Sunderland should request the judge to make findings of fact and conclusions of
              law.

   (B)   Sunderland may move for and probably has the right to obtain a new trial as a result
              of the erroneous jury instructions.

   (C)   Sunderland may move for and probably has the right to a new trial based on the
              admission of the evidence of other copyright violations.

   (D)   Sunderland may challenge the factual sufficiency of the evidence for the first time
              in a motion for new trial.

111.   If Sunderland attempted to raise the factual sufficiency of the evidence for the first time
        in the court of appeals, what result?

ANSWER:

112.   Under the same facts as in question 110, assume that the jury returns a defense verdict
        for Sunderland. Which of the following statements is most accurate?

   (A)   Clark may move for a new trial, but cannot move for judgment as a matter of law
              because he had the burden of proof on the whole case.

   (B)   Clark can move for a judgment on the basis that the jury's verdict is against the
              great weight and preponderance of the credible evidence and is clearly wrong.

   (C)   Clark may combine a motion for new trial with a motion for judgment as a matter
              of law even though these remedies are inconsistent with each other.

   (D)   None of the above.

113. What if the verdict loser has not made a proper motion for judgment as a matter of law "at the close of all of the evidence," but does make a proper challenge to the verdict (based on answers to special interrogatories) by filing a motion for new trial challenging the sufficiency of the evidence to support the jury's $1,000,000 damages award, no later than 10 days after entry of judgment? What can a reviewing court do on appeal if the trial judge overrules the motion for new trial?

ANSWER:

114. Ace Pickles (Ace) brought suit against Duke Power Co. (Duke) for damages based on a complaint that Duke had failed to promote Ace in violation of Ace's rights to equal employment opportunity under the Civil Rights Act of 1964. After Duke was served with the summons and complaint, it failed to answer and Ace obtained a default judgment against it for $100,000 based on Ace's damages allegations concerning lost income and his false affidavit concerning the differential between his current wages and the wages that he would have earned, if he had been promoted. The clerk entered the $100,000 judgment. With respect to the default judgment:

   (A) If Duke learns of the entry of judgment within ten days, Duke should move for a new trial because it was improper for the clerk to enter the default judgment.

   (B) If Duke learns of the judgment more than 10 days after its entry, Duke should move to have the default set aside in accordance with Rule 60(b) on the basis of its excusable neglect.

   (C) Regardless of when Duke learns of the judgment, the trial court should set it aside because a judgment based on false testimony is absolutely void.

   (D) (A) and (B) are both correct.

115. If less than one year has elapsed from the date that the $100,000 default judgment was entered against Duke, under what circumstances can Duke attack the judgment in the trial court?

ANSWER:

116. Four years after a take-nothing judgment became final in a diversity case, Molly obtains very clear proof that Mike deliberately withheld documents that would have defeated Mike's affirmative defense, which was the basis of the trial court's summary judgment against Molly. The documents were definitively covered by a request for production sent by Molly to Mike. Under these circumstances what would be Molly's most likely avenue for setting aside the judgment?

ANSWER:

117. Tom, from Texas, wants to sue Mark, from Mississippi, and Acme Corp., an Alabama corporation with its principal place of business in Texas, for $100,000 alleging breach of contract. Can Tom properly file his suit in federal court?

   (A) Yes. There is diversity of citizenship because Tom and Mark are citizens of different states.

   (B) Yes. There is diversity of citizenship because Mark and Acme are citizens of different states.

   (C) Yes. There is diversity of citizenship because Tom is a citizen of a different state from Mark and Acme.

   (D) No. Tom and Acme are both citizens of Texas and the diversity statute requires that no plaintiff be a citizen of the same state as any defendant.

118. Clara and Carl, from California, want to sue Ida and Irene, both of whom are citizens of Illinois, for a $500,000 personal injury claim. Can they properly file their suit in federal court?

ANSWER:

119. Pam was born and grew up in Pennsylvania. She went away to college in Massachusetts (her parents paid her tuition), but she always returned home to work in the summers. During her senior year, her parents moved to Virginia, and she lived there between college and law school. She is now a law student at a law school in Texas. She really likes it there and has decided to take the Texas bar exam and look for a job there after graduation. Where is Pam domiciled?

   (A) Pennsylvania. This is her domicile of origin and she keeps it until she is no longer a student.

   (B) Massachusetts. She changed her domicile when she went to live there to attend college.

   (C) Virginia. Her domicile changed when her parents moved there and she went to join them.

   (D) Texas. By being present there and having the intention to stay indefinitely, she has made the state her domicile.

120. Karen has always lived in Kansas. She wants to try new experiences, and so she has decided to move to New York City. She has started getting home delivery of The New York Times and is looking for a job and an apartment. Karen loads up her Audi and begins the move to New York. While on the road, she is involved in a serious automobile accident and is hospitalized in Ohio. Where is Karen domiciled at this point?

(A) Kansas. This is her domicile of origin.

(B) Ohio. Given the extent of her injuries, she will be there indefinitely.

(C) New York. She has made the decision to make New York her home.

(D) Karen is in transit — at the moment she has no domicile.

121. Mike, from Maine, enters into a contract with Monster Motors, Inc. (also from Maine) to buy a rare and extremely valuable tricked-out sports car for $100,000. Monster Motors breaches the contract, as it has decided that Mike is not cool enough to drive such a car. Mike, in the meantime, has moved to New Hampshire, bought a house, gotten a job, and considers New Hampshire his home. Mike then sues Monster Motors in federal court in Maine. Does the court have subject matter jurisdiction?

(A) No. Mike is still a citizen of Maine for purposes of diversity jurisdiction because he lived there when the cause of action arose.

(B) Yes. Mike has changed his citizenship by moving to New Hampshire with the intent to make it his home. Diversity jurisdiction is determined as of the time the suit is filed.

(C) No. Mike has changed his citizenship for other purposes, but he cannot do so in order to confer jurisdiction on the federal courts.

(D) Yes. As long as Mike owns property in New Hampshire he is a citizen there for purposes of diversity jurisdiction.

122. Greg, from Georgia, wants to sue Frank, from Florida, for personal injuries totaling $250,000. Must he file the suit in federal court?

(A) Yes. The complete diversity requirement has been met.

(B) Yes. This is necessary to protect Frank from local prejudice.

(C) No. While federal jurisdiction would be proper, it is not exclusive.

(D) No. Only federal question jurisdiction is exclusive in the federal courts.

123. Marilyn, from Minnesota, wants to sue Brotherhood of Bisons in federal court. The Brotherhood is an unincorporated association with its headquarters in Wisconsin. More than half of its members are from Wisconsin, another quarter is from Illinois, and the rest are from a smattering of states, including Minnesota. If Marilyn were to file her suit in federal court, would the diversity requirement be met?

(A) Yes. The Brotherhood is a citizen of Wisconsin because its headquarters are there.

(B) Yes. The Brotherhood is a citizen of Wisconsin because a majority of its members are domiciled there.

(C) No. The citizenship of an unincorporated association can never form the basis of diversity jurisdiction.

(D) No. Diversity of citizenship is lacking.

124. Terry, from Tennessee, wants to file a class action on behalf of all purchasers of Cheap Computers notebook computer model A1. She alleges, as named plaintiff, that this model has a design flaw that causes the hard disk to crash without warning, losing in the process all of the owner's data. In Terry's case, this happened just before her first-year law school finals and she lost all of her notes and outlines. Her proposed class would include all U.S. purchasers in the last two years. Cheap Computers, a Montana corporation with its principal place of business in Montana, sold its notebook model A1 in college bookstores in every state in the U.S. Would a federal court have jurisdiction over Terry's suit?

(A) Yes. Terry's citizenship is diverse from Cheap Computers' citizenship.

(B) No. At least some members of the class will be citizens of Montana, thus destroying complete diversity.

(C) Yes. The diversity of citizenship requirement does not apply to class actions.

(D) Yes, but only if Terry defines the class to exclude citizens of Montana.

125. An Upside Airlines (UA) jet tragically crashed in a snowstorm while flying over Idaho, killing all 86 passengers. Upside is a Delaware corporation with its principal place of business in Utah. The passengers were citizens of Utah, Idaho, and Wyoming. Larry Lawyer represents the families of several of the passengers, including some from each state. He wants to file suit against UA in federal court. Each plaintiff has damages far in excess of $75,000. Would federal jurisdiction be proper?

(A) No. Since some of the plaintiffs are from Utah, and UA is a citizen of Utah, complete diversity of citizenship is lacking.

(B) Yes. UA is a citizen of Delaware, and so it is diverse from all of the plaintiffs.

(C) Yes. There is diversity between at least some of the plaintiffs and UA, and more than 75 people died in the same location, and the accident took place in a state different from UA's residence.

(D) No. There is only minimal diversity, and substantial parts of the accident did not take place in different states.

126. Nick, from North Carolina, wants to sue Carol, from Connecticut. Nick has two claims against Carol. One claim, for $50,000, is for breach of a contract to buy Duke basketball souvenirs. The other, for $30,000, is for breach of a separate contract to buy University of Connecticut women's basketball t-shirts. Carol took delivery of the items but has failed to pay for them. If Nick filed his suit in federal court, what would be the amount in controversy?

(A) $50,000

(B) $30,000

(C) $80,000

(D) $80,000 plus interest

127. Martha and Maude, from Maryland, want to sue David and Don, from Delaware, for personal injuries. They each claim $50,000 in damages. Would their suit satisfy the federal amount in controversy requirement?

ANSWER:

128. Tom and Ted, from Texas, jointly own an obligation against Olivia, from Oklahoma, by virtue of a promissory note signed by Olivia payable to "Tom and Ted" in the amount of $100,000. Between themselves, Tom and Ted each own a one-half interest in the $100,000 note. If Tom and Ted file suit on the obligation in federal court, what is the amount in controversy?

(A) $100,000 for Ted and Tom.

(B) $50,000 for Tom.

(C) $50,000 for Ted.

(D) $50,000 each for Ted and Tom.

129. Alice, an artist from Alabama, wants to sue Truman and Theodora, from Tennessee, on two breach of contract claims arising from two separate purchases of large oil paintings of Alabama landscapes made by Truman and Theodora while visiting Alice's gallery in Tuscaloosa. The painting purchased by Truman cost $45,000, and the painting purchased by Theodora, being somewhat smaller, cost $35,000. If Alice brings suit

against Ted and Theodora in federal court seeking to recover the purchase price of the paintings from Truman and Theodora, is there federal jurisdiction over the claims made in the action?

(A) Yes, $80,000 is the amount in controversy because separate claims against multiple defendants are aggregated and there is complete diversity of citizenship.

(B) No, the $45,000 (Truman) and $35,000 (Theodora) breach claims are not aggregated; separate claims against codefendants are not aggregated.

(C) No, because Truman and Theodora are from the same state, there is no diversity jurisdiction, regardless of the amount in controversy.

(D) Both (B) and (C) are correct.

130. Calvin, from California, is the owner of a private lake in a remote part of Alaska. Unfortunately, the lake has been polluted by two separate exploration companies, Drill Deep, Inc. and Well Bore Co., Delaware corporations having their principal places of business in Texas, that have completed oil and gas wells and separate pipelines on acreage adjacent to Calvin's lake. Calvin believes that under applicable law, each defendant could be held jointly and severally liable for the entire loss although the amount of each polluter's individual harm is approximately $50,000, based on evidence concerning the amount of pollution each company added to the lake. If Calvin sues both Drill Deep, Inc. and Well Bore Co. in federal court, what is the amount in controversy?

(A) $50,000, because the claims cannot be aggregated.

(B) $100,000 if Calvin claims that Drill Deep, Inc. and Well Bore Co. are jointly and severally liable and applicable law could support joint and several liability against both defendants.

(C) $50,000, even if it ultimately is determined that the defendants are jointly and severally liable. Each will end up paying $50,000 unless one is insolvent.

(D) $100,000, but only if it is established at trial that both defendants are jointly and severally liable.

131. Susan, from South Carolina, wants to sue Nate, from North Carolina. Susan owns a beachfront lot which, but for Nate's erection of an unsightly shack on the beach, would be worth $250,000. With the shack (and its associated squatters) the land is worth only $150,000. It would cost Nate about $300 to have the shack torn down and hauled away. Susan wants to sue for an injunction ordering Nate to remove the shack. What would be the amount in controversy?

(A) $250,000

(B) $100,000

(C) $300

(D) There is no amount in controversy in injunction cases.

132. Laurel, from Louisiana, sues Olivia, from Oklahoma, for $40,000 for damages from a car wreck. Olivia files a counterclaim for $55,000 for her own damages in the same wreck. Is the amount in controversy requirement satisfied?

(A) No. The counterclaim is not counted in determining the amount in controversy.

(B) Yes. This is a compulsory counterclaim and so it is counted in determining the amount in controversy.

(C) No. The amount in controversy would be $15,000, the difference in value between the two claims.

(D) Yes. Counterclaims are always counted in determining the amount in controversy.

133. Naomi, from North Dakota, sues Sherry, from South Dakota, for breach of a $15,000 contract. Naomi is extremely annoyed by the breach, which she thinks was spiteful, and so she also includes a claim for $100,000 in punitive damages. Under the applicable state law, punitive damages cannot be recovered in cases based on contract. Is the amount in controversy requirement satisfied?

(A) No. Damage claims that are invalid on their face cannot be included in computing the amount in controversy, leaving only the $15,000 claim.

(B) No. It is extremely unlikely that a jury would award Naomi punitive damages of that size, leaving the total probable damages less than $75,000.

(C) Yes. Damages based on contract and tort theories against a single defendant should be combined in computing the amount in controversy.

(D) Yes. Because the $100,000 claim is sufficient by itself, it does not matter whether you can also add the $15,000.

134. Romeo and Juliet were married for ten years, and their marital domicile was New Jersey. Sadly, their marriage missed that spark of excitement that came from the family feud, and so they decided to divorce. Romeo moved to Rhode Island, where he had better job prospects. The marital estate is worth more than $100,000. Romeo wants to file suit for divorce in federal court. Would that be proper?

(A) No. Romeo and Juliet are both domiciled in New Jersey so there is no diversity of citizenship.

(B) Yes. The size of their marital estate satisfies the amount in controversy requirement.

(C) No. The size of the marital estate, when halved, does not satisfy the amount in controversy requirement, making each spouse's claim too small.

(D) No. This case does not fall within federal jurisdiction.

135. Heather started a new business selling Miracle Jeans. These jeans utilized a scientific breakthrough and guaranteed every wearer would look ten pounds thinner. BlueCloth

Ltd. contracted to supply Heather with all her denim needs. Unfortunately, BlueCloth breached its contract and so Heather was unable to fill her orders on time, and many customers cancelled. The delay also decreased the value of Heather's big media campaign launching her new business. Heather sued BlueCloth in federal court, seeking $500,000 in lost profits. BlueCloth filed a motion to dismiss for lack of subject matter jurisdiction, arguing that a new business such as Heather's will not be able to prove lost profits with sufficient certainty. How should the court rule on BlueCloth's motion?

ANSWER:

136. When Officer Krupke arrested Tony, a scuffle ensued. Tony believes that Krupke used excessive force in making the arrest. He wants to sue Krupke for violating his federal constitutional rights, but his injuries amount to only about $2,000 worth of medical bills and a sore jaw. Both Tony and Krupke are citizens of New York. Can Tony file his case in federal court?

(A) No. The amount in controversy is insufficient.

(B) No. There is no diversity of citizenship.

(C) No. The suit lacks both diversity and a sufficient amount in controversy.

(D) Yes. The suit would be proper under federal question jurisdiction.

137. Tony has a low opinion of federal courts. Could he file his case in state court instead?

(A) No. The federal courts have exclusive jurisdiction over federal questions.

(B) No. The federal courts have exclusive jurisdiction over federal questions based on constitutional rights.

(C) Yes. State and federal courts have concurrent jurisdiction over most federal questions, including this one.

(D) Yes, but only if Tony also joins a state law claim for battery.

138. News parody journal "The Potatoe" ran a story about a former Secretary of Defense, still a prominent national figure, suggesting that he had a personal financial stake in companies that repair infrastructure in the aftermath of U.S. wars. The Secretary wants to sue "The Potatoe" for libel under state tort law. He is aware that "The Potatoe" will assert its constitutional free press rights under the First Amendment in order to force proof of malice. Because the Constitution will play a key role in the case, the Secretary would like to file the case in federal court. Will the federal court have subject matter jurisdiction?

(A) Yes. The federal courts have a clear interest in consistent interpretation of the Constitution.

(B) Yes. An issue of federal law will inevitably be determined in the case.

(C) No. The First Amendment issue is merely a defense and therefore does not create federal question jurisdiction.

(D) No, unless the Secretary anticipates the constitutional defense by including it in his complaint.

139. Polly, from Paris, Texas, purchased some diet pills from her pharmacy because she wanted to lose a few pounds. Instead, the pills increased her blood pressure and caused her to suffer a cerebral stroke. Polly has sued the manufacturer, Megadrugs, Inc., for damages in a products liability action based on a common law negligence *per se* claim. Federal law is invoked in her complaint which rests in part on her claim that the pills were sold in violation of the Federal Food, Drug, and Cosmetic Act (FDCA). Specifically, the federal act is one of the bases for negligence *per se* liability under Polly's pleading. Is there a basis for federal question jurisdiction under these circumstances?

(A) No, the claim is a state law products liability claim, not one created by federal law. The FDCA does not provide consumers an express or implied federal right of action. Allowing federal jurisdiction over negligence *per se* claims premised in federal statutes would greatly expand federal question jurisdiction, upsetting the allocation of cases between state and federal courts.

(B) Yes, the FDCA violation is alleged, and thereby has been made an ingredient or element of the plaintiff's claim which rests in part on federal law.

(C) No, federal question jurisdiction requires the claim to be created by a federal statute or based on a recognized federal law claim grounded on a violation of Constitutional rights.

(D) Yes, federal law is a central issue in the case.

140. Hamlet sues Ivy University for breach of contract. He claims that the university wrongfully discontinued a program in Paranormal Studies before he could graduate with his P.S. degree. Hamlet has also included a claim for breach by Ivy of his right to an A average, which Hamlet believes arises out of the Privileges and Immunities Clause of the U.S. Constitution. Based on the latter claim, Hamlet has filed his case in federal court. Does the court have jurisdiction?

(A) Yes. Although his federal claim may be somewhat sketchy, Hamlet has pleaded it in good faith.

(B) Yes. Decisions about subject matter jurisdiction must be based on the issues pleaded and not on the merits.

(C) No. A claim such as Hamlet's is wholly insubstantial and frivolous and therefore cannot confer jurisdiction on the federal courts.

(D) No. When parties lose their federal claims, as Hamlet will lose this one, it ousts the court of jurisdiction.

Dorothy Woodman, a Texas resident, was treated by Dr. Kate Houston, a Texas cardiologist. Dr. Houston referred Dorothy to the National Clinic, which is located in Rochester, Minnesota, for heart bypass surgery by Dr. Jeffrey Heart. Dr. Heart is an employee of the National Clinic. Following surgery, Dorothy spent ten days at the National Clinic before being discharged to return to Texas. During this post-operative time, Dorothy noticed that the fairly large incision on her chest kept getting redder and more tender to the touch. Dr. Heart assured her that it was nothing. Following Dorothy's return to Texas, the incision remained very red and Dorothy developed a slight fever. She immediately contacted Dr. Houston, who examined her and assured her that it was just a slight infection at the incision site, prescribed a mild antibiotic, and sent Dorothy home. The redness continued to get worse, Dorothy's fever increased, and she began experiencing terrible chest pain. She returned to Dr. Houston, who ran some tests and determined that Dorothy was suffering from a fairly advanced infection of the sternum (a large bone in the chest which must be cut through in order to reach the heart). Dorothy was confined to bed for eight weeks and was administered massive doses of IV antibiotics. Dorothy believes that had the infection been prevented or caught earlier, either by Dr. Heart or Dr. Houston, this treatment would not have been necessary and Dorothy would have been spared significant pain and suffering and the possibility of permanent impairment.

141.   Dorothy sued the National Clinic in federal court. She alleges that the Clinic and its agent, Dr. Heart, were negligent in treating Dorothy and that this negligence caused her harm in the amount of $5 million. (You may assume that National Clinic would be liable for Heart's negligence, if any.) National Clinic is a Minnesota corporation with its principal place of business in Minnesota. The Clinic takes the position that it was Dr. Houston's fault that Dorothy Woodman suffered serious consequences from her infection of the sternum. The Clinic therefore added Dr. Houston to the lawsuit. The Clinic says that if it is found liable then Dr. Houston should have to pay the judgment. Does the federal court have jurisdiction over these claims?

(A)   The court has jurisdiction over Dorothy's claim against the Clinic because there is complete diversity and a sufficient amount in controversy. It does not have jurisdiction over the Clinic's claim against Houston, because Houston and Dorothy are both Texas citizens.

(B)   The court has jurisdiction over Dorothy's claim against the Clinic based on diversity and amount in controversy. It also has jurisdiction over the Clinic's claim against Houston, because it arises out of a common nucleus of operative fact with Dorothy's claim against the Clinic.

(C)   The court has lost whatever jurisdiction it might have had over these claims because of the lack of diversity of citizenship between Dorothy and Houston.

(D) The court has jurisdiction over both claims, because in both cases there is diversity of citizenship between the parties and a sufficient amount in controversy.

142. The Clinic learned that Woodman has also taken extra-legal steps in her unhappiness. She has taken a computer class and learned to create a website of her own. Using that knowledge, she launched Stop The Clinic, at www.heartattack.com. This website contains allegations of various acts of malpractice by Clinic doctors (including Dorothy's experience), provides a chat room for people to share bad Clinic experiences, and has an e-mail based newsletter that sends direct mailings to doctors, discouraging them from referring cases to the Clinic. The Clinic is not thrilled about these activities. Although the Clinic's reputation is secure enough to survive Woodman's attack, her claims have cost the Clinic at least two patients. The Clinic has therefore filed a claim against Woodman for commercial disparagement (a corporate version of libel) in the amount of $50,000. Does the court have jurisdiction over this claim?

(A) Yes, because the court always has jurisdiction over counterclaims.

(B) No, because the amount in controversy is insufficient.

(C) Yes, because the Clinic's claim is not a claim made by a plaintiff.

(D) No, because the Clinic's claim is not part of the same case or controversy as Woodman's claim against the clinic.

143. Woodman's husband Cyrus, a law professor at SMU in Dallas, Texas, also has a legally cognizable claim against National Clinic for loss of society and companionship under either Texas or Minnesota law. Because Cyrus and Dorothy don't live together and don't spend much time together, there is a real question whether Cyrus' claim exceeds $75,000, exclusive of interest and costs. Does the federal court have supplemental jurisdiction over Cyrus' claim?

(A) Yes, but only if Cyrus joins Dorothy as an original plaintiff under Rule 20.

(B) Yes, even if Cyrus intervenes in the action brought by Dorothy against National Clinic.

(C) Yes, Cyrus is a person needed for just adjudication under Rule 19.

(D) No, Cyrus' claim is not part of the same constitutional case as Dorothy's claim.

144. Consider the same facts as the preceding question, except that Cyrus had established a new domicile in Minnesota by taking a permanent job at one of the three Minnesota law schools before becoming a plaintiff in the lawsuit brought by Dorothy against National Clinic. Would the federal court have supplemental jurisdiction over Cyrus' claim?

ANSWER:

145. National Clinic is considering a third party claim against Dr. Heart for indemnity. There is no amount in controversy problem in either case, but Dr. Heart's citizenship in Minnesota appears to be inconsistent with the jurisdictional requirements of Section 1332. Does supplemental jurisdiction exist with respect to the potential indemnity claim against Dr. Heart?

    (A) No, although the indemnity claim is so related to the Woodman claim that both claims are part of the same constitutional case, Section 1367(b)'s first exception prohibits the cross-action.

    (B) No, the indemnity claim is a different case or controversy from the Woodman claim.

    (C) Yes, 1367(a) permits the claim and 1367(b) does not prohibit it, even though the Clinic and Dr. Heart are citizens of Minnesota.

    (D) No, the contamination theory created by the majority opinion in *Exxon* prohibits supplemental jurisdiction under these circumstances.

146. Woodman never paid Dr. Houston's bill, because she believed that Houston committed malpractice and deserved no payment. Dr. Houston has therefore added a claim against Woodman for her unpaid medical bill for this treatment. That claim is for $10,000. Does the court have jurisdiction over Houston's claim against Woodman?

    (A) Yes, because Rule 14 allows third-party defendants to bring claims against plaintiffs.

    (B) No, because Houston and Woodman are both from Texas and the claim is too small.

    (C) Yes, because Houston's claim is not a claim made by a plaintiff.

    (D) No, because Houston's claim is not part of the same case or controversy as Woodman's claim against the Clinic.

147. Assume that the court has decided to allow Houston's claim against Woodman. Woodman has filed a motion for leave to amend her complaint to add a claim. She was not going to sue Dr. Houston originally, since she kind of likes the doctor's bedside manner, but now that Houston is in the lawsuit, Dorothy has gone ahead and asked to amend the complaint to include a malpractice claim against Houston. She seeks the same $5 million as in the original lawsuit. If the court wanted to grant leave to amend, would it have subject matter jurisdiction over Woodman's claim?

ANSWER: (Two Paragraphs)

One spring, *Today in America* ("TA") did a show about sheets — more specifically, a show about thread count. The National Textile Association defines thread count as the number of threads running both horizontally and vertically in a square inch of fabric. For example, a sheet with a thread count of 400 would have 200 threads running vertically and 200 threads running horizontally. The higher the thread count, the more expensive the sheets, because the higher thread count sheets are softer and more comfortable for sleeping. The report on TA disclosed that a number of national retailers were knowingly selling sheets with much lower thread counts than the packages listed.

The following persons and entities have claims they would like to bring:

- Sleep Hotels, Inc. (a Texas corporation with its principal place of business in Texas) has a claim against Mall Mart (an Arkansas corporation with its principal place of business in Arkansas), claiming fraud, breach of warranty, and violations of the Texas Deceptive Trade Practices Act. Sleep Hotels has for years bought all of the sheets for its national chain of hotels from Mall Mart, paying extra so that it could advertise itself as providing a superior night's sleep to its customers. It seeks damages in the amount of $80,000.

- Alice, a resident of Texas, bought 4 sets of sheets labeled 1,000 thread count when in fact they were only 500 thread count. She seeks $200 in damages.

- Barbara, a resident of Arkansas, bought about 10 sets of sheets during the past three years, labeled as 600 thread count when they were actually 300 (she always buys sheets as wedding presents, and seeks $500 in damages).

148. Suppose Sleep Hotels and Alice join as plaintiffs to sue Mall Mart. Would the federal court have jurisdiction over the case?

    (A) Yes. Sleep Hotels (a Texas citizen) is diverse from Mall Mart (an Arkansas citizen) and has a sufficient amount in controversy, and there is supplemental jurisdiction over Alice's claim even though on its own it would be too small.

    (B) No. Alice's claim is much too small, and so it is a claim by a plaintiff inconsistent with the requirements of Section 1332.

    (C) No. Alice's claim is precluded by Section 1367(b).

    (D) Yes. The aggregated claims of Sleep Hotels and Alice exceed $75,000.

149. Suppose Sleep Hotels and Barbara join as plaintiffs to sue Mall Mart. Would the federal court have jurisdiction over the case?

(A) Yes. Sleep Hotels is diverse from Mall Mart and has a sufficient amount in controversy, and there is supplemental jurisdiction over Barbara's claim even though on its own it would lack diversity of citizenship.

(B) No. Barbara and Mall Mart are both Arkansas citizens, and so it contaminates Sleep Hotels' claim and eliminates jurisdiction.

(C) No. Sleep Hotels' claim and Barbara's claim are part of the same constitutional case or controversy, but Section 1376(b) removes jurisdiction over Barbara's claim.

(D) Yes. Minimal diversity is all that Article III requires.

150. Suppose Sleep Hotels and Alice sue Mall Mart and SheetSheet Company, Mall Mart's supplier (an Arizona corporation with its principal place of business in Tennessee). Can they file their lawsuit in federal court?

ANSWER:

151. Claire, another purchaser of mislabeled sheets, filed a class action against Bed Bath & Barrels ("BBB") (a New York corporation with its principal place of business in New York) in federal court in New Jersey, Claire's home state. Claire's complaint describes the class as "all New York and New Jersey citizens who have purchased mislabeled sheets from one of BBB's New York stores." Her complaint estimates that there are about 10,000 class members (7,000 from New York), each of whom overpaid about $55 for sheets. Under applicable state law, Claire would be entitled to recover both her $55 in damages and reasonable attorney's fees. Assume that, given the complexity of the case, the complaint's request for $150,000 in attorney's fees is a reasonable one. Does the federal court have jurisdiction over this class action?

(A) No. Claire's claim is OK, but the class members' claims are too small for federal court.

(B) No. Claire's claim is OK, but some of the class members are from the same state as the defendant and so the lack of complete diversity eliminates jurisdiction.

(C) Yes. The federal court would have jurisdiction over this case under the Class Action Fairness Act, and so complete diversity is not required.

(D) Yes. Claire is diverse from BBB and her claim is large enough. The court has supplemental jurisdiction over the class members' smaller claims.

152. Dana bought mislabeled sheets from Cotton and Things ("CT"), a Connecticut corporation with its principal place of business in Connecticut. She filed a class action against

CT in federal court in Connecticut, Dana's home state. Dana's complaint describes the class as "all Connecticut, Massachusetts, Rhode Island, Vermont, New Hampshire, and Maine citizens who have purchased mislabeled sheets from one of CT's New England stores." Her complaint estimates that there are about 100,000 class members (75,000 from Connecticut, with others scattered throughout Massachusetts, Rhode Island, Vermont, New Hampshire, and Maine). Each class member overpaid about $55 for her sheets, as did Dana. Under applicable state law, Dana would be entitled to recover only her actual damages of $55. Does the federal court have jurisdiction over this class action?

(A)   No. Dana is the class representative, and she is from the same state as the defendant.

(B)   Yes. There is sufficient minimal diversity, there are more than one hundred class members, and the amount in controversy exceeds $5 million.

(C)   Yes. The court has supplemental jurisdiction over the class members' claims because they share a common nucleus of operative fact with Dana's claim.

(D)   No. More than two thirds of the class members and the primary defendant are from Connecticut, and the damages were incurred in Connecticut. Connecticut law is also very likely to apply.

153. Martin, from Michigan, sued his employer, Blue Hat Computers, a Delaware corporation with its principal place of business in Oregon, for wrongful discharge. He filed suit in state court in Detroit, Michigan, asking for damages of $85,000. He had his lawyer draw up the lawsuit papers on May 1, but he continued to negotiate with Blue Hat. Negotiations finally broke down on July 1. As a last ditch effort at settlement, Martin's lawyer faxed a copy of Martin's potential complaint to Blue Hat on July 2. After receiving no response, Martin had his lawyer file the case and serve Blue Hat with the summons and complaint on July 15. Blue Hat would like to remove the case to federal court. When is/was its deadline for removal?

    (A) May 31

    (B) August 1

    (C) August 14

    (D) This is a trick question. There is no deadline for removal.

154. Assume the same facts as in the question above, except that Martin files suit in state court in Oregon. Is the case removable?

    (A) Yes, it can be removed at any time.

    (B) Yes, it can be removed because the diversity of citizenship and amount in controversy make it a case that could have been brought in federal court.

    (C) Yes, if Blue Hat files the proper papers by the removal deadline.

    (D) No. This case is not removable.

155. Assume the same controversy between Martin and Blue Hat with the following changes: Blue Hat is a Michigan corporation with its principal place of business in Oregon, and Martin adds a claim that he was discriminated against based on his age in violation of the federal Age Discrimination in Employment Act (ADEA). The case is filed in state court in Michigan. Is the case removable?

    (A) No. Resident defendants cannot remove cases to federal court.

    (B) No. Blue Hat is a citizen of both Michigan and Oregon, and since Martin is a citizen of Michigan complete diversity is lacking.

    (C) Yes. This case contains a federal question.

    (D) Yes. The state of incorporation is not considered in deciding whether a corporate defendant is a citizen of the state where the action is brought.

156. Assume that *Martin v. Blue Hat* is pending in state court in Detroit, and that Blue Hat is a citizen of Delaware and Oregon. To what federal district court can the case be removed?

(A) The Eastern District of Michigan (in which Detroit is located).

(B) Any judicial district in Michigan.

(C) Oregon

(D) Blue Hat can choose any of these districts.

157. *Martin v. Blue Hat* has been pending in state court in Oregon for over a year and contains only Martin's state law breach of contract claim. Eighteen months after filing suit, Martin amends his complaint to add the ADEA claim. Can Blue Hat remove the case to federal court?

(A) No. His thirty days to remove ran out a long time ago.

(B) No. Removability is based on the status of the lawsuit when it is first filed.

(C) Yes, if Blue Hat files the proper removal papers within thirty days after it receives a copy of the amended complaint.

(D) No. Federal question cases must be removed within one year of commencement of the action.

158. Assume that Martin sued Blue Hat, a Delaware corporation with its principal place of business in Oregon, for $85,000 for breach of contract in state court in Michigan. Martin also sued Marty, the former boss who fired him. Marty is a citizen of Michigan. Eighteen months after the suit was filed, Martin amended his complaint to drop the claim against Marty. Can Blue Hat remove the case to federal court now?

(A) Yes. With Marty removed, there is complete diversity, sufficient amount in controversy, and no in-state defendant.

(B) Yes, if Blue Hat files the proper removal papers within thirty days after it receives a copy of the amended complaint.

(C) No. Removability is based on the status of the lawsuit when it is first filed.

(D) No. Diversity jurisdiction cases must be removed within one year of commencement of the action.

159. Martin sued Blue Hat in state court in Michigan, and Blue Hat timely removed the case to federal court. Martin has noticed, however, that Blue Hat failed to sign its notice of removal and failed to attach the required pleadings. Can Martin get the case sent back to state court?

(A) Yes, if he files the motion to remand within thirty days of the filing of the notice of removal.

(B) Yes, if he files the motion to remand within 30 days of when he received the notice of removal.

(C) Yes. Because subject matter jurisdiction cannot be waived, Martin can file a motion to remand at any time.

(D) No. Unless there is a jurisdictional flaw in the removal process, the case will stay in federal court.

160. Martin sued Blue Hat in state court in Michigan, and Blue Hat properly removed the case to federal court. Martin would far rather be in state court, so he forms a plan to destroy complete diversity by adding his former boss, Marty, as an additional defendant. Marty is a citizen of Michigan. Martin files a motion for leave to amend his complaint to add Marty as an additional defendant. What are the court's options in ruling on Martin's motion?

ANSWER:

161. *In personam* jurisdiction:

    (A)   requires the presence of the defendant's property in the forum state.

    (B)   gives the court the power to impose personal liability on the defendant in favor of the plaintiff.

    (C)   requires the presence of the defendant in the forum state.

    (D)   gives the court the power to enter a judgment involving only the property that is the subject of the dispute.

162. *In rem* jurisdiction:

    (A)   allows the court to resolve the interest of all the world in the property that is the subject of the dispute.

    (B)   permits the court to enter judgment to the full extent of the wrong done to the plaintiff.

    (C)   allows only a judgment involving the parties' interest in the property that is the subject of the dispute.

    (D)   requires jurisdiction over the people claiming an interest in the property in order to bind them to the outcome of the litigation.

163. *Quasi in rem* jurisdiction:

    (A)   may allow a state to take jurisdiction to enforce a foreign judgment against the defendant's property, present in the state, that is unrelated to the claim that led to the foreign judgment.

    (B)   must also meet the due process requirements of *in personam* jurisdiction.

    (C)   allows the court to resolve the interest of all the world in the property that is the subject of the dispute.

    (D)   (A) and (B) are both correct.

164. Goneril and Regan enter into a contract to purchase a year's supply of heating oil from Lear Energy. The contract provides, in paragraph 25: "Any suit to collect overdue payments under this contract may be filed in any state or federal court in the State of New York." Goneril and Regan reside in Michigan, and Lear is a New York corporation with its principal place of business in New York, but it does business in a number of states and negotiated the contract with Goneril and Regan and delivered their oil from Lear's Michigan office. Goneril and Regan, who are not particularly honest, take the oil but fail to pay. Lear wants to sue them in New York. Are Goneril and Regan subject to personal jurisdiction on this claim in a New York court?

(A) No. Goneril and Regan are not domiciled in New York.

(B) Yes. This suit is about the "status" of the contract, and so jurisdiction over Lear is sufficient.

(C) Yes. Goneril and Regan have consented to jurisdiction in New York, which has some connection to the underlying dispute.

(D) No. Goneril and Regan lack sufficient contacts with New York to be sued there.

165. Goneril and her husband Albany are unhappily married and totally broke. Albany moves out of the family home and moves to Idaho to start a new life. About five years later, things are looking up for Goneril, and she wants a divorce. As the couple has no children and no assets, the divorce itself is all she needs. Can she get an enforceable divorce by filing in her home state of Michigan?

(A) Yes. Cases involving personal status are a traditional exception to the requirement that a court have personal jurisdiction over the defendant.

(B) Yes. Because Michigan was once Albany's home, it will always have personal jurisdiction over him.

(C) No. Albany has been gone too long for Michigan still to have sufficient minimum contacts with him to justify personal jurisdiction.

(D) No. Albany has not consented to jurisdiction in Michigan.

166. Cordelia, disinherited by her family, has moved to Iowa and bought a farm. She is very happy in her new home. Unfortunately, she has a difficult former business partner, Edmund, who believes that Cordelia owes him money from a failed venture in Dover, Delaware. Edmund has sued Cordelia in Iowa. At the time, Cordelia was out of state attempting a family reconciliation back in Michigan, and so Edmund arranged for

Cordelia to be served with process while she was there. Assuming this is permitted under Iowa's long-arm statute, may Iowa constitutionally assert jurisdiction over Cordelia?

(A) No. Defendants must be served with process in the forum state to be subject to personal jurisdiction.

(B) No. The transaction that is the subject of Edmund's suit has nothing to do with Iowa.

(C) Yes. Cordelia has enough contacts with Iowa to allow specific jurisdiction.

(D) Yes. Courts of human defendants' home states traditionally have personal jurisdiction over them in all cases.

167. Kent makes his home in Kansas, but he and his family have for years spent two weeks of each summer in a cabin in Estes Park, Colorado. Kent purchased gardening supplies for his Kansas home from A Thousand Acres, a mail order company headquartered in Phoenix, Arizona. Kent has refused to pay the bill, and the company has sued him in Colorado, as that is far more convenient. Knowing that Kent would be in Colorado on vacation, the company had its process server hand the lawsuit papers to Kent at the summer cabin. Does Colorado have personal jurisdiction over Kent in this case?

(A) Yes. Coming to Colorado every summer creates sufficient contacts to justify jurisdiction.

(B) Yes. Service within the state under these facts makes jurisdiction proper.

(C) No. Kent's contacts with Colorado are not related to the company's claim.

(D) No. Transient jurisdiction is no longer constitutional.

168. Under *Pennoyer v. Neff*, 95 U.S. 714 (1877), a state could assert *in personam* jurisdiction over an individual defendant who had not consented to jurisdiction only:

   (A) when the defendant was a citizen of the state.

   (B) when the defendant owned property located in the state.

   (C) when the defendant was served with process while physically present in the state.

   (D) when the judgment could be fully enforced against assets present in the state.

169. Which of the following developments helped to erode the mechanical application of the "presence" test?

   (A) The difficulty in determining where a corporation was "present."

   (B) The enactment of state statutes creating presumed consent to be sued in the state.

   (C) Changes in the national economy involving an ever greater volume of interstate commerce.

   (D) All of the above.

170. Specific jurisdiction gives the court the power to adjudicate:

   (A) causes of action arising out of or related to the defendant's contacts with the forum state.

   (B) all disputes between the plaintiff and the defendant, even if they are not related to the defendant's contacts with the forum state.

   (C) all disputes described with sufficient particularity in the plaintiff's complaint.

   (D) any cause of action between the plaintiff and the defendant, as long as one of the plaintiff's claims arises out of or relates to the defendant's contacts with the forum state.

171. Which of the following best describes the constitutional test for specific jurisdiction?

   (A) The defendant must be a resident of the forum state.

   (B) The defendant must purposefully establish a sufficient level of contacts with the forum state, and the forum's taking jurisdiction must not offend traditional notions of fair play and substantial justice.

   (C) The defendant's contacts with the forum state must be continuous and systematic.

   (D) The defendant must be present in the forum state.

172. A court has general jurisdiction over a defendant when:

    (A) the defendant does business in the forum state.

    (B) the defendant has sufficient purposeful contacts with the forum state so as not to offend traditional notions of fair play and substantial justice.

    (C) the defendant's contacts with the forum state are substantial and continuous and systematic.

    (D) the plaintiff is a resident of the forum state.

173. General jurisdiction over a defendant gives the court the power to adjudicate:

    (A) only causes of action arising out of or related to the defendant's contacts with the forum state.

    (B) all claims against the defendant, even if they are not related to the defendant's contacts with the forum state.

    (C) only causes of action involving the defendant's use of the forum as a substitute headquarters when some crisis prevents doing business in its normal location.

    (D) all claims against all the defendants properly joined in the case.

For all of the following questions, assume that the forum state has a long-arm statute that would authorize jurisdiction over the defendant.

174. Sydney Carton traveled to Paris, Texas, on vacation. While shopping at a local department store there, (a "mom and pop" establishment that has never advertised outside of Texas) he was wrongfully detained and searched. Back home in Virginia, Carton filed suit against the store. Can a Virginia court constitutionally assert jurisdiction over Carton's claim against the Texas store?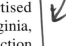

    (A) Yes. The store intentionally injured a resident of Virginia.

    (B) Yes. Plaintiffs can always file suit in their home states.

    (C) No. The store's contacts with Virginia are insufficient to permit the assertion of jurisdiction.

    (D) Yes. The store profited from selling its products to a Virginian.

175. Carton learned that the store, on several occasions in the past, sold knives and shipped them to residents of Virginia who had called the store and ordered the knives. Now can a Virginia court constitutionally assert jurisdiction over the store in Carton's case?

    (A) Yes. The store intentionally injured a resident of Virginia.

    (B) Yes. The store now has sufficient contacts with Virginia to permit the assertion of jurisdiction.

    (C) No. The store's contacts with Virginia are unrelated to Carton's claim.

    (D) Yes. The store profited from selling its products to a Virginian.

176. DeFarge, Inc. sells knitting needles in every state in the United States. It has sold 5,000 pairs of needles to customers in California over the past three years. At least one pair was defective, and it broke and injured Lucie Manette while she was knitting. Lucie, a resident of California, would like to sue DeFarge there. Can California constitutionally assert jurisdiction over DeFarge?

    (A) Yes. DeFarge has purposefully done business in California and should have anticipated being haled into court there.

    (B) Yes. By selling its products in California, DeFarge has consented to jurisdiction there.

    (C) No. DeFarge does not have continuous and systematic contacts with California.

(D) No. If the customers initiated the orders, the mere sale of goods in the forum state will not be sufficient to make the assertion of jurisdiction constitutional.

177. DeFarge also sells another product, the Super Chopper. This is a large, expensive machine used in manufacturing plants. It advertises the Super Chopper in nationally-circulated trade publications. After a DeFarge salesman made a persuasive presentation on a swing through Maine, DeFarge sold one Super Chopper to a customer there. Because of a flaw in the chopper's safety system, it cut off the hand of Jarvis Lorry, an employee of the customer. Lorry wants to sue DeFarge in Maine for his personal injuries. Can a Maine court constitutionally assert jurisdiction over Lorry's claim against DeFarge?

(A) No. This isolated transaction is not enough to be the basis for personal jurisdiction.

(B) Yes. DeFarge reached out to Maine by advertising there.

(C) No. DeFarge's customer could sue in Maine, but Lorry cannot.

(D) Yes. Lorry's cause of action arises directly out of DeFarge's contacts with Maine, which were purposeful and from which DeFarge earned profits.

178. Catherine grew up in Kentucky, where she lived for some time. While there, Catherine purchased a stepladder from Hindley's Hardware, a local store. Fleeing an unhappy love life, Catherine moved to Tennessee. After the move, she went back to Kentucky for a visit, chatted with the owner of Hindley's about her new life in Tennessee, and bought a chain saw. Back in Tennessee, Catherine was injured while standing on the ladder attempting to trim a tree with the chain saw. The stepladder collapsed and the saw cut her badly. Catherine would like to sue Hindley's in Tennessee. Could Tennessee constitutionally assert jurisdiction over Hindley's?

(A) Yes. Hindley's could foresee that its customer might take the stepladder to another state, including Tennessee.

(B) Yes. Hindley's knowingly sold the saw to a resident of Tennessee.

(C) No. Hindley's did not seek to serve residents of Tennessee.

(D) No. There is not enough profit in a saw and a stepladder to justify jurisdiction over Hindley's.

179. Catherine was quite a public figure in her day, and her injuries and litigation have caught the attention of the media. The Atlanta Journal printed a story about Catherine, dredging up all the old scandals with Heathcliff, and claiming that Catherine has become an alcoholic and that's why she is hiding out in Tennessee and that's why she fell. The Journal sells 95% of its papers within the state of Georgia, but it has about a dozen subscribers in each state in the southeast, including Tennessee. Catherine wants to sue the Journal, but even more she wants to sue Nelly Dean, the author of the story, for writing a story full of intentional lies. Nelly has never been to Tennessee herself, but she talked to Tennessee sources on the phone when researching the story and sent a

photographer there to try to get a picture of the no-longer-glamorous Catherine. As Catherine is still somewhat immobilized by her injuries, she wants to sue Nelly in Tennessee rather than going all the way to Atlanta. Can Tennessee constitutionally assert jurisdiction over Nelly?

ANSWER:

180. Online publication "TheDirt.com" picked up the story about Catherine from the Atlanta paper, added some gossip of its own about Catherine's life in Tennessee, and published the story online. "TheDirt.com" does not really have an office *per se*. Its content is supplied by a handful of freelance reporters from around the country. The stories are uploaded to the world wide web from the personal computer of Emily Haworth, a resident of South Dakota, at which point it becomes accessible to anyone in the world with internet access. Emily has had the publication incorporated so it does exist as a legal entity. Catherine wants to sue "TheDirt.com" for intentional libel. How will the court decide whether she may constitutionally do so in Tennessee?

ANSWER:

181. Nile.com is a successful e-commerce business. It sold a computer program to Crane; sadly, the program did not quite meet the expectations created by the website, and Crane wants his money back. Crane had been at home in Washington when he discovered Nile.com's business while surfing the net, and he was in Washington when he downloaded the program. Assume that the website contained no choice of forum clause, and that other than whatever sales it might make from its website, Nile.com has no contacts with Washington. Can a court in Washington constitutionally assert jurisdiction over Crane's claim against Nile.com?

(A) Even if Nile.com's website had been purely passive (just pictures of its products), that web site makes it present in Washington and Crane can sue it there.

(B) Because Nile.com's website is extremely interactive, allowing customers to learn about merchandise and to purchase it online, Washington can assert jurisdiction over Nile.com.

(C) Because Nile.com's website is constantly available in the state of Washington, it constitutes continuous and systematic contact and justifies general jurisdiction over Nile.com, even if it never makes a sale to a resident of Washington.

(D) No, internet contacts take place only in virtual space and cannot provide the basis for contact-based jurisdiction.

182. HairCo, a Montana corporation, manufactures tiny blonde wigs that are used in the manufacture of Peppy, a doll that looks like a cheerleader. The dolls, in turn, are manufactured by ToyCo, a Missouri corporation, which distributes them in the southeastern United States. HairCo has no control whatsoever over where ToyCo chooses to sell the Peppy dolls, but it knows from payments it has received over the last ten years that ToyCo has been selling 1,000 dolls a year in South Carolina. HairCo's contract with ToyCo calls for it to be paid based on the number of dolls sold. In South Carolina, a toddler chews on the wig of a Peppy doll and suffers personal injuries. Does HairCo have enough contacts with South Carolina to constitutionally be sued there?

(A)   Under Justice O'Connor's opinion in *Asahi Metal Indus. Co. v. Superior Court*, 480 U.S. 102 (1987), HairCo's knowledge of its profits from the sale of the dolls (with wigs) would be sufficient evidence of purposeful availment.

(B)   Under Justice O'Connor's opinion in *Asahi*, HairCo would have had to take some additional action such as creating a consumer advice mechanism in South Carolina (*"Trouble with styling Peppy's hair? Call our helpline at 1-800-555-HAIR."*).

(C)   *Asahi* is irrelevant to this issue because it involved a non-U.S. defendant.

(D)   Component part manufacturers can never be sued in the states where the finished products are sold unless they control the chain of distribution.

183.   In addition to the existence of sufficient purposeful contacts, the exercise of personal jurisdiction over a defendant must be fair. Which of the following factors is considered in doing the due process fairness analysis?

(A)   whether the forum state's procedural rules resemble the Federal Rules of Civil Procedure

(B)   whether the forum state has good judges

(C)   how sincere the plaintiff seems in explaining his desire to sue there

(D)   the forum state's interest in adjudicating the dispute

184. Mining Corporation (MC) was located in West Virginia and did all of its business there. Unfortunately, after a major mine collapse, MC had to suspend its mining operations. Due to local hostility, the company's management decided to temporarily move the company headquarters to Vermont. The CFO opened a bank account in Vermont and paid all the bills there. The CEO bought a house in the mountains of Vermont, and any board meetings and management team conferences that happened after the collapse occurred there. It is unknown at this time when MC will be able to re-open the mine and move back to West Virginia. Morgan, a miner who worked for MC, was killed when the mine collapsed. His widow has moved to New Hampshire, so the possibility of suing MC in Vermont is very appealing. Could Vermont constitutionally assert jurisdiction over MC for a claim arising out of the collapse of the mine?

   (A) Yes. MC has a level of contacts with Vermont that would satisfy the Supreme Court's test in *Burger King v. Rudzewicz*, 471 U.S. 462 (1985).

   (B) Yes. MC now has continuous and systematic contacts with Vermont.

   (C) No. MC's contacts with Vermont do not involve mining.

   (D) No. Morgan's injuries did not arise out of MC's contacts with Vermont.

185. Coaster Country is an amusement park in North Dakota. Word of mouth among coaster enthusiasts is that Coaster Country has the biggest, fastest, most amazing roller coasters of any theme park in the world. For years, Coaster Country has purchased all of the food sold in the park from Acme Packing, a Texas company. Dave, a resident of New Mexico, loves roller coasters, and so he goes to Coaster Country on vacation. While there, he is injured when a coaster goes faster than planned and flies off the track. Recuperating back home in New Mexico, Dave would like to sue Coaster Country in Texas, as that is closer than North Dakota. Can a Texas court constitutionally assert jurisdiction over Coaster Country?

   (A) Yes. Coaster Country has created continuous and systematic contacts with Texas by purchasing food there over a long period of time.

   (B) Yes. Dave's cause of action is related to Coaster Country's contacts with Texas.

   (C) No. Coaster Country's contacts with Texas are insufficient to justify general jurisdiction.

   (D) No. Dave must sue either in New Mexico or in North Dakota.

186. Really Big Eggs (RBE) is a multinational corporation that owns fast food outlets throughout the United States and the world. The company believes in concentrating its management structure in a single location, however, and so despite the far flung nature of its business all company officers work in the company's Illinois headquarters. The company is also incorporated in Illinois, and Illinois has more outlets per capita than any other state in the nation. Little, a resident of Nebraska, gets salmonella while on vacation in San Diego, and she thinks she got it from undercooked eggs at an RBE outlet. Little has heard that juries in Illinois are really sympathetic. Can Illinois courts constitutionally assert jurisdiction over RBE on Little's claim that they caused her food poisoning in California?

(A)   No. RBE's contacts with Illinois are not related to Little's cause of action.

(B)   No. There is no such thing as general jurisdiction over corporations.

(C)   Yes. Although there is some question about the extent of contacts that justifies a finding of general jurisdiction over a corporation, the contacts here are enough.

(D)   Yes. Because RBE is a huge corporation it can be sued anywhere.

187. Peter sues Dan in federal court in Arizona. Dan believes that he has insufficient contacts to be sued there, and he immediately files a motion to dismiss for lack of personal jurisdiction. Assuming the court agrees with Dan, what action should it take?

(A) The court should ask Peter where he would like the case transferred.

(B) The court should dismiss the case. Peter may refile it where personal jurisdiction over Dan would be proper.

(C) The court should dismiss the case with prejudice. Peter may not refile it.

(D) The court should keep the case. By appearing, Dan has waived any objection he may have had to personal jurisdiction.

188. Paul sues Dick in federal court in Wyoming. Dick answers the complaint, and 40 days later he realizes that he may have insufficient contacts to be sued in Wyoming and files a motion to dismiss for lack of personal jurisdiction. Assuming the court agrees with Dick, what action should it take?

(A) The court should ask Paul where he would like the case transferred.

(B) The court should dismiss the case. Paul may refile it where personal jurisdiction over Dick would be proper.

(C) The court should dismiss the case with prejudice. Paul may not refile it.

(D) The court should keep the case. By answering, Dick has waived any objection he may have had to personal jurisdiction.

189. Pam sues Donna in federal court in Wisconsin. Donna is from Pennsylvania, and she does not think the Wisconsin court has the power to make her defend herself there, so she does not respond. Pam takes a default judgment against Donna. Because Donna has no assets in Wisconsin, Pam brings her Wisconsin judgment to Pennsylvania to try to collect from Donna. What defenses can Donna raise?

(A) None. When Donna failed to respond to the lawsuit she lost the right to complain about jurisdiction or defend on the merits.

(B) Donna can still complain about the Wisconsin court's lack of jurisdiction over her. If she is right, the judgment is not enforceable.

(C) Donna can still complain about the Wisconsin court's lack of jurisdiction over her. If she is wrong, then she can still assert her defense on the merits.

(D) Donna can assert her defenses on the merits, but she has lost the right to complain about personal jurisdiction by failing to make a special appearance.

190. Woolf, who resides in the Northern District of Texas (N.D. Tex.), wants to sue Austen, who resides in the Western District of Louisiana (W.D. La.), for negligence resulting in an automobile accident. The accident occurred in Oklahoma (E.D. Okla.). Where would venue be proper?

 (A) N.D. Tex.

 (B) W.D. La.

 (C) E.D. Okla.

 (D) W.D. La. or E.D. Okla.

191. Woolf (N.D. Tex.) wants to sue Austen (W.D. La.) and Bronte (E.D. La.) for violating her federal civil rights in an incident that took place in Oklahoma (E.D. Okla.). Where would venue be proper?

 (A) W.D. La., E.D. La., or M.D. La.

 (B) E.D. Okla.

 (C) W.D. La., E.D. La., M.D. La., or E.D. Okla.

 (D) W.D. La., E.D. La., or E.D. Okla.

192. Woolf (N.D. Tex.) wants to sue Austen (W.D. La.) and Bronte (E.D. La.) for theft of trade secrets. The alleged theft arose out of a series of events: (1) Austen approached Woolf in New York City (S.D.N.Y.) while Woolf was there to see a Broadway play and got access to the secret; and (2) Bronte wrongfully used the secret in her business in Hartford (D. Conn.). Aside from Louisiana, where would venue be proper?

 (A) D. Conn.

 (B) S.D.N.Y.

 (C) N.D. Tex.

 (D) D. Conn. or S.D.N.Y.

193. Dickinson (D. Mass.) wants to sue Alcott (D.N.H.) and Montgomery (D. Me.) for trespassing on Dickinson's property in Massachusetts. Where would venue be proper?

 (A) D.N.H.

 (B) D. Me.

 (C) D.N.H. or D. Me.

(D)   D. Mass.

194. Fast Ride Co. is a Delaware corporation with its principal place of business in King of Prussia, Pennsylvania. It is in the business of selling motor scooters throughout the United States and has contracted with independent regional distributors, which have separate contracts with independent retailers in many markets, including all districts and divisions in California. Lance Racer purchased a scooter in Los Angeles (C.D. Cal.) and wants to sue Fast Ride Co. for breach of warranty. Because Lance lives in San Francisco, he would like to sue Fast Ride Co. there, if possible. What are Lance's options?

    (A)   Lance can sue Fast Ride Co. in San Francisco because Fast Ride Co. is a corporation and it is subject to personal jurisdiction in any district in California.

    (B)   Lance can sue Fast Ride Co. in San Francisco because Lance resides there and Fast Ride Co. is a corporation that does business in all districts in California "sufficient to subject it to personal jurisdiction if that district were a separate state."

    (C)   Regardless of where Lance resides, Fast Ride can be sued in any district in California because its contacts are sufficient to subject it to jurisdiction in each one as if that district were a separate state.

    (D)   Lance must sue in Los Angeles.

195. Wow Chemicals is a Delaware corporation with its headquarters in Houston, Texas (S.D. Tex.). All of Wow's management team works out of the Houston office. Wow also has a manufacturing plant in Amarillo, Texas (N.D. Tex.) that manufactures the company's entire line of its best selling chemical, Titanic Chloride. It otherwise does no business in Texas. Jack Dawson (S.D. Cal.) wants to sue Wow for personal injuries he believes were caused by the company's Titanic Chloride. He has heard that the federal courts in Texas are good, so he wants to file suit there. Where would venue be proper? What if Wow Chemicals obtained a certificate of authority to transact intrastate business in Texas from the Texas Secretary of State?

ANSWER:

196. Kathy (D. Kan.) goes to England where she is involved in a three-car accident with Otis, a resident of the Northern District of Oklahoma, and Nancy, a resident of Nebraska. (All of them were confused about driving on the left.) Kathy knows that Otis and Nancy will be changing planes at Kennedy Airport in New York on their way home. Kathy therefore files suit in New York and has her process server deliver process to them at the airport. Assume that the airport is in the Eastern District of New York. Is venue proper in E.D.N.Y.?

    (A)   No. It is only proper in N.D. Okla.

    (B)   Yes. E.D.N.Y. is a place where Otis and Nancy may be found.

(C) No. E.D.N.Y. is not a judicial district in which Otis and Nancy were subject to personal jurisdiction at the time the action was commenced.

(D) Yes. E.D.N.Y. is a judicial district in which Otis and Nancy were subject to personal jurisdiction at the time the action was commenced.

197. Bloomer sued Pankhurst (D. Utah) for breach of a contract to deliver 100 widgets to Bloomer's business in Boulder (D. Colo.). Bloomer's summer home is in Cheyenne, Wyoming, and she filed her suit in the federal court in the District of Wyoming. Pankhurst knows that she is subject to personal jurisdiction in Wyoming, but she does not think this particular lawsuit should be there. What can Pankhurst do, and do you expect it to succeed?

ANSWER:

198. Wendy's husband, Peter, was killed in the crash of a private plane in Iowa. The plane was manufactured by Pepper Corp., which is headquartered in St. Louis, Missouri, where the planes are assembled (E.D. Mo.). Wendy (who lives in southern Minnesota), as Peter's surviving spouse, filed a wrongful death lawsuit against Pepper in federal court in Iowa. Pepper knows that it is subject to personal jurisdiction in Iowa, but it would rather defend at home in Missouri. What motion could Pepper file to achieve this, and what factors will the court consider?

ANSWER:

Wow Chemicals is a Delaware corporation with its principal place of business in Delaware. All of Wow's pesticide development team works out of the company's Houston office. During the 1980s, Wow manufactured, in New Jersey, a chemical designed to enhance the productivity of banana growing by eradicating a worm that otherwise destroys a sizeable portion of the banana crop. The chemical is very effective because it sterilizes the worms, making them unable to reproduce. Unfortunately, the chemical has the same effect on banana workers — they were also rendered sterile, unable to have children. Use of the chemical was banned in the United States. Wow, however, had already produced large quantities of the chemical and sold it to banana growers outside the United States, including some in Costa Rica.

Juan Alfaro was a worker on a Costa Rican banana plantation. He was 25 years old, newly married, and wanted to have many children. However, he was exposed to the chemical at work and is now medically sterile. He and a number of his coworkers filed suit against Wow in state court in Harris County, Texas. Wow removed the case to the federal district court for that area, the Southern District of Texas. Wow admits that it is subject to personal jurisdiction in Texas, but it has filed a motion to dismiss the case based on the doctrine of forum non conveniens, saying that the case would be far better handled in Costa Rica where the plaintiffs live and where they were exposed to the chemical. Alfaro opposes this motion.

199. What test should the court apply in deciding whether to dismiss Alfaro's case?

   (A) Whether the defendant resides in the Southern District of Texas.

   (B) Whether Alfaro's claim accrued in the Southern District of Texas.

   (C) Whether considerations of party and forum convenience override Alfaro's choice of forum.

   (D) Whether Costa Rica uses U.S.-style discovery in civil cases.

200. How will the judge in *Alfaro v. Wow Chemicals* probably rule on the motion to dismiss, and why?

ANSWER:

201. Roadway sued Marriott on a state-law contract claim in a Texas state court seeking contract damages based on Marriott's failure to pay Roadway for the construction of a parking lot at Marriott's new facility in Bandera, Texas. Roadway suffered a take-nothing judgment because the trial court ruled that Roadway failed to substantially perform the contract. Roadway then sued Marriott in federal court in the Western District of Texas seeking to receive the reasonable value of its construction services on a state-law *quantum meruit* (quasi contract) theory. Marriott's defense of *res judicata* in the federal court action is most likely to succeed if:

   (A) the federal courts sitting in Texas use the "same rights" approach to the definition of particular causes of action for claim preclusion purposes.

   (B) Texas follows the "transactional" approach to the definition of particular causes of action for claim preclusion purposes.

   (C) the federal Fifth Circuit, which includes the entire state of Texas, follows the "transactional approach" to the definition of particular causes of action for claim preclusion purposes.

   (D) the Fifth Circuit has embraced the "same evidence" approach to the definition of particular causes of action for claim preclusion purposes.

202. As a result of Roadway's failure to substantially perform its paving contract with Marriott, Marriott was unable to open its hotel facility in Bandera, Texas, on time and lost a substantial amount of hotel revenue that would have been earned during the two-week Bandera County Rodeo. After obtaining a favorable result in Texas state court and after the commencement of the federal action by Roadway against Marriott, Marriott counterclaimed in federal court against Roadway for breach of the paving contract seeking more than $75,000 in compensatory damages. Assuming that proper procedural steps are followed by the parties, how should the federal court dispose of the counterclaim filed by Marriott?

   (A) The trial judge should render judgment in Marriott's favor as a matter of law based on common law principles of claim preclusion.

   (B) The trial judge should render judgment in Roadway's favor as a matter of law based on common law principles of claim preclusion.

   (C) The trial judge should determine whether Texas procedural law required Marriott to file a compulsory counterclaim in the first action and, if so, render judgment as a matter of law for Roadway.

   (D) The counterclaim should be litigated to conclusion in federal court in the normal way without regard to the first action.

203. Nathaniel, while under the care of Dr. Uncas for heart trouble, was advised that he could resume his strenuous occupation of professional wrestling on a full duty — full contact — no holds barred basis. During Nathaniel's first match, in the second period, he experienced chest pains and, according to him, suffered a heart attack. Nathaniel filed a diversity action against New Jersey Health and Accident Ltd. for medical and disability benefits based on the heart attack. Upon trial before a jury, the federal judge submitted Special Interrogatory No. 1 to the jury inquiring whether Nathaniel sustained a heart attack. According to the judgment rendered, the jury found that Nathaniel had not suffered a heart attack. Nathaniel next sued Dr. Uncas in the New York Supreme Court for Suffolk County for medical malpractice, claiming that Dr. Uncas' negligence in advising him to resume wrestling proximately caused Nathaniel to suffer a heart attack. Dr. Uncas' counsel has invoked the affirmative defense of issue preclusion, sometimes known as estoppel by judgment. Does issue preclusion apply in the these circumstances?

(A) No, mutuality of estoppel is lacking.

(B) Yes, the heart attack question was actually litigated, the judgment in the first case rests on the jury's finding, and Nathaniel had a full and fair opportunity to litigate the issue.

(C) No, New Jersey Health and Accident and Dr. Uncas are not in privity with one another.

(D) (A) and (C) are both correct.

204. Henrietta brought a wrongful death action on her own behalf and as next friend of her daughter, Polly, against Wings-Are-Up, the manufacturer of a single engine airplane, claiming that a design defect and a marketing defect caused the plane to crash causing the untimely death of Henrietta's husband, Harry. The action was tried to a jury that found that the airplane was defective as designed, unreasonably dangerous, and that the defect proximately caused the crash and Harry's death. The trial judge rendered judgment on the verdict for Henrietta and Polly for $6,300,000. Thereafter, another death action was filed against Wings-Are-Up by the parents of Harry's dead co-pilot, Larry, who suffered the same fate as Harry. What effect, if any, will the judgment in the first action brought by Harry's relatives have on the second action brought in federal court by Larry's parents?

(A) The judgment in the first case will have no effect on Wings-Are-Up's liability in the federal action.

(B) Larry's parents will probably not be able to use the liability findings in the first action against Wings-Are-Up because they were not parties in the first action.

(C)   Larry's parents may be able to use the liability findings obtained in the first action against Wings-Are-Up to estop it from contesting liability in the federal case.

(D)   Larry's parents will be barred from prosecuting the second wrongful death action because it involves the same strict product liability claim against Wings-Are-Up that was the basis for the first judgment in favor of Harry's relatives. If they had knowledge of the action they could have intervened, but instead purposely bypassed the proceeding.

205. Albert took his 1957 Chevrolet Belair to Classic Cars for a tune-up. Albert accompanied Classic Cars' chief mechanic, Jones, on a road test. Jones was killed in the accident and Albert was seriously injured. Albert brought suit against Classic Cars in the Pennsylvania Court of Common Pleas for Erie County contending that Jones' negligence caused the accident. Judgment was rendered in Albert's favor based on findings of negligence and causation against Jones. Thereafter, Jones' administratrix brought suit against Albert under the Pennsylvania Wrongful Death and Survival Act in federal district court. The federal court granted Albert's motion for judgment on the grounds that any recovery would be barred by the prior finding in the first action that Jones was guilty of negligence, which was conclusive under the doctrine of collateral estoppel. This judgment is on appeal. Should it be affirmed or reversed?

(A) The judgment should be affirmed on appeal because the derivative liability of an employer for the tortious actions of an employee established the employee's privity to the employer and binds Jones' administratrix to the findings in the first case.

(B) Because Jones' administratrix had not had her day in court on the critical issues in the first action, she is not bound and the judgment should be reversed.

(C) Although Jones' administratrix may be regarded as in privity with the decedent Jones, neither the administratrix nor Jones was a party in the former action. Because they derived no rights from any party and had no voice in the conduct of the prior suit, the judgment should be reversed.

(D) Although there is no generally prevailing definition of privity, an employer-employee relationship establishes privity for preclusion purposes and otherwise. Consequently, the judgment should be affirmed.

206. Williams and Spencer brought a class action against the City of Akron claiming that allegedly discriminatory policies violated their civil rights and the rights of black police officers and black applicants for employment in the Akron Police Department (APD). After the class was certified, white, Hispanic, and female members sought to intervene. Shortly before trial, Williams and Spencer announced a settlement with Akron and the APD and submitted a comprehensive consent decree to the district judge for approval. The district court approved the consent decree but denied the intervention. The court subsequently granted partial intervenor status to other members of the department for the limited purpose of challenging the consent decree. Both the consent decree and the order denying full intervenor status were appealed to the court of appeals, which affirmed the order denying full intervenor status and remanded the case to the trial court for further action. On remand, intervention was again attempted and again denied. On further appeal, the court of appeals probably will:

(A) deny relief to the intervenors under the law of the case doctrine because all subsequent proceedings in a case must follow prior appellate rulings.

(B) consider the intervenor's request for relief under a *de novo* standard of review.

(C) deny relief unless the appellate record shows substantially different evidence, a change in controlling legal authority, or that the earlier appellate decision was clearly erroneous and would work a manifest injustice.

(D) dismiss the appeal for want of jurisdiction.

Franklin and Jefferson were involved in an automobile accident in Pennsylvania, while Jefferson was sightseeing in Philadelphia. Because Jefferson was injured as a result of Franklin's negligence in the operation of his motor vehicle, Jefferson brought suit against Franklin in Jefferson's home state of Virginia and had Franklin served with process there.

207. Assuming that there are material differences between the substantive laws of Pennsylvania and Virginia, whose law will the Virginia court probably apply?

(A) Virginia will apply its own substantive tort law because the case is pending in Virginia.

(B) Virginia will apply its own choice of law rules in determining whether Virginia or Pennsylvania substantive law should be applied.

(C) Because the accident occurred in Pennsylvania, Virginia must apply Pennsylvania law under the Full Faith and Credit Clause of the Constitution.

(D) The trial judge has unfettered discretion to apply Pennsylvania law or Virginia law.

208. What law will Virginia apply if neither Franklin nor Jefferson requests the trial court to apply Pennsylvania law to the adjudication of the action?

ANSWER:

Franklin and Jefferson were involved in an automobile accident in Pennsylvania while Jefferson was sightseeing in Philadelphia. Because Jefferson was injured as a result of Franklin's negligence in the operation of his motor vehicle, Jefferson brought suit against Franklin in Jefferson's home state of Virginia and had Franklin served with process there.

209. Because more than two years elapsed from the date of the accident and Jefferson's injuries before he commenced the Virginia action and had Franklin served in Virginia, one key question is whether Pennsylvania's two-year limitations statute for negligence actions or Virginia's three-year statute applies. Which of the following statements is correct?

    (A) If Pennsylvania substantive law must be applied, the Pennsylvania statute of limitations must be applied and the action is barred.

    (B) Even if Pennsylvania substantive law must be applied, the action is not barred because general limitations statutes are considered to be procedural and Virginia's general three-year statute governs actions filed in Virginia.

    (C) Virginia's statute of limitations applies only if Virginia law is applied generally.

    (D) The answer depends on whether the case is litigated in federal court or in state court because the federal court will apply general principles of equity to determine which statutory bar to apply.

210. Fearing how a Virginia trial judge would act in the course of adjudicating Jefferson's case against Franklin, Franklin removes the case to federal court. Another byproduct of removal will involve:

    (A) the application of federal substantive common law principles by the federal court, rather than Virginia law or Pennsylvania law.

    (B) the application of Virginia choice of law rules by the federal judge under the rule of *Erie RR v. Tompkins*, 304 U.S. 64 (1938).

    (C) the application of Virginia substantive tort law because the federal court sitting in Virginia must apply Virginia law in diversity cases.

    (D) the application of Pennsylvania tort law because a federal court located in Virginia cannot constitutionally apply its own substantive laws to an event that happened in Pennsylvania.

211. Bush filed a diversity action against Gore in a federal court in Kansas, but did not serve the complaint until after the Kansas two-year statute of limitations had expired. Because the pertinent Kansas statute clearly and expressly states that a civil action is not deemed to have been commenced until service is accomplished under Kansas law, the action would have been barred if filed in a Kansas state court. Federal Civil Procedure Rule 3, however, provides: "A civil action is commenced by filing a complaint." Under this approach, the action would have been commenced in time. Which approach is the proper one?

(A) Federal law should be followed because the action is pending in federal court and the Federal Rules of Civil Procedure adopted in conformity with the Rules Enabling Act (28 U.S.C. § 2072) govern the proceeding.

(B) Kansas law must be applied under the Rules of Decision Act (28 U.S.C. § 1652) and the Constitution because the Kansas approach is "outcome determinative."

(C) Kansas law must be applied because no countervailing federal policies outweigh the *Erie* policy of avoiding different outcomes in state and federal courts.

(D) (B) and (C) are both correct.

212. Paul Payne sued Harris County Hospital (HCH) and Dr. Mel Practer in federal court in Houston, Texas, for providing Payne with negligent medical care after he suffered a cerebral stroke in 2006. Payne's federal complaint was prepared and filed in accordance with the federal rules. Similarly, Payne has complied with all federal procedural requirements in prosecuting his claims in federal court. Under Texas law, if a plaintiff fails to serve an expert report on each physician or health care provider not later than the 120th day after the claim was filed, the trial court must, on motion of the affected physician or health care provider, "enter an order of dismissal" with prejudice to the refiling of the claim. Expert report means a written report that provides a fair summary of the expert's opinions regarding applicable standards of care, how those standards were violated and the causal relationship between the violation and the injury, harm, or damages claimed. Tex. Civ. Prac. & Rem. C. § 74.301. Because Payne did not file any reports, both HCH and Dr. Practer have moved to dismiss Payne's claims with prejudice. How should the federal judge rule on the motion to dismiss?

(A) The federal judge cannot dismiss the case because Payne's compliance with the Federal Rules of Civil Procedure adopted in conformity with the Rules Enabling Act (28 U.S.C. § 2072) precludes dismissal under *Hanna v. Plumer*, 380 U.S. 460 (1965).

(B) Texas law must be applied because no federal policies outweigh the *Erie* policy of avoiding different outcomes in state and federal courts. Case dismissed.

(C) Texas law must be applied under the Rules of Decision Act (28 U.S.C. § 1652) and the Constitution because the Texas law is "outcome determinative" in the sense of having an important effect on Payne's choice of forum.

(D) (B) and (C) are both correct.

Paul Payne sued Harris County Hospital (HCH) and Dr. Mel Practer in federal district court in Houston, Texas, for providing Payne with negligent medical care after he suffered a heart attack in 2006. Payne did not file expert reports with the district court or serve them on the defendants in compliance with Texas Civil Practice and Remedies Code Section 74.301, which requires claimants to serve an expert report on each affected physician or health care provider or suffer a dismissal with prejudice to the refiling of the claim.

213. Because Payne did not file any reports, the district judge dismissed Payne's complaint with prejudice by signed written order on Monday, June 11, 2007. Payne timely filed his notice of appeal. Which of the following statements is correct with respect to the appealability of the dismissal order?

   (A) The order is appealable as a final judgment under 28 U.S.C. § 1291.

   (B) The order is appealable as a final judgment under 28 U.S.C. § 1291 and Fed. R. Civ. P. 54(b).

   (C) The order is not appealable because it is not a final judgment on the merits of Payne's malpractice claim.

   (D) The order is appealable under the collateral order doctrine.

214. Now assume that Payne filed a sufficient report concerning Dr. Practer in compliance with Texas law, but that Payne's separate report for HCH was deficient. Thus, on the defendants' motions to dismiss, the district judge ordered Payne's case dismissed as to HCH and in a separate order denied Dr. Practer's motion to dismiss. If Payne files a notice of appeal complaining of the dismissal of HCH, does the court of appeals have jurisdiction of the appeal?

   (A) Yes, the dismissal of HCH is a final order that is appealable under 28 U.S.C. § 1291.

   (B) No, because Federal Rule 54(b)'s requirements were not satisfied and no severance order was entered, the dismissal order is not final and appealable under 28 U.S.C. § 1291.

   (C) No, the order is not appealable because it is not a final judgment on the merits of Payne's malpractice claim.

   (D) Yes, the order is appealable under the collateral order doctrine.

215. Paula Prisoner sues Sergeant Ducote and Officer Mary Jane in federal court in the Northern District of Texas, Dallas Division, claiming that Paula's constitutional rights were violated after she was arrested and incarcerated in the city jail on the day of the

Texas/Oklahoma football game. Paula claims that she was denied medical treatment as a result of the deliberate indifference of Ducote and Jane to Paula's serious medical needs, which were obvious. Paula's summary judgment evidence shows that she requested medical treatment from the police, who told her that because she wasn't concerned about the safety of the public the police weren't concerned about her medical needs. If a motion for summary judgment made by the defendants is denied by the district judge, which of the following statements is correct?

(A) The order is not appealable before final judgment on the merits.

(B) The order is appealable under the collateral order doctrine if the motion is based on the officers' defense of qualified immunity.

(C) The order is immediately appealable if the judge issues a written order for interlocutory appeal under 28 U.S.C. § 1292(b), unless the court of appeals refuses permission to appeal.

(D) (B) or (C), alternatively.

Paul Payne sued Harris County Hospital (HCH) and Dr. Mel Practer in federal district court in Houston, Texas, for providing Payne with negligent medical care after he suffered a heart attack in 2006. Payne did not file expert reports with the district court or serve them on the defendants in compliance with Texas Civil Practice and Remedies Code Section 74.301, which requires claimants to serve an expert report within 120 days after commencement of suit on each affected physician or health care provider or suffer a dismissal with prejudice. Because Payne did not file any reports, the district judge dismissed Payne's complaint. Assume that the first order concerning HCH was signed and entered on Monday, June 11, 2007, and that the second order concerning Dr. Practer was signed and entered on Wednesday, June 13, 2007. Assume further that neither the district judge nor the court clerk prepared a separate judgment embodying both dismissal orders.

216. What must Payne do to commence an appeal?

    (A) Payne must file a notice of appeal in the trial court within 30 days after June 11, 2007.

    (B) Payne must file a notice of appeal in the trial court within 30 days after June 13, 2007.

    (C) Payne must file notices of appeal in the trial court within 30 days after June 11 and within 30 days after June 13, 2007.

    (D) Payne must file a notice of appeal within 30 days after 150 days have run from entry of the last dismissal order (June 13) in the civil docket.

217. If Payne filed a motion for new trial on Friday, June 15, 2007, and the motion was overruled by a signed written order entered in the civil docket on Friday, June 22, 2007, what must Payne do to commence an appeal?

    (A) Payne must file a notice of appeal within 30 days after June 11, 2007.

    (B) Payne must file a notice of appeal within 30 days after June 13, 2007.

    (C) Payne must file a notice of appeal within 30 days after June 22, 2007.

    (D) Payne must file a notice of appeal within 60 days after June 22, 2007.

218. Under the same facts as the preceding question, if Payne does not receive notice of the entry of the trial court's order overruling Payne's motion for new trial until July 23, 2007, because the court clerk did not mail notice of the entry of the order to Payne's counsel, what, if anything, can Payne do to prosecute an appeal to the court of appeals?

    (A) Payne can do nothing; the time to commence an appeal has expired.

(B)   Payne can file a motion for extension of time to commence the appeal within 60 days after entry of the order denying Payne a new trial.

(C)   Payne can move the trial court to reopen the appeal if the motion is filed within 180 days after the judgment or order is signed.

(D)   Payne can use Rule 60(b) to ask the trial court to vacate the order denying the new trial so that the same order can be entered again to restart the appellate timetable.

219.   Once Payne has properly given notice of appeal, what must Payne do to prosecute the appeal to judgment in the court of the appeals?

ANSWER:

PRACTICE FINAL EXAM: QUESTIONS

Instructions: **This exam consists of 48 multiple choice and short answer questions. Try to answer these questions in no more than two hours.**

Charley, Donald, and Mark met to try to finalize the formation of a joint venture to obtain a Mini Cooper dealership for New Britain, Connecticut. Unfortunately, the meeting went from bad to worse, with all of the parties blaming the others for the collapse of the deal. Donald and Mark stormed out immediately, heading for their cars while still fuming about the meeting. Charley followed several minutes later, still preoccupied over what he saw as the lack of vision of his business partners. No one is quite sure what happened next, but the result was a serious accident in the parking lot in which Charley, while walking to his car, was caught between Mark and Donald's cars as they collided. Charley was seriously injured. Donald and Mark escaped without physical injury, but both suffered significant damage to their cars.

Because of a longstanding business relationship, Charley does not want to sue Donald for breach of contract, and Donald does not want to sue Charley for breach of contract. Charley does, however, sue Donald for his injuries, claiming that Donald was driving negligently, causing the accident. The suit is filed in federal court based on diversity jurisdiction (Charley is from Connecticut, Donald is from Delaware, and Mark is from Maine).

For questions 220-224, consider only issues arising under the federal joinder rules. For questions 225-227, consider whether the federal court would have subject matter jurisdiction over the claims in question.

220. Donald wants to bring Mark into this lawsuit. What procedural vehicles could he use?

ANSWER:

221. Donald decided to use Rule 14 to bring Mark into the lawsuit, alleging that Mark drove negligently and requesting contribution and indemnity. Can Donald also add a claim against Mark for negligence to seek damages for the damage to Donald's car?

(A) Yes, he can do that under Rule 13.

(B)   Yes, he can do that under Rule 18.

(C)   No, that is not a derivative claim.

(D)   Yes, but only if it arises out of the same transaction or occurrence as the Rule 14 claim.

222.   Assume that Donald used Rule 14 to bring Mark into the lawsuit. Can he add a claim for breach of contract?

(A)   Yes, he can do that under Rule 20.

(B)   Yes, he can do that under Rule 18.

(C)   No, that is not a derivative claim.

(D)   Yes, but only if it arises out of the same transaction or occurrence as the Rule 14 claim.

223.   Assume that Donald used Rule 14 to bring Mark into the lawsuit. Mark in turn has filed a claim against Charley for negligence. Can Mark bring a claim against Charley for breach of contract?

(A)   Yes, he can do that under Rule 18.

(B)   No, it does not arise out of the same transaction or occurrence as Charley's claim against Donald.

(C)   Yes, Rule 14 permits the third-party defendant to bring any and all claims against the original plaintiff.

(D)   No, not unless he also brings a claim against Charley alleging that his negligence caused the accident and the damage to Mark's car.

224.   Assume that Donald filed a counterclaim against Charley for negligence, claiming that Charley dashed out from between parked cars and caused the accident. Can he use that counterclaim to bring a breach of contract claim against Mark?

(A)   Yes, but only if he also brings a negligence claim against Mark.

(B)   Yes, Rule 13 provides complete authorization for the contract claim alone.

(C)   No, defendants can only bring in new parties through impleader.

(D)   No, the contract claim is not part of the same transaction or occurrence as Charley's claim against Donald.

225.   Assume that Charley has sued Donald for negligence for $500,000. Donald has filed a counterclaim for damages to his car for $10,000. Does the court have jurisdiction over the counterclaim?

(A)   Yes, Charley and Donald are from different states.

(B)   No, the amount in controversy is less than $75,000.

(C)   No, this would be inconsistent with the requirements of 28 U.S.C. § 1332.

(D)   Yes, the counterclaim is part of the same constitutional case as Charley's claim, and Donald is not a plaintiff.

226.   Assume that Charley sued Donald for negligence for $500,000, and that Donald impleaded Mark for contribution and indemnity. Donald also added a negligence claim against Mark for his own damages ($10,000) and a breach of contract claim for $50,000. Over which of Donald's claims does the federal court have jurisdiction?

(A)   Only the contribution and indemnity claim.

(B)   The contribution and indemnity claim and the negligence claim.

(C)   The contribution and indemnity claim, the negligence claim, and the breach of contract claim.

(D)   None of the claims; two are clearly too small, and Mark's percentage of causation might make the indemnity claim too small as well, so the amount in controversy requirement is not satisfied for any of the claims.

227.   Assume that Charley sued Donald for negligence for $500,000, and that Donald impleaded Mark for contribution and indemnity and added a negligence claim for $10,000. Mark wants to file a breach of contract claim against Charley for $100,000. Does the federal court have jurisdiction over this claim?

(A)   Yes, it meets the requirements of the diversity statute.

(B)   No, it does not share a common nucleus of operative fact with Charley's claim against Donald.

(C)   No, it is a claim by a person made a party under Rule 14.

(D)   Yes, because Mark is not a plaintiff within the meaning of 28 U.S.C. § 1367.

Charley v. Donald v. Mark went to trial including the following claims:

- Charley v. Donald for negligence (personal injuries)

- Donald v. Charley for negligence (damage to car) (counterclaim)

- Donald v. Mark for negligence (damage to car) and breach of contract (additional party to counterclaim)

- Mark v. Donald for negligence (damage to car) and breach of contract (counterclaim)

The court entered a judgment for Donald on his negligence claim against Mark, based on jury findings that the accident was caused 100% by Mark's negligence. It entered a take-nothing judgment on Charley's and Donald's negligence claims against each other. It also entered a take-nothing judgment on Mark's and Donald's claims against each other for breach of contract, based on jury findings that neither Mark nor Donald breached the contract. No one appealed.

228. One year later, the trial has taken a toll on the parties' remaining relationships, and no one feels a reluctance to sue anyone. Assume that no statute of limitation bars any potential claims. Donald got a judgment for damage to his car, but he has decided that his persistent backaches must also be a result of the accident. He wants to sue Mark for personal injury damages resulting from the accident. May he?

(A) Yes. This issue was not actually litigated in the first case.

(B) No. That claim is barred by the judgment in the first case.

(C) No. That claim is merged into the judgment in the first case.

(D) Yes. That claim is not the same cause of action as the property damage claim.

229. Donald is also feeling peevish about losing the Mini Cooper dealership, and he no longer cares whether he offends Charley. Can he now sue Charley for breach of contract?

(A) Yes. The contract claim was not the same cause of action as Donald's negligence claim against Charley.

(B) No. The contract claim against Charley was a compulsory counterclaim in the first case.

(C) No. It is barred by the results of Donald's claim against Mark.

(D) Yes. The judgment in the first case was not final because there was no appellate court decision.

230. Although Charley, Donald, and Mark were too wrapped up in themselves to notice at the time, a fourth person also suffered injuries due to the parking lot accident. Donald ricocheted backward after hitting Charley and ran his car into a parked car belonging to Ed. Now Ed sues Donald for the damages. There is no claim that Ed was negligent in any way. Donald claims that his lack of negligence was established in the first case, and asks the court to dismiss Ed's case. Should the court dismiss the case?

(A) No. The finding of Donald's lack of negligence was not necessary in the first case.

(B) Yes. The issue of negligence was actually decided and Donald was found not to be liable.

(C) It depends on whether the jurisdiction allows non-mutual collateral estoppel.

(D) No. Ed was not a party to the first case.

Steven Stress was a first year law student at Elite University School of Law (EUSL). During the fall semester, he purchased a book called "The Ultimate Study Guide," a 200-page text that promised that it contained the secret to law school success. The book's publisher, DTPA Press, went so far as to guarantee that those who purchased and studied the book would be guaranteed a spot on law review. Steven bought the book, studied it religiously, took his exams, and ended up with a very respectable B average but no spot on law review. (At EUSL the only road to law review is grades.) He sued DTPA Press for fraud and breach of warranty, seeking actual and punitive damages for himself individually and for a class composed of all law students in the United States who purchased DTPA's book but failed to make law review. His suit is now pending in federal court, based on diversity of citizenship. (Steven is a citizen of California, and DTPA Press is a Nevada corporation with its principal place of business in Nevada, and Steven seeks damages in excess of $75,000 for himself and each class member.)

231. Steven's complaint, with regard to the fraud claim, reads as follows: "DTPA Press guaranteed law review membership, and DTPA knew this promise was false. Plaintiff Stress relied on this promise, and carefully read the book, but did not make law review. He has suffered severe mental anguish and lost significant future income due to this reliance." Does this pleading satisfy the federal pleading rules?

ANSWER:

232. Steven's case is moving forward, and the parties have begun to engage in discovery. Steven has sent an interrogatory to the Elite University campus bookstore, asking for the names of all persons who purchased The Ultimate Study Guide from 1990 to the present. The bookstore has objected to answering it. Should the court order an answer?

(A) No. This question is too burdensome.

(B) Yes. These names, while not themselves admissible, might lead to the discovery of admissible evidence, because they too may have failed to make law review.

(C) No. The bookstore is not a party to the lawsuit.

(D) Yes, but the court should narrow the question to only require information since 2000.

233. Steven has also sent a request for production of documents to DTPA Press. One request asks for "all documents constituting or referring to research done by DTPA Press to substantiate the claim that all readers of The Ultimate Study Guide would make law review." DTPA Press has objected that this information is a trade secret and need not be disclosed to anyone. Should the court order production of these documents?

(A) No. The company's research is not relevant to the reason Steven failed to make law review.

(B) Yes. It is unlikely that this information is a trade secret. Even if it is, it is highly relevant to Steven's fraud claim.

(C) No. The trade secret privilege is absolute.

(D) Yes. Trade secrets, if relevant, are not protected in litigation.

234. DTPA Press has retained William Blackstone as a non-testifying expert to help it prepare for trial. Steven thinks that Blackstone has a lot of helpful information about the proper use by law students of study guides and wants to take his deposition. Can he do so?

(A)   Yes. Blackstone's information is relevant to both the warranty claim and the fraud claim.

(B)   No. Consulting experts can never be deposed by opposing parties.

(C)   No. Blackstone is a consulting expert, and there are many such experts available.

(D)   Yes. Blackstone is really famous, so Steven can show exceptional circumstances allowing the deposition.

235.   Steven has retained Oliver Holmes as a testifying expert. Holmes makes his living as an educational expert witness, working primarily for plaintiffs, and Steven would prefer not to disclose Holmes' list of prior cases. He says this is confidential information and has refused to reveal it. Will DTPA Press be successful in its motion to compel Steven to comply with the automatic disclosure provisions by revealing all the cases on which Holmes has worked?

(A)   Yes. The automatic disclosure rules require parties to reveal all of the cases that a testifying expert worked on.

(B)   Yes and no. Steven will have to reveal all the cases in which Holmes testified as an expert at trial or deposition, but only for the last four years.

(C)   Yes and no. Steven will have to reveal only the cases in which Holmes testified at trial during the last four years.

(D)   No. Information about Holmes' other cases is not relevant to his opinion in Steven's case.

236.   DTPA Press has taken Steven's deposition. Steven refused to answer questions regarding the names of his friends, the extent of his law school social life, his health (physical and mental), and the names of his health care providers. He believes that this information is private and therefore protected from discovery. DTPA has moved to compel answers to these questions. How should the court rule on DTPA's motion?

(A)   The court should order answers. This information is relevant to issues of causation and damages, and Steven has waived his privacy interest by bringing suit.

(B)   The court should not order answers. Disclosure of this information would violate Steven's privacy rights and possibly even lead to an invasion of doctor-patient privilege.

(C)   The court should order answers. Privacy interests are not listed in Rule 26 and are therefore not protected in discovery.

(D)   The court should not order answers. Steven's friends should have an opportunity to object to information about them being revealed.

237.   Steven has had a number of conversations with fellow law students regarding his case. DTPA Press asked Steven at his deposition to describe these conversations. He objected. Should the court order him to answer?

(A) No. These conversations were in anticipation of litigation and are therefore protected as work product.

(B) No. Steven reported these conversations to his attorney, and those communications are protected by the attorney-client privilege.

(C) Yes. Informal venting with friends does not become work product simply because the speaker is a party to a lawsuit.

(D) Yes. DTPA Press will be able to show substantial need and undue hardship if this question is not answered, because Steven's friends will not be as honest with them as they would be with Steven.

238. DTPA Press employs Charles Clark as general counsel. DTPA's President had a conversation with Clark back when they were beginning to market The Ultimate Study Guide. It went like this:

President: "Charley, we need a big seller in the law student market. How can we get students to buy this new study guide?"

Clark: "Tell them it will guarantee they make law review. That will make them buy it."

This conversation is:

(A) protected by the attorney-client privilege. The President would be the "client" under either a control group or subject matter test.

(B) protected by work attorney-client privilege. The President was asking his lawyer for advice, and he gave it.

(C) not protected by attorney-client privilege. The conversation was not made in anticipation of litigation.

(D) not protected by attorney-client privilege. The President was not seeking legal advice.

239. Steven has filed a motion to certify his lawsuit as a class action. Which of the following will he *not* have to demonstrate to achieve class certification?

(A) The class is so numerous that joinder is impracticable.

(B) The class action would be superior.

(C) DTPA Press acted or refused to act on grounds generally applicable to the class.

(D) Steven's claim is typical of those of class members.

240. The court has held a hearing on class certification. Steven has established that 2,500 copies of The Ultimate Study Guide have been sold to U.S. law students since August 1, 2000. He also introduced evidence regarding the qualifications of his lawyers, his own serious devotion to the case, and the adoption by 49 U.S. states of the Uniform

Commercial Code provisions regarding breach of warranty. Steven stated that the case would be manageable because the same written representations were made to each class member (on the back of the book). DTPA Press introduced evidence of differing legal standards regarding warranty and, especially, fraud in the fifty states. They also argued that class members (who cannot be individually identified) must each prove that they relied on DTPA Press' representations, and must individually prove their damages from failure to make law review and that this failure was caused by the defendant. Should the judge certify this class?

ANSWER:

241.   The court also needs to rule on another issue in the case. Assume that under the law of California, the state in which this case is pending in federal court, plaintiffs claiming punitive damages must swear to their complaints. This rule is intended to make litigants think hard before bringing claims for punitive damages. The federal pleading rules contain no such requirement. DTPA Press moved to dismiss Steven's complaint (which is not sworn to), arguing that the federal court must apply the state procedure here.

The court, in ruling on this motion, should first consider:

(A)   whether Federal Rule 11 is broad enough to cover this issue.

(B)   whether the state rule is outcome determinative.

(C)   whether the state rule is judge-made.

(D)   whether the federal rule is outcome determinative.

242.   If the court determines that the relevant federal rules cover the issue of whether pleadings must be sworn to, it should next ask:

(A)   whether the federal rule is proper under the Rules Enabling Act.

(B)   whether the difference between the rules is outcome determinative.

(C)   whether there is a strong federal interest.

(D)   whether the federal rule is proper under the Rules of Decision Act.

Maria Rodriguez is a 66-year-old woman living in Houston, Texas. She has a modest income, and her first language is Spanish. Rodriguez shops regularly at Alpha Omega, a grocery store in her neighborhood. One day she had a serious fall there -Rodriguez went to pull out a grocery cart, but the carts stuck together, the whole line of carts came toward her and pushed her down, and she fell on her right wrist, causing severe pain and permanent incapacity. Rodriguez has sued Alpha Omega in federal court on a theory of premises liability. This will require her to prove that the grocery store was negligent and, more specifically, that: (1) the stuck grocery carts constituted a dangerous condition; (2) Alpha Omega knew or should have known of the condition; (3) the condition caused her fall; and (4) she suffered damages as a result.

243. One month after Rodriguez filed her lawsuit, Alpha Omega filed a motion for summary judgment. The motion read, "Plaintiff will not have any evidence that Alpha Omega knew or should have known that the carts were stuck together. It would be wasteful to force Alpha Omega to spend time and money defending this case. Alpha Omega is entitled to judgment as a matter of law." This motion:

(A) satisfied Alpha Omega's burden as movant because it identified the issue on which Rodriguez was said to lack evidence.

(B) failed to satisfy Alpha Omega's burden as movant because in the summary judgment context it must disprove its state of knowledge.

(C) was filed too soon under Rule 56.

(D) failed to satisfy Alpha Omega's burden because it did not point to the record or otherwise demonstrate Rodriguez's lack of evidence.

244. Assume that the court denied Alpha Omega's initial motion for summary judgment. Alpha Omega then deposed Rodriguez about her accident. After she described the circumstances of her fall, the following exchange occurred:

Q: Tell me what happened on the occasion in question.

A: I walked in the store, and I was going to get my basket. And they were all stuck together. And I pulled with my right hand and they were all, at the beginning -

Q: In other words, they were inside each other, as store employees customarily stack baskets?

A: Yes.

Q: Do you know what caused the baskets to adhere to each other?

No. A:

Q: And every week when you patronize the store, the baskets are stacked in an identical manner?

A: Yes, sir.

Q: You don't have any particularized knowledge regarding the reason the two or three or four of them stayed together?

A: No, sir.

Q: Did you ever make a close inspection of the baskets?

A: No, sir.

Q: Do you have any reason to believe that any employee was knowledgeable with regard to any defect in these particular baskets?

A: No.

Alpha Omega re-filed its motion for summary judgment, arguing that Rodriguez admitted that she did not look at the baskets, did not know why they stuck together, and did not have any reason to believe that Alpha Omega employees knew of a problem with the baskets. Rodriguez responded with an affidavit that states: "I had a hard time understanding the questions I was asked at my deposition. I want to make it clear that I did not carefully examine the baskets on the day that I fell, but I did look at them generally, the way anyone looks at baskets when shopping.

I have shopped in that store for five years and I know that the baskets are often bent and in bad condition. The wheels don't roll straight. The neighborhood kids crash the carts into each other in the parking lot. I think the store people must be aware of the bad condition of their carts." How should the court rule on the motion?

(A) The court should grant the motion. Rodriguez admitted in her deposition that she had no knowledge of the condition of the baskets or the defendant's knowledge, and she cannot take that back that admission.

(B) The court should grant the motion. Rodriguez has no direct evidence that the baskets that caused her fall were dangerous.

(C) The court should deny the motion. The circumstances here make Rodriguez's clarification of her deposition testimony permissible. Her affidavit provides some evidence of the dangerous condition and Alpha Omega's knowledge.

(D) The court should deny the motion because Rodriguez's affidavit constitutes a scintilla of evidence on her behalf.

245. Assume that the court denies the motion for summary judgment and the case goes to trial. During the plaintiff's case in chief, she testifies as follows:

Q: Did you look at the baskets?

A: I looked at them just like that, that is all, when I went to get one.

Q: What was the condition of the baskets on the day you fell?

A: I didn't see the baskets then, but I know they were pretty old in that store. They don't seem to fix up the store in our neighborhood very often.

Q: How long have you shopped at this particular Alpha Omega store?

A: About five years.

Q: Did you ever see the grocery carts taken outside onto the parking lot?

A: Yes. Some of the kids take them outside and play with them and crash them together.

Q: Did you ever see anyone abandon a cart out there and leave it out in the parking lot?

A: Yes.

Q: Did you ever notice carts at this store that were bent?

A: Yes. I've seen other people have trouble getting carts out of the line. Sometimes I have to ask my granddaughter for help with the carts when they stick together.

At the close of the evidence for Rodriguez, Alpha Omega moved for judgment as a matter of law, arguing that Rodriguez presented no evidence that it knew or should have known of a dangerous condition. In considering this motion, the court should canvass the entire record and then:

(A) only give credence to direct evidence in favor of Rodriguez.

(B) refuse to rule. This motion is premature.

(C) only give credence to evidence and reasonable inferences in favor of Rodriguez.

(D) weigh the evidence and decide whether a reasonable jury could find for Rodriguez.

246. Assume that the judge denied Alpha Omega's motion for judgment as a matter of law at the close of Rodriguez's evidence. Alpha Omega, therefore, presented its own case. Former store manager Hugh Cumber testified that he inspected the grocery carts 30 minutes after Rodriguez fell, and there was nothing wrong with any of the carts that would cause them to stick together. On cross-examination, Cumber testified that he has worked for Alpha Omega for ten years and that just after his deposition in this case he was assigned to manage a bigger store in a wealthier neighborhood at a big increase in salary. He also testified that he is on probation at this new assignment. Alpha Omega also called Kay Rett, who testified that she works for Alpha Omega and is the supervisor in charge of repairing baskets in all Houston area stores. During the year that Rodriguez fell, each store was visited for basket repairs every 90 days. About 25 damaged baskets would be repaired or replaced on each visit. On cross-examination, she testified that the store where Rodriguez fell was a "high loss" store, meaning that there was a high rate of basket damage and disappearance. High loss stores are not visited for repairs as often as other stores because the damage is seen as inevitable. She further testified that basket frames become bent when hit by cars or damaged by children, and that this could cause a row of baskets to stick together.

At the close of all the evidence, Alpha Omega once again moved for judgment as a matter of law. What evidence and what inferences may the court consider in ruling on the motion?

ANSWER:

247. Assume that the court denied the motion and sent the case to the jury. The jury found that the baskets were a dangerous condition, that Alpha Omega knew or should have known of the condition, that the condition caused Rodriguez to fall, and that she was damaged in the amount of $125,000. Alpha Omega filed a timely motion for new trial arguing only that the jury verdict was not supported by the evidence. In ruling on the motion:

(A) the judge should decide whether he thinks the verdict was correct. If not, he should grant a new trial.

(B) the judge should decide whether a reasonable jury could have found for Rodriguez. If so, he should deny the motion for new trial.

(C) the judge should question the jurors as to the basis for their verdict.

(D) the judge should decide whether the jury verdict was clearly contrary to the weight of the evidence. If not, he should enter judgment on the verdict.

Robert Builder runs a construction company in West Virginia, although Builder lives in Ohio. Builder is currently involved in a large road construction job in West Virginia. Pilchard Supplies is a Pennsylvania company (incorporated and with its principal place of business there) that sells construction materials. Builder called Pilchard, and after negotiations involving more than a dozen phone calls between Builder in Ohio and Pilchard in Pennsylvania, Pilchard accepted Builder's offer and they entered into a contract. The contract obligated Pilchard to deliver $1 million worth of materials to Builder's job site in West Virginia. Pilchard defaulted on the contract, failing to deliver any materials. This caused Builder to lose a $500,000 early-completion bonus and to incur $1 million in missed deadline penalties.

Under the law of Ohio, Pilchard would be liable to Builder for both the lost bonus and the penalties. Under the law of West Virginia, Pilchard would be liable to Builder for the penalties but not the lost bonus. Under the law of Pennsylvania, Pilchard would be liable only for any higher price that Builder had to pay for replacement materials, in this case only $100,000.

Builder wants to sue Pilchard and is trying to decide where to file suit. *Assume that any of the three states would apply its own law to Builder's claim against Pilchard.* Help Builder think through the consequences of choosing where to sue.

248. Builder likes the law of Ohio best and would love to sue at home. Suppose Builder sues Pilchard in federal court in Ohio. The Ohio long-arm statute provides for service on anyone who enters into a contract with an Ohio resident. Under these circumstances:

 (A) Builder's claim is proper under the Ohio statute, but he has a weak claim for personal jurisdiction over Pilchard there and venue is incorrect.

 (B) Builder's claim is proper under the Ohio statute, and he has a strong claim for personal jurisdiction over Pilchard but venue is incorrect.

 (C) Builder's claim is proper under the Ohio statute, he has a strong claim for personal jurisdiction over Pilchard, and venue is correct.

 (D) Builder's claim exceeds the scope of the Ohio statute, and he has a weak claim for personal jurisdiction over Pilchard, although venue is correct.

249. Suppose Builder files in Ohio. Pilchard files a motion to dismiss or, in the alternative, to transfer the case to the Eastern District of Pennsylvania under 28 U.S.C. § 1406. The court decides that both venue and personal jurisdiction are improper in Ohio. What could the court do that would make Builder especially unhappy?

 (A) Dismiss the case.

 (B) Transfer the case to E.D. Pa.

 (C) Remand the case to state court.

(D)   Transfer the case to N.D. W.Va.

250.   Would a federal court in Pennsylvania have jurisdiction over Pilchard and proper venue in Builder's case? Why?

ANSWER:

251.   Builder really does not want his claim to end up in Pennsylvania. What would happen if he filed his suit in federal court in West Virginia (N.D. W.Va.) and Pilchard filed a motion to transfer to Pennsylvania, alleging that venue is improper?

(A)   The court would probably grant the motion. Pilchard does not reside in West Virginia.

(B)   The court would probably deny the motion. Pilchard does reside in West Virginia for venue purposes.

(C)   The court would probably deny the motion. A substantial amount of the acts or omissions giving rise to Builder's claim took place in West Virginia.

(D)   Both (B) and (C) are correct.

252.   If you represented Builder (who is a very risk-averse client), what would you advise him about the advantages and disadvantages of his potential choices of forum?

ANSWER:

Imagine that Builder has filed his claim against Pilchard in state court in Ohio. Pilchard, who was served with process a week ago, believes that Ohio lacks personal jurisdiction over him. He is trying to decide whether to file a motion to dismiss in state court or whether to remove the case to federal court and *then* file an immediate motion to transfer the case to Pennsylvania. The statute of limitations is not even close to running out. Help Pilchard consider the consequences of these options.

253.   If Pilchard were to file a motion to dismiss in state court in Ohio, what would be the probable result?

(A)   The court would dismiss the case and Builder would refile in West Virginia.

(B)   The court would dismiss the case and Builder would be precluded from refiling it.

(C)   The court would transfer the case to a state court in Pennsylvania.

(D)   The court would keep the case.

254. If Pilchard wanted to remove the case from state court to federal court in Ohio, would this be permissible under the federal removal statutes?

ANSWER:

255. If Pilchard first removed the case, and then filed a motion to transfer the case to Pennsylvania because of lack of personal jurisdiction, improper venue under 28 U.S.C. § 1406, and also in the interests of justice under 28 U.S.C. § 1404, what would be the probable result?

   (A) The court would keep the case. Pilchard has waived his complaints about personal jurisdiction and venue by filing the removal notice first.

   (B) The court would transfer the case because both personal jurisdiction and venue are improper.

   (C) The court would transfer the case because it lacks personal jurisdiction and because most of the witnesses and most of the evidence is in Pennsylvania rather than Ohio.

   (D) The court would keep the case because venue is correct in a removed case in the district that includes the location of the state court.

256. In addition to Pilchard's complaint that Ohio lacks personal jurisdiction over him with regard to Builder's claim, what other argument could Pilchard make to try to get the case dismissed from state court?

ANSWER:

257. If you represented Pilchard, and it was sued in state court in Ohio, what action would you recommend?

ANSWER:

258. Builder has just learned that five years ago, Pilchard was sued in Ohio state court by another customer. In that case, Pilchard was accused of delivering substandard materials to an Ohio building site. Pilchard challenged Ohio's personal jurisdiction in that case, but the court found that Pilchard had sufficient purposeful contacts with Ohio and that it was fair to subject Pilchard to suit there. Builder wants to argue that Pilchard is now bound by this finding of personal jurisdiction and cannot contest the Ohio court's jurisdiction over *Builder v. Pilchard Corp.* Is Builder correct?

   (A) No. This would be offensive non-mutual collateral estoppel and that is not allowed in any court in the United States.

(B) Yes. Pilchard had a chance to litigate this issue and lost.

(C) No. Personal jurisdiction in one specific jurisdiction case is not generally the same issue as specific jurisdiction in another case.

(D) Yes. The issue of Pilchard's contacts with Ohio was necessarily decided in the first case.

259. What limits exist on the plaintiff's ability to choose a forum?

ANSWER:

260. Amy, a purchaser of "Dietaid" diet drink, filed a class action in federal court in California, Amy's home state, against Smith Pharmaceuticals (a California corporation with its principal place of business in California), the manufacturer of Dietaid. Amy's complaint alleges that Dietaid actually has no weight loss benefits and alleges breach of implied warranty claims against Smith Pharmaceuticals. The complaint seeks recovery of the amount that Amy and each class member paid for the pills. The complaint describes the class as "all citizens and legal residents of the United States who have purchased Dietaid from Smith Pharmaceuticals from January 1, 2003, to December 31, 2006. Approximately 60,000 class members each paid $100 for Dietaid, which was sold in California, Texas, New York, and Florida. There are about 15,000 class members in each of the four states. Amy's individual claim is for $225 in out-of-pocket expenses. Does the federal court have jurisdiction over this class action?

(A) No. Amy is the class representative and she is from the same state as the defendant.

(B) Yes. The court has supplemental jurisdiction over the class members' claims because they share a common nucleus of operative fact with Amy's claim.

(C) Yes. There is sufficient minimal diversity, there are more than one hundred class members, and the amount in controversy exceeds $5 million.

(D) Both (B) and (C) are correct.

261. Lance, a resident of Louisiana, has filed suit against Legalstuff, a New York corporation with its principal place of business in New York, seeking $200,000 in damages resulting from inaccurate legal advice he obtained from the company's website, legalstuff.com. A search of the Better Business Bureau website revealed that previous customers have complained about the inaccurate legal information on legalstuff.com. Lance believes the company was aware of the problem, but failed to correct it. He has requested discovery of the e-mails and computer files of all management-level employees since January 2007. The parties do not agree on the proper format for the production of electronically stored information ("ESI"). Legalstuff maintains that, as the producing party, it gets to designate the format and has the right to choose to produce the information printed out in hard copy. Is Legalstuff correct?

(A) Yes. Rule 34 provides that the responding party may indicate the form it intends to use for production.

(B) No. Rule 34 allows the requesting party to specify the format in which ESI should be produced.

(C) No. Legalstuff must produce the information both in the desired format of the requesting party and the format indicated by the responding party.

(D) No. Absent agreement or court order, Legalstuff must produce ESI in the form in which it is normally maintained or which is reasonably usable.

262. Oliver Smith filed suit against Hayden Corp., his former employer, based on federal discrimination law. Smith has requested discovery of all of Hayden Corp.'s e-mails concerning Smith's treatment by his supervisors sent between January 1, 2006, and May 1, 2007, contending that various e-mails exchanged among Hayden Corp. employees contain evidence of gender discrimination. Hayden Corp. stores old e-mails on backup tapes with other computer files that are difficult and expensive to access and search. In contrast, the e-mail messages from January 1, 2007, through May 1, 2007, are currently stored on the company's computers and are easily accessible. Hayden Corp. has asked the court to shift the cost of production of the e-mails from January 1, 2006, through December 31, 2006, to Smith, as production would be unduly burdensome because Hayden Corp. would have to search 392 backup tapes to locate the requested e-mails at an estimated cost of $175,000. What will the court likely order?

(A) The court will probably shift the cost of production of all e-mails from January 1, 2006, through May 1, 2007, to Smith because the requesting party should bear the cost of production.

(B) The court may not shift the cost of production of any of the requested information to Smith, because the producing party should bear the cost of production.

(C) The court may shift some of the cost to Smith, but Hayden Corp. will bear the cost of producing the e-mails currently stored on the company's computers.

(D) The court will not order Hayden Corp. to produce the 2006 e-mails because production would place an undue burden on Hayden Corp.

263. Robin Roberts brought suit in federal district court in Philadelphia against Harry Anderson and Ashburn Sports Products, Inc. ("Ashburn Sports") for damages based on fraud claims against Anderson and Ashburn Sports, coupled with a breach of contract claim against Ashburn Sports. Roberts claimed that Anderson made false representations concerning the future profits that Roberts would probably receive as a franchisee of Ashburn Sports to induce Roberts to enter into a franchise agreement with Ashburn Sports to operate a sporting goods store in Montgomery County, Pennsylvania. Unfortunately, instead of making a profit, Roberts' store operated at a loss and had to be closed. Roberts' breach of contract claim alleged that Ashburn Sports violated the terms of the franchise agreement in a number of ways. (Anderson was not sued for breach of contract because he was not a party to the contract.)

Anderson and Ashburn Sports filed motions for summary judgment based on the defense that the representations alleged by Roberts could not be fraudulent because they were statements of opinion or predictions that could not be a basis for fraud claims. Ashburn Sports also moved for summary judgment on Roberts' contract claim against it based on the defense of failure of consideration. The trial court granted Anderson's motion, but denied Ashburn Sports' motion concerning the breach of contract claim against it. If Roberts chooses to appeal the summary judgment, does the court of appeals have jurisdiction of the appeal?

(A) Yes, the order is appealable under the collateral order doctrine.

(B) No, the order is not appealable because it is not a final judgment disposing of all claims.

(C) No. Because Federal Rule 54(b)'s requirements were not satisfied and no severance order was entered, the summary judgment is not final and appealable under 28 U.S.C. § 1291.

(D) Answers (B) and (C) are correct.

264. Assume the same facts as in the preceding question, except this time the court granted summary judgment in favor of both defendants on all claims. Summary judgment in favor of Anderson was signed and entered on July 24, 2007, and summary judgment in favor of Ashburn Sports was signed and entered on July 26, 2007. Assume that neither the district judge nor the court clerk prepared a separate judgment indicating the successful disposition of both summary judgment motions. What may or must Roberts do to commence an appeal?

(A) Roberts must file a notice of appeal in the trial court within 30 days after July 26, 2007.

(B) Roberts must file a notice of appeal in the trial court within 30 days after July 24, 2007.

(C) Roberts may file a notice of appeal within 30 days after 150 days have run from entry of the last dismissal order (July 26) in the civil docket.

(D) Roberts must file notices of appeal in the trial court within 30 days after July 24 and within 30 days after July 26, 2007.

265. Marsha Kent sued Dr. Lane for medical malpractice in a federal district court in Texas. Kent failed to serve an expert report regarding Dr. Lane's actions, as required by Texas law. The district judge, therefore, dismissed Kent's complaint with prejudice. Kent filed a motion for new trial on June 5, 2007, but the district judge overruled Kent's motion in a signed order entered in the civil docket on June 12, 2007. Kent, however, did not receive notice of the district court's entry of the order denying her motion for new trial until July 24, 2007, because the court clerk did not mail notice of the entry of the order to Kent's attorney. What, if anything, can Kent do to prosecute an appeal to the court of appeals?

(A)   Because the time to commence an appeal has expired, Kent cannot do anything.

(B)   Kent can file a motion for extension of time to commence the appeal within 90 days after entry of the order denying Kent's motion for new trial.

(C)   Under Rule 60(b), Kent can ask the trial court to vacate the order denying the new trial so that the same order can be entered again to restart the appellate timetable.

(D)   Kent can move the trial court to reopen the appeal if the motion is filed within 180 days after the judgment or order is signed.

266.   Builder, Pilchard, and Wendy each have a claim against Pickles for work each separately performed in connection with the construction of Pickles' new farm house. Travis Bank supplied the financing for the construction of the new farm house and now holds a deed of trust, executed by Pickles, to the farm and farm house. Builder, Pilchard, and Wendy join together as plaintiffs under Rule 20, seeking a judgment to foreclose their mechanics' and materialmen's liens. If Travis Bank is not joined as a party and its absence is not raised in the trial court by Pickles or by any other party, and judgment is rendered for the plaintiffs, can Pickles challenge the judgment on appeal on the basis of Travis Bank's nonjoinder?

(A)   Yes, the nature of Travis Bank's lien interest in the farm house makes it a person that "should be regarded as indispensable" under Rule 19(b).

(B)   Yes, Travis Bank's deed of trust lien represents a substantive right that makes it indispensable to the trial court's exercise of jurisdiction.

(C)   No, Travis Bank's deed of trust lien is inferior to the plaintiffs' liens; therefore, Pickles cannot challenge the judgment based on Travis Bank's nonjoinder.

(D)   No, Pickles' failure to raise Travis Bank's nonjoinder in the trial court eliminates Pickles' ability to attack the judgment foreclosing the plaintiffs' liens on Pickles' property.

267.   ASAP Delivery's driver, Rick, was killed when his delivery vehicle collided with Paula's car. Paula has filed a diversity action against ASAP in federal district court in Wyoming, seeking personal injury damages in the amount of $150,000. Paula also joined Hybrid Cars, the manufacturer of Paula's car, under a manufacturing defect theory, because Paula's brakes failed during the collision. ASAP's truck was badly damaged in the accident, so ASAP filed a cross-claim against Hybrid Cars. May Hybrid Cars make a claim for contribution against ASAP in the same action?

(A)   No, contribution claims are premature until judgment in the underlying action. Thus, Hybrid Cars cannot make a cross-claim against ASAP for contribution under Rule 13(g).

(B)   Yes. ASAP became an "opposing party" by claiming against Hybrid Cars, making Hybrid Cars' contribution claim against ASAP a compulsory counterclaim.

(C) Yes. Although Hybrid Cars cannot make a counterclaim for contribution because its contribution claim is premature until judgment in the underlying action, Rule 13(g) expressly permits Hybrid Cars to file a cross-claim against ASAP.

(D) Yes. Hybrid Cars can file a contribution claim against ASAP either as a counterclaim or a cross-claim because Hybrid Cars' contribution claim is mature.

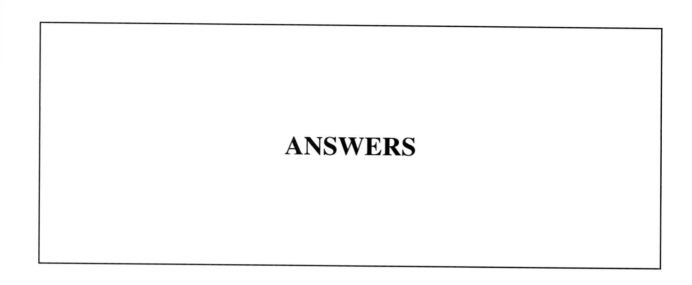

ANSWERS

1. **Answer (D) is the best answer.** This is the language of Rule 8 of the Federal Rules of Civil Procedure, and the language is significant because it was deliberately chosen by the drafters to eliminate some of the technicalities and disputes about pleadings that occurred under pre-FRCP practice.

   Answer (A) is incorrect. This is the rule that was applied under the rules of "code pleading," which predated the FRCP. This rule led to a very technical approach to analyzing pleadings that the FRCP drafters wanted to avoid.

   Answer (B) is incorrect; it is not a correct statement of the test in federal court. Its language is also a part of the requirements of the old "code pleading" standards.

   Answer (C) is incorrect. Under pre-FRCP pleading practice, it was difficult to determine the difference between facts, which a pleader was supposed to allege, and evidence, which a pleader was not supposed to allege. The language of Rule 8 was intended to avoid this kind of dispute.

2. In the federal court system, pleadings are designed to accomplish three purposes. First, the complaint gives notice to the defendant of what the plaintiff is complaining about, at least in a general way, and allows the defendant to prepare a response. Second, pleadings are designed to provide an outline for the court that will guide the development of the case as it goes along. For example, the scope of discovery will be largely determined by the issues set forth in the pleadings. Third, in some cases the pleadings may be used to determine the merits of the case, as when the face of the complaint shows that the plaintiff has no right to relief, even if the plaintiff's version of the facts is taken as true. Early merits decisions based on the pleadings alone are rare, however, as they are generally inconsistent with the philosophy of the FRCP that disputes should usually be decided based on evidence presented at a trial on the merits rather than on the pleadings.

3. This complaint does satisfy the requirements of Rule 8. In fact, it is very similar to the complaint included in Federal Form 9. The Forms were included by the framers of the FRCP to demonstrate for the bench and bar the meaning of their new system of pleading, and they are attached as an Appendix to the FRCP. By providing information about the general nature of the plaintiff's complaint, this meets the requirement of being a "short and plain statement of the claim." Unlike the practice in some states and in other common law jurisdictions, the plaintiff is not required to plead the specific factual basis for his negligence claims. In such jurisdictions, Crockett would likely have to plead that Boone "was negligent due to speeding" or "was negligent in that he failed to keep

a proper lookout" or the like, but federal courts do not use the pleadings as the vehicle to supply this type of information.

In 2007, the Supreme Court sent somewhat mixed messages about pleading. In one case, *Bell Atlantic v. Twombly,* 2007 U.S. LEXIS 5901 (May 21, 2007), the majority held that an antitrust conspiracy claim had to plead specific facts showing that illegal conspiracy, and not legal parallel conduct, was a plausible inference. Further, the majority limited the reach of *Conley v. Gibson,* 355 U.S. 41 (1957), the Court's classic pleading case. In *Conley* the Court stated: "a complaint should not be dismissed for failure to state a claim unless it appears beyond doubt that the plaintiff can prove no set of facts in support of his claim which would entitle him to relief." 355 U.S. at 45-46. In *Twombly* the majority characterized this as merely "an incomplete, negative gloss on an accepted pleading standard: once a claim has been stated adequately, it may be supported by showing any set of facts consistent with the allegations in the complaint. *Conley* described the breadth of opportunity to prove what an adequate complaint claims, not the minimum standard of adequate pleading to govern a complaint's survival." A few weeks later, the Court decided a second case. In *Erickson v. Pardus,* 2007 U.S. Lexis 6814 (June 4, 2007), the *pro se* plaintiff brought a civil rights claim against prison officials for their wrongfully terminating his medical treatment for hepatitis C, alleging that this action endangered his life. The Tenth Circuit affirmed the dismissal, on the ground that the plaintiff had pleaded the substantial-harm element in a "conclusory" fashion. The Supreme Court summarily vacated because that "holding departs in so stark a manner from the pleading standard mandated by the Federal Rules of Civil Procedure." It cited *Twombly* for the propositions that notice pleading does not require alleging of "specific facts" and that the "judge must accept as true all of the factual allegations contained in the complaint," but it made no reference to any plausibility test. Outside of certain kinds of complex, expensive cases disfavored by the Court (particularly antitrust and securities fraud), in which the substantive law may require greater factual particularity, it appears that a pleading like Form 9 will be sufficient.

4.   **Answer (C) is the correct answer.** General damages follow "naturally" and "necessarily" from the occurrence made the basis of the action. Because the only damage that would meet this test "necessarily" is past physical pain and mental suffering resulting from a serious injury, it is the only general damage allegation, i.e. the only one that did not need to be "specifically stated." Of course, it is routine for plaintiffs to claim both past and future pain and suffering with specificity.

      Answer (A) is not correct because pain and suffering "naturally" and "necessarily" will result from a serious injury, such as a broken hip suffered in an automobile accident. The others might "naturally" occur, but that is not "necessarily" true. For example, Crockett might not have suffered any loss of earnings or earning capacity or incurred medical and hospital expenses.

      Answer (B) is not correct because future pain and suffering will not necessarily be suffered by Crockett. By the time of trial, when the fact finder will decide whether to award damages for future pain and suffering, Crockett might have completely recovered.

Answer (D) is not correct because future pain and suffering and lost earnings or earning capacity are considered to be special damages.

5. **Answer (D) is correct.** Rule 8(e)(2) allows a party to "set forth two or more statements of a claim or defense alternately or hypothetically. . . . A party may also state as many separate claims or defenses as the party has regardless of consistency." [Restyled Rule 8(d)(2) provides that a "party may set out 2 or more statements of a claim or defense alternatively or hypothetically" and 8(d)(3) states that a "party may state as many claims or defenses as it has, regardless of consistency."] The claims that Boone was the driver and that Travis was the driver, although factually inconsistent, are therefore allowed.

Answer (A) is incorrect because inconsistent claims can be proper. It is true that Crockett's ability to plead inconsistently is subject to the requirement of Rule 11 that the allegations be made in good faith. If Crockett knew who was driving the car, the alternative pleading would not be proper. Because Crockett does not know, the alternative pleading is allowed.

Answer (B) is incorrect because, as noted, Rule 8 allows the pleading of inconsistent claims.

Answer (C) is incorrect. Although it may be strategically difficult or unwise to maintain the alternative pleading through trial, the rules do not require an election before going to the jury. Imagine, for example, that at trial of this case Boone claimed that Travis was the driver and Travis claimed that Boone was the driver. Crockett will be allowed to leave the decision to the jury.

6. **Answer (A) is correct.** Although generally speaking the federal pleading rules are quite forgiving, a plaintiff must sue for a cause of action that is recognized under the applicable substantive law. Your neighbor, for example, could not sue you for being a law student and adding to some kind of perceived national oversupply. Similarly, Crockett cannot invent a cause of action for "annoyance" and pursue it against Boone based on his bad taste in bumper stickers. Rule 8 does provide that the complaint must show "that the pleader is entitled to relief."

Answer (B) is incorrect. Although, as you will learn when you study subject matter jurisdiction, there are situations in which jurisdiction over one claim will justify jurisdiction over others, stating one legally valid claim does not give a party the right to add into the same lawsuit claims that have no legal basis.

Answer (C) is also incorrect. Plaintiffs may combine "as many claims or defenses as the party has." There is no longer a rule in federal court requiring separate suits for different types of claims, even claims that in earlier times would have been brought in different types of courts.

Answer (D) is incorrect. A "short and plain statement" of a nonexistent claim is not salvaged by providing the required amount of detail.

7. **Answer (A) is correct.** Rule 12(b) provides certain defenses that a party may assert even before filing an answer, if it wishes, or that may be included in the party's answer. Rule 12(b)(6) is the one directed at legally insufficient allegations. It allows the determination, based on the pleadings alone, that all or part of a case should be dismissed because it "fails to state a claim upon which relief can be granted." The court, in ruling on such a motion, must assume that all the facts pleaded by the plaintiff are true, and should not consider matters outside the pleadings. In this case, Crockett has alleged that Boone's car has a bumper sticker containing a bad pun, that this bothered Crockett when he read it, and that Crockett therefore sues for damages based on his annoyance. The court should assume that those allegations are correct (Boone has such a bumper sticker; Crockett saw it; Crockett was annoyed) but can still dismiss the allegation because there is no cause of action for "annoyance." This will eliminate the claim at the outset without further expenditures for discovery on these issues.

    Answer (B) is incorrect. Although an invalid claim could be disposed of by summary judgment, where, as here, it can be eliminated earlier through a 12(b)(6) motion based on the plaintiff's allegations alone, the latter motion is the more efficient procedural vehicle.

    Answer (C) is incorrect. Boone does not want more detail about the annoyance claim, he wants to get rid of it, and there is no likelihood that greater detail about the bumper sticker or Crockett's reaction will be helpful to the court in disposing of this claim.

    Answer (D) is incorrect. The general demurrer was abolished for the federal courts by the Federal Rules of Civil Procedure.

8. **Answer (B) is correct.** Rule 11 is designed to require good faith in pleading, and a pleader must have a basis both in law and in fact for the contents of its pleadings, motions, and other papers filed with the court. Rule 11 has often been amended. Under the current version of the rule, there are four listed certifications that a party makes to the court when presenting a pleading, written motion, or other paper. Signing a complaint that does not live up to these certifications is a violation of Rule 11, and potentially subjects the violator to various types of sanctions. This question focuses on the requirements of Rule 11(b).

    Rule 11(b)(2) is aimed at pleadings that bring claims that are warranted neither by existing law nor by a nonfrivolous argument for its modification. Assuming that the annoyance claim does not exist under applicable substantive law, and that there is no indication Crockett's lawyer can point to, not even a dissenting opinion or a law review article, advocating such a cause of action, the annoyance claim violates Rule 11(b)(2). Note that if Crockett were actually advocating a change in the law (as opposed to just failing to research it), Rule 11 does not require him to identify it as such, but the Advisory Committee Notes to the 1993 amendments point out that "a contention that is so identified should be viewed with greater tolerance" under Rule 11.

Answer (A) is incorrect. Rule 11(b)(1) prohibits presenting the pleading for an improper purpose. Crockett and his lawyer appear to fall more into the "empty head, warm heart" category: their conduct still violates Rule 11, but not because of their subjective motives.

Answer (C) is incorrect. This is not a pleading in which the problem is lack of factual basis. Crockett knows and has alleged the facts surrounding the bumper sticker. Rule 11(b)(3) is aimed at parties who file claims without having evidentiary support for them.

Answer (D) is incorrect because there is no need for more factual investigation — more detail would not improve Crockett's non-existent cause of action. (Note also that even if this were the case, the rule calls for contentions lacking evidentiary support to be "specifically so identified.")

9. Boone should not file the Rule 11 motion immediately. The current version of Rule 11 contains so-called "safe harbor" provisions. A party who believes her opponent has violated Rule 11 may not go straight to the court for sanctions. She must first serve on the opposing party a motion describing the offending conduct, giving that party an opportunity to withdraw or correct the challenged claim. Only after this is done, and the pleading is *not* withdrawn, may a Rule 11 motion be filed with the court. The drafters hoped that this would encourage the parties to work out these disputes among themselves, reducing the number of hearings required. If the motion causes a party to drop the challenged contention, it also eliminates that contention from the lawsuit without further expenditure of attorney time. Boone must therefore give that kind of advance notice to Crockett before going to the court.

10. **Answer (D) is correct.** The flaw in Crockett's pleading in this case is a legal one — the annoyance claim is legally frivolous. This is therefore a violation of Rule 11(b)(2), as you learned in question 7. When it comes time for sanctions, Rule 11(c)(2)(A) provides that monetary sanctions may not be awarded against a represented party for a violation of subsection (b)(2). Thus, any award in this case would have to be made against Crockett's lawyer, not Crockett himself. Rule 11(c) provides that sanctions may be imposed on the attorneys, law firms, or parties that have violated Rule 11(b) or are responsible for the violation.

Answer (A) is not completely correct, and therefore not the best answer. Rule 11(c)(1)(A) allows the court to award the party prevailing on the Rule 11 motion the reasonable expenses and attorney's fees incurred in presenting the Rule 11 motion, but that does not include any other fees incurred that were caused by the wrongful pleading itself.

Answer (B) is also not the best answer. Answer (B) is correct to point out that generally monetary penalties (beyond fees incurred in presenting or opposing the Rule 11 motion itself) are paid to the court rather than to the parties. See Rule 11(c)(2). The rule, however, allows the court to award monetary sanctions to the movant including "some or all of the reasonable attorney's fees and other expenses incurred as a direct result of the violation." These are only proper "if imposed on motion and warranted for effective deterrence." The statement in Answer (B) that penalties *must* be paid to the court is therefore incorrect.

Answer (C) is incorrect. It correctly recognizes that the sanction can be paid to the moving party if warranted for effective deterrence. It likewise notes that the court may choose to award all or only part of the attorney's fees — Rule 11(c)(2) provides that a sanction "shall be limited to what is sufficient to deter repetition of such conduct." In other words, it is deterrence rather than compensation that is to guide the court's decision about the amount or nature of any sanction. Answer (C), however, overlooks one point that makes it wrong and makes Answer (D) correct: when the Rule 11 violation stems from a frivolous legal position, the sanctions must be assessed against the attorney rather than against a represented client.

11. **Answer (B) is correct.** Boone did not have to file a pre-answer motion, but once he did so he had to include certain defenses or waive them. Boone filed a motion to dismiss for insufficiency of service of process under Rule 12(b)(5) but did not include in it a motion to dismiss for lack of personal jurisdiction under Rule 12(b)(2). The consequences of this sequence of events are governed by Rules 12(g) and (h). Rule 12(g) provides that a party who makes a motion under Rule 12 but omits from that motion any defense or objection then available to the party "shall not thereafter make a motion based on the defense or objection so omitted" except as permitted in Rule 12(h)(2), which does not apply to Boone's situation here. Rule 12(h)(1) provides that a defense of lack of jurisdiction over the person is waived "if omitted from a motion in the circumstances described in subdivision (g)." Thus, Boone has lost the right to complain about personal jurisdiction being asserted over him in Texas, even if his complaint would have been valid. Crockett's case should therefore go forward.

Answer (A) is incorrect. Boone waived the defense of lack of personal jurisdiction, as explained above.

Answer (C) is incorrect. Rule 8(b) provides that if "a party is without knowledge or information sufficient to form a belief as to the truth of an averment, a party shall so state and this has the effect of a denial." It is quite likely that Boone lacks information concerning the nature and extent of Crockett's injuries, so his response to the damage allegations was proper.

Answer (D) is incorrect. When a defendant denies the allegations of the plaintiff's complaint, it shows that there is a factual dispute requiring that the case go forward. Defendants cannot achieve dismissal of the claims against them merely by denying those claims.

12. **Answer (D) is correct.** The defense of lack of personal jurisdiction is a disfavored one, subject to waiver if not raised in a timely way. However, Boone has managed to hold on to his defense this time. Rule 12(h)(1) provides that a defense of lack of jurisdiction over the person is waived if it is neither made by motion under this rule (true in this case) nor included in a responsive pleading (also true — it was not in the answer) or an amendment to the responsive pleading permitted by Rule 15(a) to be made as a matter of course. This is the provision that saves Boone. Rule 15(a) allows one amendment as a matter of course "if the pleading is one to which no responsive pleading is permitted" [true of answers — see Rule 7(a)] and "the action has not been placed on the trial calendar" [very likely so early in the case] and the amendment is made "within 20 days after it is served." [Restyled Rule 15(a)(2) allows amendments as a matter of course "within 20 days after serving the pleading if a responsive pleading is not allowed and the action is not yet on the trial calendar."] Because Boone amended his answer only a week after serving it, it is very likely that he meets the requirements of Rule 15(a). Thus, Boone's defense of lack of personal jurisdiction was included in an amendment to the answer permitted to be made as a matter of course and, therefore, was *not* waived under Rule 12(h).

Answer (A) is incorrect because pre-answer motions are optional. A party need not make one at all if it does not want to. If, however, Boone had filed a pre-answer motion that omitted the personal jurisdiction defense, that defense would have been waived.

Answer (B) is incorrect because the timely amendment to the answer saved the defense. Had Boone not amended his answer within 20 days of the time his original answer was served, (B) would be the correct answer.

Answer (C) is incorrect. While complaints about subject matter jurisdiction (the power of the court to hear the type of case involved) may be raised at any time under Rule 12(h)(3), Boone's concern was jurisdiction of the court over him as a defendant. This kind of defense is indeed subject to waiver.

13. This question highlights the issue of affirmative defenses. Formerly called a "plea in confession and avoidance," an affirmative defense asserts some independent reason that the plaintiff cannot prevail. It is, thus, different from a denial. The most common affirmative defenses are listed in Rule 8(c). The defenses themselves are often governed by state law [see Topic 44]. The pleading of the defenses, though, is governed by Rule 8. Here, Boone is attempting to raise the affirmative defense of contributory negligence. In most states, this affirmative defense acts as a complete or partial bar to the plaintiff's recovery, even when the defendant is negligent. A defendant cannot raise this issue at trial unless he has pleaded it. The allegation that the plaintiff's own negligence is to blame for the accident in question is different from a mere denial that the defendant was negligent.

14. When a defendant wants to bring a claim for his own damages against the plaintiff, the pleading device that is used is called a "counterclaim." Counterclaims are governed

by Rule 13 of the FRCP. Counterclaims are either "compulsory" or "permissive." A counterclaim is compulsory if it arises out of the same transaction or occurrence as the plaintiff's claim against the defendant. This may be considered under a test of whether there is a "logical relationship" between the complaint and counterclaim, or whether the two claims would involve the "same evidence." Under either test, Boone's counterclaim against Crockett would be a compulsory one.

15. **Answer (C) is correct.** Rule 7(a) provides for "a reply to a counterclaim denominated as such." [Restyled Rule 7(a) lists "an answer to a counterclaim designated as a counterclaim."] This means that a reply containing Rule 8 defenses is required to join issue on the allegations of the counterclaim and to avoid them.

   Answer (A) is incorrect because denial defenses must be included in the reply. See Rule 8(d). [Restyled Rule 8(b)(6) provides that an "allegation . . . is admitted if a responsive pleading is required and the allegation is not denied."]

   Answer (B) is incorrect because affirmative defenses to the counterclaim must be made to avoid waiver of the defenses.

   Answer (D) is incorrect because the reply is to the counterclaim, not the entire answer.

16. This is a tricky question and requires both an appreciation of contract law defenses and Rule 8(c). Under contract law, there is a contract based on mutual promises. There is no want of consideration. But because Boone breached the contract, the consideration failed. Rule 8(c) lists failure of consideration as an affirmative defense, so it must be alleged by Crockett specifically. Crockett probably should allege that the consideration failed completely because the bargain required authentic long rifles. Out of an abundance of caution, Crockett might also plead want of consideration alternatively. A weak argument can be made that there was no consideration, not merely that the consideration failed. In many jurisdictions, want of consideration is also considered an affirmative defense in cases involving written contracts because written contracts are presumed to be supported by consideration.

17. **Answer (B) is correct.** The drafters of the Federal Rules of Civil Procedure wanted to eliminate the prolonged 'back and forth' of pleadings that characterized the common law pleading system. Therefore, Rule 7 put limits on the pleadings allowed. It does not normally allow a reply to an answer. Further, Rule 8(d) [Restyled Rule 8(b)(6)] provides the party with an automatic denial *and avoidance* of matters raised in a pleading to which no responsive pleading is required — which would include the answer. It therefore relieves Crockett of the need to plead fraud in response to Boone's pleading of release. Some state court systems would have a different rule, requiring the pleading of defenses that 'avoid' affirmative defenses, in order to provide notice to the defendant that the plaintiff intends to raise this issue.

   Answer (A) is incorrect. Fraud is an affirmative defense, and a defendant who wishes to raise a defense of fraud to the plaintiff's complaint would indeed have to plead it.

However, when it appears in the context of an affirmative defense to an affirmative defense, Rule 8(d) [Restyled Rule 8(b)(6)] relieves the plaintiff of the need to plead it, as explained above. In fact, the plaintiff is not allowed to file a reply to the answer without the court's prior permission.

Answer (C) is incorrect. Rule 7 does not usually allow responsive pleadings to answers; it certainly does not require them.

Answer (D) is incorrect. The pleading of issues in avoidance — the essence of an affirmative defense — generally is required. A defendant who fails to plead an affirmative defense in response to the plaintiff's complaint may easily have waived that defense.

18.   **Answer (A) is correct.** The basic requirements for the level of pleading specificity are set out in Rule 8(a). Rule 9 lists certain kinds of issues that must be alleged with a greater degree of detail, usually called "pleading with particularity" or "heightened pleading requirements." There are also certain statutes, such as the Private Securities Litigation Reform Act, that require more fact-specific pleadings before a plaintiff is allowed to proceed. Beyond that, however, the Supreme Court has repeatedly interpreted the rules to prevent individual judges from creating their own heightened pleading rules for categories of cases. *See, e.g., Leatherman v. Tarrant County Narcotics Intelligence & Coordination Unit*, 507 U.S. 163 (1993); *Swierkiewicz v. Sorema N.A.*, 534 U.S. 506 (2002).

       Answer (B) is not correct. It is probably true that judges have some amount of flexibility in individual cases in determining what constitutes a "short and plain statement of the claim showing that the pleader is entitled to relief." This does not, however, justify any kind of across-the-board rule like the one used by the judge in this question.

       Answer (C) is not correct either. In the particular circumstance of certain kinds of good faith immunity claims in civil rights cases, the Fifth Circuit has used the device of a Reply as a substitute source of particularized information from the plaintiffs. *See, e.g., Schultea v. Wood*, 47 F.3d 1427 (5th Cir. 1995) (en banc). The special policy concerns that apply in those cases do not apply in garden-variety tort claims, however, making it unlikely that the Supreme Court would approve of wholesale adoption of the Reply to get around the language of Rule 8(a).

       Answer (D) is also incorrect. *Leatherman* may have left a tiny hole for civil rights cases against individual government officials, but it did not give permission to require heightened pleadings generally. Similarly, *Bell Atlantic v. Twombly*, based on antitrust law, has required the pleading of specific facts that support a persuasive inference of conspiracy, but neither case supports *ad hoc*, across-the-board heightened pleading requirements. *See Erickson v. Pardus*, 2007 U.S. Lexis 6814 (June 4, 2007).

19.   **Answer (C) is correct.** Fraud claims must be alleged specifically because Rule 9(b) provides that in averments of fraud, a party must state with particularity the circumstances constituting fraud or mistake. This means that the plaintiff must plead who individually has done or said what, when, where, and why.

       Answer (A) is incorrect for the same reason that answer (C) is correct.

       Answer (B) is incorrect because Rule 9(b) also provides that malice, intent, knowledge, and other conditions of a person's mind may be alleged generally. This contrasts with the PSLRA which requires factual support for scienter allegations.

Answer (D) is incorrect. The liberal Rule 12(b)(6) standard is read in conjunction with the specific requirements of Rule 9.

20. At least in certain kinds of cases, a change from the current version of Rule 8(a) to a requirement of pleading facts with particularity would work to the disadvantage of plaintiffs. This would be particularly true if no discovery were allowed until a plaintiff satisfied the requirement of the pleading rule. There will be cases in which a plaintiff does not have access to the kind of information required for a fact-specific pleading, and while those cases can go forward under a notice pleading system, they would be dismissed under a heightened pleading standard. Also, because pleadings provide the outlines for development of the case through discovery, more specific pleadings would mean a narrower scope of discovery and less opportunity for a plaintiff to gain information with the help of the court. In cases in which both parties have fairly equal access to all relevant information before any litigation is filed, a change in the pleading rule would have less effect on the parties' comparative advantage.

21. **Answer (D) is the best answer, although Answer (A) is also correct.** Pretrial amendments to pleadings are governed by Rule 15(a). Once the period allowing amendments as a matter of course passes, amendments require permission from the court, but amendments are generally still favored: "leave shall be freely given when justice so requires." [Restyled Rule 15(a)(2) says that the court "should freely give leave when justice so requires."] Courts have interpreted this rule to mean that an amendment should be allowed unless the party opposing the amendment shows that it will be prejudiced in some way by the delay, as when relevant evidence has been lost, witnesses have become unavailable, or an amendment that makes a significant change in the nature of the lawsuit comes too late in the case. In the hypothetical, the defendant seeks to amend its answer only six weeks after it originally served its answer, and less than two months after suit was filed. It is unlikely that a change coming so early in the case would prejudice the plaintiff. Under other circumstances, the result could be different. Because of the pro-amendment attitude of the FRCP, Answers (D) and (A) are correct in that the amendment should be allowed. However, amended pleadings are subject to the requirements of Rule 11 as are other pleadings, and the defendant should not make this change unless the denial is "warranted on the evidence" as provided in Rule 11(b)(4). Because Answer (D) includes this caution, it is a better answer.

    Answer (B) is incorrect because January 15 is outside the time period in which pleadings can be amended without permission under Rule 15(a). For defendants, this time expires 20 days after its original answer is served, and in this question the request to amend came six weeks after the answer.

    Answer (C) is incorrect because parties are allowed to change their factual contentions as well as their legal theories. The FRCP's emphasis on using the entire pretrial process to develop the case assumes that as discovery and informal investigation progress the pleadings may need to be amended and that this is preferable to freezing the allegations to the parties' state of knowledge at the outset of the case.

22. Question 22 focuses only on whether Boxer's proposed amendments are proper as amendments; question 23 will add the problem of the statute of limitations. In this case, the court should allow the amendments. As in question 21, it is early in the lawsuit. Mastiff has not lost access to any kind of proof by virtue of the slight delay in correctly naming his business or in adding a claim for an additional type of damages. Thus, neither change would prejudice Mastiff, and both amendments should be allowed.

23. **Answer (B) is the best answer.** This question, based on the same facts, is more difficult. Now you are asked to assume that the original complaint was timely, but the amended

complaint standing alone would be barred by the statute of limitations. Boxer's new damage claim and indeed any claim against Mastiff will be barred unless the amendments "relate back" to the filing of the original complaint. The answer, thus, depends on the application of Rule 15(c). In order to relate back, the new damage claim must arise out of the conduct, transaction, or occurrence set forth in the original complaint. Here, Boxer's claim for consequential damages is alleged to be a consequence of the defect in the dog food, as was her original damage claim. "Same conduct, transaction, or occurrence" under Rule 15 is more concerned with notice to the defendant than to the evidence overlap and trial efficiency sought when a similar phrase is used in other rules. The different types of damages, although they will not involve the same evidence, will be considered part of the same transaction or occurrence and will be allowed to relate back. Boxer's amendment changing the naming of defendant from "BBD, Inc." to "Martin Mastiff, doing business as BBD Products" must meet additional tests. These tests are incorporated into Answer (B). Under Rule 15(c)(3), this type of amendment also requires timely notice to the new defendant so that he will not be prejudiced in maintaining a defense on the merits. Notice of the institution of the action is timely if it is given "within the period provided by Rule 4(m) for service of the summons and complaint," i.e. within 120 days after the filing of the complaint. In this case, Mastiff himself was served with the original complaint before limitations ran and thus had notice of the allegations in the suit, avoiding prejudice due to late notification of the claim. Rule 15(c)(3) also requires that within the same period the new defendant knew or should have known that, but for a mistake concerning the identity of the proper party, the action would have been brought against the new defendant. Here, Mastiff knew or should have known the name and legal status of his company, and therefore he should have known that but for Boxer's mistake he would have been sued individually. Answer (B) comes closest to including all of these requirements.

Answer (A) is incorrect. The consequential damage claim *does* arise out of the same conduct, transaction, or occurrence as Boxer's original claims. The original complaint puts the defendant on notice that he is being sued for the harm caused to Boxer by alleged defects in his dog food, and this new damage claim should not come as an unfair surprise to Mastiff.

Answer (C) is incorrect. This is exactly the kind of mistaken identity that Rule 15(c) was designed to rectify. A known defendant has been inadvertently misnamed.

Answer (D) is incorrect because it omits so much important information. While lack of prejudice is a factor to consider in whether to allow amendments and in whether they may relate back, a number of other tests must be met, leaving this answer fatally incomplete.

24. Boxer needs for her amendment to relate back in order to defeat the bar of the statute of limitations. This is more difficult when the amendment changes the party against whom a claim is asserted. Here it would change from ABC Corporation to PoroCal Company. Even if PoroCal had timely notice of the suit, Boxer will have difficulty

proving that this was a "mistake" within the meaning of Rule 15(c). A few courts have held that any situation in which a party is renamed, including situations such as this one and those involving "John Doe" defendants, involves a mistake. Boxer, however, was not mistaken in the sense that she actually thought the chemical manufacturer was called "ABC Corporation." Therefore, a majority of federal courts have refused to allow relation back in circumstances such as these as no "mistake" is involved. A number of commentators have called for Rule 15(c) to be amended to allow relation back under these circumstances as long as the other requirements are satisfied.

25. The drafters of the Federal Rules of Civil Procedure tried to shift merits determinations of lawsuits from the initial pleadings to a later point in time, allowing an opportunity for discovery, and resolving fact issues through trial. They envisioned a system in which the true issues in dispute between the parties would become clearer as the lawsuit progressed. Some issues would disappear, either because the plaintiff dropped them for lack of evidentiary support or because the defendant admitted the plaintiff's claims. Other issues would be added, as the plaintiff gathered evidentiary support for additional factual or legal theories. In order to facilitate this process, amendments to the pleadings are encouraged. These amendments, however, should not be allowed when they will prejudice one of the parties. This could happen when a significant amendment is allowed after evidence has been lost, or very shortly before trial. The trial court, therefore, has discretion to deny permission to amend to avoid prejudice to a party.

26. **Answer (D) is correct.** The trial judge has broad discretion to order separate trials for convenience, to avoid prejudice, or to expedite and economize. Rule 42(b). Similar discretion exists to sever claims, even in cases involving one plaintiff and one defendant, to avoid prejudice. *Cf.* Rule 21.

Answer (A) is probably not correct. Although Rule 18(a) places no limit on joinder of claims, regardless of their type or relationship to one another (so that they cannot be "misjoined"), courts have concluded that severance orders may be issued under Rule 21 (entitled Misjoinder and Nonjoinder of Parties) as a matter of judicial discretion, to facilitate the administration of justice.

Answer (B) is incorrect. Unlike Rule 20 (Permissive Joinder of Parties), which contains a nexus requirement, Rule 18(a) has no such requirement.

Answer (C) is incorrect because there is no misjoinder of claims and because severance is within the court's discretion to avoid prejudice and does not depend on misjoinder.

27. **Answer (C) is correct.** In fact, it is the type of situation envisioned by the rule drafters. While Paris could not collect on his claim until it matures, he is permitted to join it.

Answers (A) and (B) are incorrect because substantive legal principles don't control the procedural issue of the circumstances under which a claim can be stated in a complaint.

Answer (D) is incorrect because the issue does not involve the court's discretion.

28. **Answer (B) is the best answer.** The claims against Boris and Doris do not satisfy all three of the procedural requirements imposed by Rule 20 [1. claim asserted against defendants "jointly, severally, or in the alternative;" 2. with respect to or arising out of "the same transaction, occurrence or series of transactions or occurrences;" and 3. "If any question of law or fact common to all defendants will arise in the action."]. Because the claim against Boris is unrelated to the claim against Doris, there is a misjoinder of parties. But misjoinder of parties is not a ground for dismissal of an action. It is a ground for a separate trial to prevent delay or prejudice (Rule 20(b)) or severance (Rule 21).

Answer (A) is incorrect. Rule 21(a) expressly states that misjoinder of parties is not ground for dismissing an action.

Answer (C) is incorrect for the reasons stated above.

Answer (D) is also incorrect. Although trial judges have broad discretion in this context, it is not unlimited.

29. **Answer (D) is correct.** Although the original version of Rule 18(a) contained a sentence that suggested that Rule 20 imposed limits on the joinder of claims in cases involving multiple parties, as amended in 1966 the sentence was deleted. The effect of the amendment is to permit joinder of unrelated claims in multiple party cases as long as the parties are properly joined, i.e. as long as one common claim links the defendants together. *See* Kaplan, *1966 Amendments of the Federal Rules of Civil Procedure*, 81 Harv. L. Rev. 591, 597 (1968). In this case, Mantle and Maris are properly joined as parties under the breach of contract claim. The remedies available to Mantle are an order of severance [Restyled Rule 21 — "The court may also sever any claim against a party"] or a separate trial of the related contract claims from the libel claim (Rule 20(b)).

Answer (A) is incorrect. Mantle's remedy is severance or a separate trial.

Answer (B) is correct as explained above.

Answer (C) is correct as explained above.

30. **Answer (C) is the best answer.** The claims of Albert, Barbara, Clarence, and David satisfy the three procedural requirements of Rule 20, because they each claim liens on Edward's summer house. Because of the nature of their claims, they should be litigated in the same action if there are no jurisdictional impediments to doing so. The same reasoning applies to Foxworth. Rule 19 makes Foxworth a "person to be joined if feasible" because he "claims an interest relating to the subject of the action" and disposing of the action in his absence may "impair or impede" the person's ability to protect the interest.

   Answer (A) is incorrect for the reasons stated above.

   Answer (B) is incorrect because Foxworth is a person needed for just adjudication under Rule 19(a), even though he might not be "regarded as indispensable" under Rule 19(b), particularly if none of the parties raised his nonjoinder in the trial court.

   Answer (D) is incorrect because Foxworth is not jurisdictionally "indispensable" to the adjudication of the claims of the other parties. If for some reason Foxworth is not or cannot be joined, the question will be whether the action should proceed in his absence, not whether the court has jurisdiction to do so.

31. **Answer (C) is correct.** Based on the Supreme Court's analysis and application of Rule 19(b) in *Provident Tradesmens Bank & Trust Co. v. Patterson*, 390 U.S. 102 (1968), Edward's attempt to obtain a windfall escape from his defeat at trial is foreclosed.

   Answer (A) is incorrect because under modern Rule 19, the issue is procedural, not substantive or jurisdictional.

   Answer (B) is incorrect because Foxworth did not need to be joined in order for the court of appeals to shape or frame relief to protect his lien interest, which probably can be enforced anyway.

   Answer (D) is incorrect. Even if Foxworth's lien is inferior, that is not an issue that the court of appeals would resolve *de novo*.

32. Because Foxworth was not a party to the first action, his lien was not extinguished and he is not bound by any judgment foreclosing the mechanics' and materialmen's liens on Edward's property. Assuming no jurisdictional problems exist, Foxworth can bring suit against Albert, Barbara, Clarence, and David to establish the priority of Foxworth's lien under applicable law. All of them can be joined under Rule 20 and each of them probably is a person to be joined, if feasible, under Rule 19. Edward should also be

joined under Rules 19 and 20, along with any subsequent purchasers who acquired the summer home at the sale foreclosing the mechanics' and materialmen's liens. Of course, Foxworth may lose the case on the merits because his lien is inferior under applicable law, or because the subsequent purchasers can avoid the deed of trust lien under applicable property law.

33.   **Answer (D) is probably the correct answer.** Rule interpleader is a device for joining rival claimants. Cookie and Dorothy are rival claimants to the same fund. Although the second phase of the case, after interpleader is permitted, will involve litigation between Cookie and Dorothy, who are both Texans, case law holds that there is no jurisdictional problem if diversity exists between the plaintiff bringing the interpleader action and the claimants. *See Aetna Life & Cas. Co. v. Spain*, 556 F.2d 747, 479 (5th Cir. 1977).

   Answer (A) is incorrect for the same reason.

   Answer (B) is correct as stated above.

   Answer (C) is correct as stated above.

34.   **Answer (D) is the correct answer.** Statutory interpleader requires only minimal diversity between "[t]wo or more adverse claimants, of diverse citizenship" and money or property in the amount of $500 or more. 28 U.S.C. § 1335. Both of those requirements are met in this question. In addition, 28 U.S.C. § 2361 provides for nationwide service of process, so that Cookie's current lack of contacts with Texas is not a problem and 28 U.S.C. § 1397 makes venue proper "in the judicial district in which one or more of the claimants reside."

   Answer (A) is correct as stated above.

   Answer (B) is correct as stated above.

   Answer (C) is correct as stated above.

35.   Confederation Life probably can still interplead Dorothy and Cookie in either Texas or New Mexico and request injunctive relief against Cookie (and Dorothy) "restraining them from instituting or prosecuting any proceeding in any State or United States court affecting the property, instrument or obligation involved in the interpleader action." 28 U.S.C. § 2361. An interpleader claim might even be regarded as a compulsory counterclaim. Confederation Life probably could obtain interpleader by way of counter-claim in Connecticut, joining Dorothy as an additional party to the interpleader counterclaim, although venue would not ordinarily be proper there as to Dorothy. Some courts don't consider venue issues to be relevant to counterclaims. Still others recognize a concept of "ancillary" venue that might cover Dorothy.

36. **Answer (C) is the best answer** because Albert "claims an interest" in the deed and his "ability to protect that interest" could be "impaired or impeded" by a delivery of the deed to Clarence. Thus, Albert is a person needed for just adjudication (Rule 19) and must be permitted to intervene in accordance with Rule 24(a).

    Answer (A) is incorrect. If a federal statute confers a right to intervene, intervention is appropriate, but it may also be appropriate in the absence of a statute.

    Answer (B) is incorrect. Permissive intervention requires only that an intervenor's "claim or defense and the main action have a question of law or fact in common." Because the standard is low (*cf.* Rule 20's more complex requirements) the trial judge has considerably more discretion to grant or deny permissive intervention.

    Answer (D) is incorrect. Although the trial court has some discretion to deny intervention to persons like Albert, the discretion is not broad.

37. **Answer (B) is the correct answer.** Third-party actions are derivative actions in the sense that they are brought to recover from third parties on the basis of the third party's derivative or secondary liability. Under Rule 14(a), a third party complaint is appropriate only in cases where the third-party defendant would be secondarily liable to the original defendant in the event the latter is held liable to the plaintiff. In other words, third-party actions are for contribution or indemnity.

    Answers (A), (C), and (D) are incorrect for the same reason that answer (B) is correct.

38. **Answer (A) is the best answer** because the contribution claim is a proper basis for Nelson's third-party complaint. Nelson should be able to add any additional claims against Rios under Rule 18(a), which specifically references a "third party claim."

    Answer (B) is plausible, but it is probably not necessary to engage in a two-step process before Nelson can add his personal injury claims.

    Answer (C) is incorrect for the same reason that answer (A) is correct.

    Answer (D) is incorrect for the same reason that answers (B) and (C) are incorrect.

39. **Answer (D) is correct, because Answers (A), (B), and (C) are all correct.** As stated in Answer (A), if the federal lawsuit proceeds to judgment first, the subsequent Connecticut action could be barred because Rule 13(a) probably makes Duds' counterclaim a compulsory claim in federal court. The preclusive effect of the federal judgment will be determined under federal common law, which in turn incorporates state preclusion law under most circumstances. *See Semtek Int'l Inc. v. Lockheed Martin Corp.*, 531 U.S. 497 (2001); *see generally* WILLIAM M. RICHMAN & WILLIAM L. REYNOLDS, UNDERSTANDING CONFLICT OF LAWS § 113(a) (3d ed. 2002). **Answer (B) is correct, too.** Nelson is an "opposing party" because Nelson sued Duds. This is significant because it invokes the compulsory counterclaim rule. **Answer (C) is also correct** because compulsory counterclaims are within a federal court's supplemental jurisdiction. [For further information about supplemental jurisdiction, see Topic 29.]

40. **Answer (A) is correct.** Under Rule 13(g), cross-claims against co-parties are not compulsory, they are permissive, even though they must arise out of the transaction or occurrence that is the subject matter of the original claim.

Answer (B) is incorrect for the reasons stated above.

Answer (C) is incorrect because defendants' cross-claims arising from the same constitutional case are within a federal court's supplemental jurisdiction. [See Topic 28].

Answer (D) is incorrect because Answer (C) is not correct.

41. **Answer (C) is the best answer.** Although counterclaims for contribution must be mature, cross-claims for contribution need not be mature at the time the cross-claim is filed. Hence, the unavailability of a counterclaim should not prohibit a cross-claim within the scope of Rule 13(a).

Answers (A), (B), and (D) are incorrect for the same reason.

42. **Answer (A) is correct.** Of the four threshold requirements in Rule 23(a), the only one that is problematic here is "typicality." To be "typical" the class representative must "possess the same interest and suffer the same injury." *See East Texas Motor Freight v. Rodriguez*, 431 U.S. 395 (1977). This means that the claims must be based on the same legal theory and generally arise from the same event or course of conduct giving rise to the claims of other class members.

    Answer (B) is incorrect. Although there is no exact numerical threshold, clearly 1,000 purchasers, who live throughout the country, are too numerous to be joined as a practical matter. **Answer (C) is incorrect.** The qualifications of class representatives are not rigorous. A willingness to serve coupled with the retention of experienced counsel capable of handling the case and financing its prosecution should be sufficient.

    Answer (D) is incorrect. In this case, common questions will not be lacking.

43. **Answer (B) is correct.** This type of case would most likely be a Rule 23(b)(3) action requiring the trial court to find that there are common questions, that the common questions predominate in the sense that they will be the object of most of the effort of the litigants and the court, and that the classwide resolution of the issues is superior, both as a matter of judicial economy and fairness to the parties.

    Answer (A) is incorrect. Multiple money damage claims, even if trial results are inconsistent, do not subject the defendant to incompatible standards of conduct.

    Answer (C) is incorrect because the claimants are seeking money damages, not an injunction.

    Answer (D) is incorrect. Individual cases would not have a preclusive or a practical effect on absent parties and so could not prejudice the interest of other class members.

44. **Answer (B) is correct.** The Supreme Court, in *Eisen v. Carlisle & Jaquelin*, 417 U.S. 156 (1974), held that regardless of the cost of providing notice to the class members, the plaintiff should bear the cost.

    Answer (A) is incorrect. Unless the defendant would not incur any additional expense or the expense would be insubstantial because, for example, notices could be included in normal periodic mailings, as a general rule, the fact that a defendant can better afford notice costs does not matter.

    Answers (C) and (D) are incorrect, as there is no authority to order these methods of allocating the costs of notice.

45. **Answer (D) is correct.** Rule 26(a)(1) describes categories of information that must be disclosed at the outset of the case without the need for a discovery request. This includes, in Rule 26(a)(1)(A), the name and location information for "each individual likely to have discoverable information that the disclosing party may use to support its claims or defenses, unless solely for impeachment."

Answer (A) is incorrect. Disgruntled former clients are unlikely to support Nanny Nation's case, and so they need not be identified in initial disclosures.

Answer (B) is incorrect. The rule does not require that witness e-mail addresses be provided, although it does specify that address and telephone numbers must be given if known.

Answer (C) is incorrect. While some parts of Hibbins' file might come under the disclosure requirements of Rule 26(a)(1)(B), this rule also is confined to information that "the disclosing party [Nanny Nation] may use to support its claims or defenses." The troublesome evaluation from the former employer is not something Nanny Nation would use, and so automatic disclosure of this document is not required.

46. **Answer (B) is correct.** Rule 26(a)(1)(C) governs the disclosures required concerning the claim for damages. It requires "a computation of any category of damages claimed by the disclosing party, making available for inspection and copying as under Rule 34 [requests for production of documents from parties] the documents or other evidentiary material, not privileged or protected from disclosure, on which such computation is based, including materials bearing on the nature and extent of injuries suffered." Thus, although the pleading rules do not require an itemization of damages (See Topic 1), the automatic initial disclosure rules provide the defendant with that information.

Answer (A) is incorrect. The requirements of this rule are not limited to economic harm.

Answer (C) is incorrect. While the rule requires documents on which a computation of damages is based, it excludes material that is privileged. Correspondence with the attorney on this topic would be protected by the attorney-client privilege as well as work product protection.

Answer (D) is not as good as Answer (B). While a computation of out-of-pocket expenses would be included in the required response, it omits a number of required types of damages.

47. August 23. Rule 26(a)(1)(E) requires the automatic initial disclosures to be made at or within 14 days after the Rule 26(f) conference. The Rule 26(f) conference must be held at least 21 days before a scheduling order is due under Rule 16(b). Thus, in this case, the Rule 26(f) conference must be held by August 9. The automatic initial disclosures, therefore, must be made within 14 days after that, or by August 23. In cases in which each step is taken on the last possible day, the disclosures will be due 7 days before the scheduling order. However, note that the deadlines in Rules 26(a)(1)(E) and 26(f) run from when the scheduling order is actually due, or from when the Rule 26(f) conference is actually held, so that the exact timing will vary from case to case.

48. **Answer (A) is correct.** Rule 26(a) also governs automatic disclosures concerning testifying expert witnesses, although these disclosures take place at a later stage of the proceedings. The rule requires a report and other information relevant to examination and impeachment of the expert. Although Rule 26(a)(2)(C) encourages a case-specific court order, in the absence of an order the rule provides the timing and sequence of disclosure. Generally the disclosures are required "at least 90 days before the trial date or the date the case is to be ready for trial." Prynne's expert information is therefore due at this time. On the other hand, expert evidence "intended solely to contradict or rebut evidence on the same subject matter identified by another party" only needs to be made within 30 days after the disclosure made by the other party. Nanny Nation's expert testimony, which would be intended to rebut that of Prynne, probably falls under this category. As the Advisory Committee Notes indicate, in most cases the party with the burden of proof on an issue (usually the plaintiff) should disclose its expert testimony on that issue before other parties are required to make their disclosures with respect to that issue.

Answer (B) is incorrect. A defendant's disclosures, absent a counterclaim or an affirmative defense, generally do not need to be made simultaneously with the plaintiff's disclosures.

Answer (C) is incorrect. These disclosures are required in cases such as this and it requires a court order or stipulation to eliminate the requirement, not to impose it.

Answer (D) is incorrect. The disclosure requirement applies to all experts who are retained or specially employed to provide expert testimony, or whose duties as an employee of the party regularly involve giving expert testimony. The reference to "a witness" does not imply that the disclosures are limited to one person.

49. **Answer (C) is the correct answer.** While Rule 26(a)(2) requires significant disclosures from testifying experts, it does not cover employee-experts unless their duties regularly involve giving expert testimony.

Answer (A) is incorrect. Although a report from an employee-expert might indeed be helpful in providing the information needed to depose, and later cross-examine, the expert, the rules do not require it from an expert like Bobbins.

Answer (B) is incorrect. The degree of litigant control over the expert is not the criterion used by Rule 26.

Answer (D) is incorrect. Even though an employee, Bobbins has special training or expertise and will be testifying to her opinions, not to the facts surrounding the recruitment and training of Hibbins.

50.   **Answer (B) is the best answer.** In cases involving voluminous document production, and especially cases involving extensive discovery of electronically-stored information, parties sometimes agree on a procedure such as that described in (B) (which is sometimes referred to as a "claw back" or "snap back" process). This benefits the producing party, in that it can reduce the cost in time and attorney fees associated with pre-screening documents for privilege, and can avoid the serious problem of privilege waiver. It can benefit the discovering party, in that it is likely to get access to the documents more quickly if it need not wait for a painstaking pre-production privilege review. On the other hand, in particular cases one party might prefer to leave the possibility of privilege waiver on the table. If an agreement is reached, asking the court to include it in a pretrial order has the advantage of greater clarity as to what exactly was agreed to, and is easier to enforce.

Answer (A) is not a probable choice. No party is likely to agree that any production of privilege, no matter how accidental, will automatically waive privilege.

Answer (C) is highly unrealistic. Even if the parties wanted their document production to be watched by a judge, they cannot agree between themselves as to what the judge will do, and it is extremely unlikely that a judge would be willing to spend his or her time in this way.

Answer (D) is close to the default rule in federal court in the absence of an agreement. Note that it makes the outcome of inadvertent production so unpredictable that it is unlikely that parties would negotiate for such a deal.

51.   Yes, Federal Rule of Civil Procedure 26(a)(2)(B) now provides for the disclosure of information "considered by" an expert in forming an opinion. The Advisory Committee notes state that "[g]iven this obligation of disclosure, litigants should no longer be able to argue that materials furnished to their experts to be used in forming their opinions — whether or not ultimately relied on by the expert — are privileged or otherwise protected from disclosure when such persons are testifying or being deposed. Advisory Committee Notes to 1993 Amendments; *see TV-3 Inc. v. Royal Ins. Co.*, 194 F.R.D. 585, 588 (S.D. Miss 2000) (". . . when an attorney hires an expert both the expert's compensation and 'marching orders' can be discovered and the expert cross-examined thereon.").

52.   **Answer (C) is correct.** This answer tracks the language of Rule 26(b)(1), including the final sentence regarding information reasonably calculated to lead to the discovery of admissible evidence.

Answer (A) is incorrect. This was the test for relevance until the 2000 amendments to Rule 26(b), but it is no longer correct.

Answer (B) is incorrect. Information need not be admissible in evidence to be discoverable.

Answer (D) is incorrect. Information relevant to the claims and defenses of the parties is discoverable without a showing of good cause. It is only for information that goes beyond "claims and defenses" but is still relevant to the "subject matter" involved in the action that a showing of good cause is required.

53.   **Answer (C) is correct.** Prynne's sexual history, however fascinating, is not related to the issues in the lawsuit. Relevance requires a relationship between the information to be discovered, the elements of claims and defenses, and the facts that tend to prove or disprove those claims or defenses. In this case the issues are whether Nanny Nation was negligent or grossly negligent in hiring and training Hibbins, whether it defrauded the plaintiffs, whether that conduct was the cause of the plaintiff's damages, and the extent of those damages. In order for the information about Prynne's sex life to be "relevant," it would have to make some fact of consequence to those issues more likely or less likely than it would be without the information about Prynne's sex life. Because that is not the case, the information is not relevant and therefore not discoverable.

Answer (A) is incorrect. Some information that bears on the credibility of a witness' testimony is relevant for discovery purposes. For example, information that might show a bias, or information that shows that a person is untruthful, might be relevant for purposes of impeachment. A person's sexual history is not, in a case unrelated to that history, apt to shed any light on the accuracy of the person's testimony and so is not discoverable for purposes of impeachment.

Answer (B) is incorrect. While a party waives certain privileges and privacy interests by bringing a lawsuit, the waiver extends only to things relevant to the issues in the action, not to any facet of her life.

Answer (D) is incorrect. If the possibility that a witness might answer any random question untruthfully made that question relevant, because the untruthfulness would be a basis for impeachment, then there would be no limits to discovery relevance.

54. **Answer (C) is correct.** Rule 26(b) requires that discoverable material be relevant to the claims and defenses of the parties. The plaintiffs' claims require proof of causation — that Nanny Nation's alleged wrongful acts were the cause of the harm to Pearl and to her parents. One part of causation is that Hibbins' behavior caused the traffic accident that harmed Pearl. Witnesses to the accident may have information relevant to whose behavior caused the accident. Access to these witnesses, whether by informal interview or by deposition, will allow Nanny Nation to ask questions concerning causation. Some or all of them may be called to testify at trial. This discovery request is, thus, relevant in that it is reasonably calculated to lead to the discovery of admissible evidence.

Answer (A) is incorrect. While the extent of Hibbins' intoxication may be relevant to the cause of the accident, and to the link between Nanny Nation's hiring and training practices and the accident, it is not the only relevant issue in the case.

Answer (B) is incorrect. The names themselves do not need to be admissible. As noted above, they are reasonably calculated to lead to the discovery of admissible evidence.

Answer (D) is incorrect. It overstates the scope of discovery. Prynne's lawyers may talk to people who end up knowing nothing of relevance to the case. In addition, a question phrased in terms of "whom did you interview while investigating this case" would be an improper request for attorney work product. [See Topic 15.]

55. Under Rule 26(a)(1), Prynne will have had to disclose the names and contact information for individuals who may be used to support *Prynne*'s case. This might include witnesses to the car wreck, but only if those witnesses' version of events is helpful to Prynne. Only by sending an interrogatory asking for *all* persons with knowledge of this information can Nanny Nation be sure that Prynne has disclosed the identity of people of whom Prynne is aware with both favorable and unfavorable information.

56. **Answer (B) is correct.** Because Holgrave's claim for damages includes lost income from his law practice, documents that might tend to support or rebut that claim are relevant. This request, however, is not well tailored to discover those documents. Every piece of paper ever generated by Holgrave's law practice will not be relevant to income; most, in fact, will not. The request thus, on its face, requests documents that do not relate to any of the claims or defenses in the case.

Answer (A) is incorrect. While some of the requested documents will be relevant, most will not be.

Answer (C) is incorrect. Information relevant to damages is discoverable through the normal discovery devices.

Answer (D) is incorrect. All of the documents are not relevant. It is correct, however, that some of the documents called for by the request will take the form of communications between attorney and client and will thus be protected by attorney-client privilege. [See Topic 16.]

57. The definition of relevance for discovery purposes creates a direct tie to the pleadings. Discoverability requires relevance to the "claims and defenses" of the parties, and those claims and defenses will be contained in their pleadings. Because the pleadings are permitted to be fairly general, discovery is designed to provide the parties with further information to prepare their claims and defenses for trial, and to further refine the issues in dispute between the parties. This approach is consistent with the philosophy of the FRCP that cases should be disposed of on the merits and that all relevant information should be available to all of the parties.

58. **Answer (B) is correct.** Rule 26(b)(3) protects such material from discovery absent a showing of substantial need for the information and the party's inability to secure the substantial equivalent of the information without undue hardship. The rule derives from the Supreme Court's landmark case, *Hickman v. Taylor*, 329 U.S. 495 (1947), which recognized protection for trial preparation materials. Rule 26(b)(3), however, is only a partial codification of *Hickman* because it does not cover intangible work product (such as the attorney's thoughts that have not been reduced to writing). *Hickman* itself continues to cover such information.

Answer (A) is incorrect. Materials must have been prepared in anticipation of litigation to qualify as work product. Confidentiality alone is not enough.

Answer (C) is incorrect. This answer describes attorney-client privilege. Some of this material may not qualify as work product. For example, work product protection would be lacking if the material is not prepared in anticipation of litigation.

Answer (D) is incorrect. Although the list of persons who may prepare work product is broad ["prepared . . . by or for another party or by or for that other party's representative (including the other party's attorney, consultant, surety, indemnitor, insurer, or agent)"], material prepared by a person who is not the party's agent, prepared for his own purposes, would not meet the requirements of Rule 26(b)(3).

59. **Answer (C) is correct.** The material was prepared in anticipation of litigation by a party's agent, and so it is work product. Because the notes were prepared by the private investigator and appear to record only facts, they would be ordinary rather than opinion work product. Had they included opinions and strategies, they would instead qualify as opinion work product. Ordinary work product can be overcome by a showing of substantial need/undue hardship, and so it is also significant that Nanny Nation could itself interview or depose these neighbors and thereby get the substantial equivalent of the information in the notes. It does not matter that the neighbors might be more forthcoming to Prynne's representative than to Nanny Nation.

Answer (A) is incorrect. Work product can be created by persons other than a party's lawyers.

Answer (B) is incorrect. As set out above, unless these notes reflect mental impressions and opinions, they are ordinary rather than opinion work product.

Answer (D) is incorrect. It is the time and purpose for making the notes, not the timing of the events they describe, that is important to whether the "anticipation of litigation" test is met.

60. This information is relevant and not privileged. While you might at first think this would be covered by the work product doctrine, work product protection shields "material" prepared in anticipation of litigation. It also protects intangible thoughts and strategies a party or its agents may have. Work product does not protect underlying information from discovery. In *Hickman v. Taylor*, 329 U.S. 495 (1947), the original work product case, the Supreme Court noted that the doctrine did not shield relevant information from litigation because a party could ask "searching interrogatories" to get the needed information. Prynne could not ask "what did you learn from investigating our claims." But she can ask about the nature of Hibbins' training and her reaction to it.

61. **Answer (A) is correct.** Nanny Nation's recruiting policies are relevant to Prynne's claims of negligent screening of nannies. This review was done before Pearl's injury — clearly before Prynne anticipated a lawsuit. Sometimes an investigation done in anticipation of a particular type of litigation will qualify as work product, even though it was not done in anticipation of this particular plaintiff's claim. But nothing in this question suggests that the review was done for any purpose other than internal quality control, so it fails the "anticipation of litigation" test and is therefore not work product.

Answer (B) is incorrect. As noted above, it was not done in anticipation of litigation and so it is not work product.

Answer (C) is incorrect. If the report were work product, Prynne would not be able to satisfy the substantial need/undue hardship test to overcome the protection. The information about Nanny Nation's hiring practices is available to Prynne through other discovery devices, such as deposing people with knowledge and requesting documents that would reveal those practices. Prynne would therefore not be able to show that she was unable to get the substantial equivalent of the information without undue hardship.

Answer (D) is incorrect. It is unlikely that locating a single report made a little over a year ago would be so burdensome as to preclude discovery.

62. **Answer (C) is correct.** The investigator was hired to investigate Hibbins' background in anticipation of litigation, and therefore the tape of his interview with Pyncheon would qualify as work product. Because it is a verbatim transcript of a fact-based interview, it would most likely be ordinary rather than opinion work product. However, Pyncheon has become unavailable to provide this information to Prynne. This is the kind of case in which the discovering party may be able to meet the test for overcoming the protection normally provided to ordinary work product. Pyncheon can neither be interviewed nor deposed to get access to the information on the tape. Nor could other residents of the village be compelled to give evidence against their wishes. It is quite likely that the tape would be ordered produced.

Answer (A) is incorrect. It is protected as ordinary work product, but the substantial need/undue hardship override makes the "no" part of the answer incorrect.

Answer (B) is incorrect. Assuming that this tape does not reveal any mental impressions or strategies, it would be categorized as ordinary rather than opinion work product.

Answer (D) is incorrect. Relevant information is only discoverable if it is not protected by a privilege — the discovery privileges shield from discovery information that would otherwise be relevant and discoverable.

63. **Answer (B) is correct.** These interview notes, taken by the lawyer in anticipation of litigation, reveal his thoughts and strategies about the suit, so they are opinion work product.

Answer (A) is incorrect. The evaluative comments make these notes opinion rather than ordinary work product.

Answer (C) is incorrect. Even if they were ordinary work product (and it might be possible to redact the evaluative comments, leaving a portion of the notes that do not disclose mental impressions), the substantial need/undue hardship test could not be met. Prynne could herself interview or depose Holgrave's former boss. If anything, this non-party witness is more available to Prynne than to Nanny Nation.

Answer (D) is incorrect. The fact that Holgrave's boss was not the client of the interviewer means that the notes are not protected by the attorney-client privilege. It does not prevent them from being protected as work product.

64. The Supreme Court in *Hickman v. Taylor*, 329 U.S. 495 (1947), gave several reasons for protecting work product. The Justices argued that if work product were discoverable, parties would engage in various kinds of undesirable behavior such as: (1) sharp practices like withholding documents or producing "red herrings"; (2) inadequately preparing cases for trial due to fear of discovery or lazy appropriation of opposing counsel's work; and (3) inadequate documentation of investigations. The court also feared that discovery of work product materials would have a demoralizing effect on lawyers, damaging the "welfare and tone" of the legal profession. The doctrine protects communications generated in anticipation of litigation and parties' litigation strategies. The existence of the doctrine, however, increases the cost of trial preparation for both sides, increases the cost to parties and the courts of disputing work product issues, and in some cases hides important information from discovering parties.

65.   **Answer (C) is correct.** While work product protection requires anticipation of litigation, communications between attorney and client can be privileged even when litigation is far from their minds if the communication is for the purpose of securing legal advice.

      Answer (A) is incorrect. Confidentiality *is* a requirement for attorney-client privilege to apply. The communication in question must be made in confidence, and it must remain in confidence or the privilege will be lost.

      Answer (B) is incorrect. In order to receive the protection of the attorney-client privilege, the communication must have been made in order to secure legal advice. So, for example, a communication with an attorney made in order to get business advice would not be protected by the privilege.

      Answer (D) is incorrect. Communications that were privileged when made can lose their privileged character if they are revealed to persons outside the attorney-client relationship. For example, if a client writes a memo to his attorney, asking for legal advice, and then later shows that memo to a friend to see the friend's reaction, the privilege has been waived.

66.   **Answer (C) is correct.** When the "client" in question is a corporation rather than a human, it is sometimes difficult to identify which employees of the corporation can qualify as the "client" for purposes of the attorney-client privilege. Different states have adopted different tests. In a state-law based claim in federal court, the federal court will apply state privilege law; in federal question cases, it will apply a federal rule. Some states use a "control group" test: only employees who are high enough in the corporate hierarchy to seek legal advice and act on it qualify as "clients." Other states use a "subject matter" test. Lower level employees can also generate privileged communications as the "client" if these communications are necessary for the lawyer to get the information needed to properly advise the client. Matthew Maule, the Vice President for Human Resources, would probably qualify as a "client" under either test. He is probably high enough up in Nanny Nation's hierarchy to be a member of the control group, and his information about the recruitment and training of nannies makes him a person whose information is important to the lawyer in representing Nanny Nation. If this were a federal claim, it would be governed by *Upjohn Co. v United States*, 449 U.S. 383 (1981), which did not specifically adopt either the control group or subject matter test, but it did extend the privilege to cover corporate communications involving lower level employees who have the information needed by the lawyer to advise the client.

Answer (A) is incorrect, because it implies that Maule would not be a client under the control group test.

Answer (B) is incorrect, because it implies that Maule would not be a client under the subject matter test.

Answer (D) is incorrect, assuming that the questionnaire process meets the other requirements for attorney-client privilege, including confidentiality.

67. **Answer (D) is correct.** In a majority of jurisdictions, a communication between an attorney and the corporate client's *former* employee is not covered by the attorney-client privilege. The Supreme Court reserved this question in the *Upjohn* case, but most courts would hold that Chillingworth is not a "client." Because he is not a client, the communication is not protected by attorney-client privilege. Note that the questionnaire may be protected under the work product doctrine. [See Topic 15.]

Answers (A), (B), and (C) are incorrect because each one assumes that the Chillingworth questionnaire is protected by some version of the attorney-client privilege.

68. Because the direct question is ruled out by discovery privileges, Prynne must use ingenuity and determination to identify alternative sources of the information she wants. She will need to identify persons with knowledge of the hiring of Hibbins through automatic initial disclosures and interrogatories asking for this information. She will then need to depose some or all of them to see what they know, and to ask them who else might have relevant information. Prynne will need to request the production of documents that might relate to Hibbins' recruitment and hiring, and she will need to draft the request specifically enough to elicit the information she wants without being so specific that Nanny Nation can interpret the request not to include relevant documents. She may also try informal investigation (not using the power of the court to compel answers) about Hibbins, her background, and her hiring.

69. Parties sometimes retain experts not to testify at trial but to assist them in preparation of their cases for trial. This type of witness is protected by a privilege contained in Rule 26(b)(4), and generally may not be deposed. Hawthorne is such an expert. However, the rule also recognizes that under certain unusual circumstances it may be unfair to protect a consulting expert witness from discovery. For example, a party may have retained all of the experts in a narrow field, or the consulting expert may have done destructive testing on an item at issue in the lawsuit. Under these kinds of "exceptional circumstances," discovery concerning the consulting expert is allowed. There is no indication that these exceptional circumstances apply here, however.

70. **Answer (A) is correct.** The protections from discovery provided by Rule 26(b)(4) only apply to experts retained in anticipation of litigation. Here, Bellingham has worked for Nanny Nation for a long time, and her information and opinions were not developed in anticipation of litigation but as part of the normal course of Nanny Nation's business.

Answer (B) is incorrect. Although not the type of expert protected by Rule 26(b)(4), Bellingham is a person whose experience and training qualify her as an expert. Some of her testimony will be factual — for example, her knowledge of Nanny Nation's practices and the recommendations she made — but that does not negate her expert status. She would still be allowed to testify as to opinions, a privilege not generally accorded to lay witnesses.

Answer (C) is incorrect. As noted above, because Bellingham was not retained in anticipation of litigation, her knowledge cannot be shielded from discovery by designating her as a consulting expert.

Answer (D) is incorrect. While employees may sometimes, prospectively only, be designated as consulting experts for purposes of their work in assisting with the lawsuit, it is certainly not true that this may always be done. And even when such designation is allowed, pre-existing knowledge remains discoverable.

71. Parties use experts for different reasons in the litigation process. Often the substantive law requires expert testimony in support of a cause of action, and even when it is not so required, it may aid the trier of fact. Parties therefore retain expert witnesses in order to testify on their behalf. It is important to maximize the reliability of this testimony. Opposing parties will therefore cross-examine the expert. In order to make this cross-examination meaningful, parties are allowed considerable discovery about the expert's opinion, the information underlying that opinion, and any biases that the expert might have. Other experts are used only to aid the parties in their preparation for trial. In technical areas, the expert may help the lawyer frame discovery requests and interpret information as it comes in. Because these experts will not testify, and therefore will not be cross-examined, their assistance falls within the zone of privacy provided for trial preparation.

72. **Answer (C) is the best answer.** The kind of information Prynne seeks can be effectively discovered by framing accurate questions and getting the answers under oath. Interrogatories can be sent to Nanny Nation, as it is a party to the lawsuit, and they are well suited to this type of specific background information.

Answer (A) is not the best answer because it suggests using a request for admission. This device would be less effective, because if Prynne is incorrect in the request Nanny Nation's only response will be "denied," not accurate substitute information.

Answer (B) is not the best answer because it suggests using a request for production of documents. While this might succeed in developing some of the desired information, it also might fail to do so. Parties are not required to create documents that did not exist in order to produce them. Nanny Nation, therefore, would only need to produce whatever it has in the way of corporate documents and organizational charts. They might be incomplete or outdated. Or they might not exist at all. So while such a request would be helpful, it would not be sufficient.

Answer (D) is not the best answer because it suggests deposing Nanny Nation's Director of Human Resources (DHR). Such a deposition might result in the information desired, if the DHR knows the information. He might or might not have accurate information about the company's official name and organizational status. He might or might not know the names and job titles of all relevant employees and contact information for them. An interrogatory, by contrast, can require an answer based on the collective knowledge of Nanny Nation's personnel. In addition, there are limits on the length of any one deposition, and Prynne might prefer to use her time with the DHR for narrative information more directly related to her claims. Finally, a deposition would be far more expensive than an interrogatory as a way to acquire this kind of specific information.

73. **Answer (D) is the best answer.** Sometimes a party's physical or mental condition is very important to the issues in the lawsuit. When it is, Rule 35 allows the court to order that person to submit to a medical examination tailored to the condition in question, by a doctor to be named in the order. An examination will only be ordered if the party's condition is "in controversy" and if the party desiring the examination can show "good cause" for the examination. In this case, Pearl's injuries and current condition are central to most of the plaintiffs' claims for damages. It is likely that a judge would order the examination to take place.

Answer (A) is not the best answer because it suggests a request for admission. This would not be as helpful. The most likely response — "denied" — leaves Nanny Nation without any further information about Pearl's condition.

Answer (B) is not the best answer because it suggests a request for production of Pearl's medical records. Such a request would be helpful. However, the reports are likely to record only the observations and opinions of Pearl's treating physician. If Nanny Nation wants an independent evaluation, it will want an examination in addition to the reports, so the Rule 35 examination will be necessary.

Answer (C) is not the best answer because it suggests interrogatories. Specific interrogatories might elicit specific information about Pearl's medical condition and treatment. However, the answers are likely to be brief (they are generally drafted with the aid of counsel) and will again be based on plaintiffs' perception of Pearl's injuries. Also keep in mind that the rules limit the number of interrogatories that can be sent to any one party.

74. Holgrave must produce these documents. The rules require parties to produce not only documents currently in their possession but also documents in the party's "control." This includes any documents that the party has the legal right to obtain on demand. Documents held by a party's attorney, expert, insurance company, accountant, or agent have been held to be within the party's control. In this case, Holgrave can get the documents from his accountant and, therefore, the request to Holgrave to produce the documents is proper.

75. **Answer (B) is the best answer.** When information is held by an entity rather than a human, it may be difficult for an outsider to know the identity of the persons within the organization who have the information they are seeking. Forcing an opposing party to repeatedly notice individuals for deposition, only to be told that that individual does not have the required information, would be extremely inefficient for all concerned. Therefore, Rule 30(b)(6) allows a party to "name as the deponent a public or private corporation or a partnership or association or governmental agency and describe with reasonable particularity the matters on which examination is requested. In that event, the organization so named shall designate one or more persons who consent to testify on its behalf, and may set forth, for each person designated, the matters on which the person will testify." This allows Prynne to depose witnesses with knowledge of all the topics she names. The disadvantage of this procedure is that Nanny Nation is likely to name, insofar as possible, only individuals whose testimony will help Nanny Nation.

Answer (A) is less correct. Prynne could notice individual Nanny Nation employees by name. The danger, as noted above, is that she will waste time and money deposing people who do not have the needed information and will fail to depose people who do.

Answer (C) is incorrect. Prynne can depose the DHR. However, the DHR at his deposition will not be compelled to acquire information he does not have. He can instead answer that he does not know.

Answer (D) is less correct. Hibbins is not a party to the lawsuit. If Hibbins remains in England, Prynne cannot take her deposition without her consent. And even if Hibbins consents, she may not be aware of all of the individuals within Nanny Nation who know about her hiring and training, so her answer might be incomplete.

76. **Answer (B) is correct.** Poppins is not a party to the lawsuit, and so in order to depose its DHR a subpoena must be issued and served on the witness. Prynne could choose to subpoena "Poppins Ltd." and include a list of topics for the deposition, forcing Poppins to identify the relevant witnesses. Or Prynne could subpoena the DHR personally. In neither case would a notice of deposition suffice. The subpoena can also include a document list that, like a request for production of documents, must describe the desired documents with "reasonable particularity." See Rule 34.

    Answer (A) is incorrect. Because Poppins is not a party, a notice will not compel the attendance of a witness at a deposition.

    Answer (C) is incorrect. Nanny Nation does not control Poppins, Poppins is not an employee of Nanny Nation, and so there is no way to compel Nanny Nation to produce another company's employee for deposition.

    Answer (D) is incorrect. There are devices to secure information from non-parties before trial, and subpoenas for deposition (with or without documents) are the most common.

77. Rule 30(d)(2) provides that absent stipulation or court order a person's deposition is limited to a single day of seven hours.

78. Rule 33(a) provides that a party may serve 25 interrogatories, including subparts, on any other party. Additional interrogatories can be served if allowed by stipulation or court order.

79. Prynne should begin by researching the substantive law to see what she will need to prove in order to prevail, both on liability and on damage claims. She should then consider what information will be needed to prove each element of each claim and each item of damages. Some of the information will be available to her outside the formal discovery process (e.g., information about her own actions and her own damages). Other information requires formal discovery. She will first receive automatic initial disclosures from Nanny Nation. She must then strategize, as to each type of information required, what discovery device(s) will best secure this information. In many cases, a party begins by sending interrogatories to identify persons with knowledge and relevant documents, as well as basic background information. The party then follows this with a request for production of the documents identified, and finally takes the depositions of the persons with the most crucial knowledge (depositions being expensive forms of discovery, and time being limited). During the process, Prynne should continue to compare the information she is getting with the information needed, in light of the proof requirements of the substantive law.

TOPIC 19:
DISCOVERY: ELECTRONICALLY-STORED
INFORMATION

ANSWERS

80. It is likely that a company like Kliban, which does extensive business over the internet, maintains a number of its files in electronic form. In addition, a majority of modern businesses of any kind maintain significant amounts of digital information such as word processing documents, data files, e-mail, text messages, voice mail, internet search records, and the like. To search only for hard copy documents would ignore significant sources of information. However, discovery of the electronically-stored information raises logistical issues that are best dealt with early. Eliot's lawyer should therefore do his or her best to learn, before the discovery conference, what formats Eliot (or the firm) is best able to handle. Before and during the conference, the lawyer would want to learn what kind of records Kliban maintains, whether they are accessible in the everyday course of business, and the various formats that the data is kept in. Eliot will want Kliban to agree to produce the data in a searchable format. He will also want Kliban to agree to cease destruction of any data relevant to this case, whether routine or intentional. Given the allegations of dishonest behavior in this case, Eliot will likely want Kliban to produce records in a format that includes embedded data, including information about changes in documents and their authors, rather than a format such as .pdf files that strips out such information.

81. **Answer (B) is the best answer.** While the rule allows the requesting party to ask for a format, and the producing party to suggest a format, neither is absolute and in the absence of agreement it is the judge rather than any particular party who makes the decision. Answer (B) states the default rule.

    Answers (A) and (C) are incorrect for the same reason. While the requesting party can specify a format that it prefers, the producing party may object to the requested format.

    Answer (D) is incorrect. There is no absolute right to convert documents to .pdf format. (It is correct, however, that conversion of documents to hard copy is objectionable since a non-searchable format is not reasonably usable. As the Advisory Committee notes point out, "If the responding party ordinarily maintains the information it is producing in a way that makes it searchable by electronic means, the information should not be produced in a form that removes or significantly degrades this feature."

82. **Answer (D) is the best answer.** Once Kliban knew that documents were likely to be relevant to the litigation, and certainly once the "litigation hold" was agreed to, it had a duty to preserve the data. This means that both tech support personnel, and company employees generally, need to be notified to preserve information. The ignorance of

badly-instructed technical employees is not a valid excuse. Here, where the plaintiff's complaint alleges that the stock sale was circumstantial evidence of the company's knowledge of tainted food, it should have been obvious that documents relating to the stock sale would be relevant to the litigation. Kliban may try to rely on the "safe harbor" provision of new Rule 37(e): "Absent exceptional circumstances, a court may not impose sanctions under these rules on a party for failing to provide electronically stored information lost as a result of the routine, good-faith operation of an electronic information system." However, Pound's deletion of his information is not the type of operation envisioned by this rule, and there is also a strong argument that his deletions were not done in good faith. The court may order Kliban to pay the cost of the more expensive production from the less accessible files, because its actions made that access necessary. Eliot's request is sufficiently targeted, is relevant to his claims, and its centrality to the dispute between the parties makes it appropriate for the court to order production at Kliban's expense.

Answer (A) is inapplicable for the reasons stated above. In addition, the Advisory Committee notes point out that even routine, good faith deletion may still justify the court — not as a "sanction" but as a discovery management tool — in requiring the responding party to make greater efforts to provide relevant information.

Answer (B) is not as correct. It is true that the producing party normally pays the costs of production, but in situations involving ESI that is not reasonably accessible, courts have the discretion to allocate some of the costs of production to the discovering party, and may also order a preliminary sampling of information rather than a full search. Neither the scope of production nor the cost allocation is automatic.

Answer (C) is also less correct. Kliban will, undoubtedly, claim that the ESI is not reasonably accessible. However, its culpability in creating that situation means that it may be required to shoulder the cost of the more expensive search and production.

83.   **Answer (A) is correct.** Nanny Nation has responded to Prynne's request but has not complied fully. Rule 37 controls the tools available to the court to encourage parties to comply with the discovery rules. Prynne must file a motion to compel production of the documents, but Rule 37(a)(2)(B) requires the motion to contain "a certification that the movant has in good faith conferred or attempted to confer with the person or party failing to make the discovery in an effort to secure the information or material without court action." Prynne must, thus, begin by attempting in good faith to contact Nanny Nation and work out their disagreement. If no agreement can be reached, Rule 37 provides for a motion to compel. The rule further allows the successful party to recover the expenses of making the motion, including attorney's fees, unless Nanny Nation's opposition was substantially justified or other circumstances make the award of expenses unjust.

Answer (B) is incorrect. Prynne must first at least attempt to confer with Nanny Nation or risk the wrath of the court and the loss of expenses even if she prevails.

Answer (C) is incorrect. A serious sanction such as striking an answer (sometimes referred to as a "death penalty" sanction) is not allowed when a party has merely objected to making certain discovery. The more severe sanctions of Rule 37(b) do not become available until a party has failed to comply with a court order, or if a party completely fails to appear at a properly noticed deposition or completely fails to respond to interrogatories or document production requests. In addition, Supreme Court case law has placed limits on death penalty sanctions based on the due process clause of the U.S. Constitution. *See, e.g., Societe Internationale Pour Participations Industrielles et Commerciales v. Rogers*, 357 U.S. 197 (1958). A party must be guilty of willfulness, bad faith, or other fault before the court may order litigation-ending sanctions.

Answer (D) is incorrect both because it omits the required conference and because it goes too quickly to severe sanctions.

84.   Rule 37(c) describes the sanctions available for failure to make required disclosures under Rule 26(a). Note first that these disclosures must be supplemented, as provided in Rule 26(e), if the party learns that the information disclosed was incomplete or incorrect. At some point, Nanny Nation must have realized that it had failed to disclose this "very important witness," making its previous answer incomplete. This will often be the case, as the automatic initial disclosures come very early in the litigation. By failing to include the witness' name initially or in a supplemental response, Nanny Nation has violated the disclosure rules. Unless such failure to disclose is harmless, which is unlikely in the case of a key witness, Rule 37(c) provides that the party is

not permitted to use the witness not disclosed as evidence. The rule further provides that in addition (or instead), the court may impose other appropriate sanctions, and Rule 37(c) incorporates by reference the other sanctions in Rule 37, including both attorney's fees and the more severe sanctions of Rule 37(b)(2). Rule 37(c) also allows the court to inform the jury of the failure to make disclosures.

85. **Answer (C) is correct.** A summary judgment ruling is a prediction. The court, by looking at discovery products plus affidavits must predict whether, if the case were allowed to go to trial, there would be a genuine issue of material fact to be tried. At trial, on the other hand, the parties have actually presented live testimony, documents, and other physical evidence and the judge is deciding whether this evidence is sufficient for a reasonable jury to find in favor of the party with the burden of production.

Answer (A) is incorrect. The movant in either case must convince the court that there is or will be no legally sufficient evidence in favor of the non-movant.

Answer (B) is incorrect. The question in both cases is whether the party with the burden has produced a record on which a reasonable jury could find in its favor.

Answer (D) is incorrect. In both cases, the court is to view the evidence and take inferences in the light most favorable to the non-movant. In neither case is the court supposed to make decisions about credibility or to weigh the evidence.

86. **Answer (B) is correct.** For many years after the adoption of the FRCP, the summary judgment motion was disfavored. This attitude was reflected in the movant's burden. Although at trial the plaintiff will have the burden of production on every element of her cause of action, for summary judgment purposes that burden was flipped. In order to show that the defendant was entitled to summary judgment based on the weakness of the plaintiff's case, the defendant had to assume a burden he would not have at trial. He had to *disprove* some element of the plaintiff's claim before he would be entitled to summary judgment.

Answer (A) is incorrect. Demonstrating the existence of a fact issue on the plaintiff's cause of action merely demonstrates that the plaintiff is entitled to have her case decided by the jury.

Answer (C) is incorrect. Negating a single element sufficed. Because the plaintiff has to prove every element of her cause of action, eliminating one was enough to show that the plaintiff could not prevail and the defendant was entitled to summary judgment.

Answer (D) is incorrect. Merely pointing out the likely weaknesses in the plaintiff's case, while sufficient at trial, was not enough in the summary judgment context.

87. **Answer (A) is correct.** Referring to the movant's burden, Justice Harlan seemed to indicate that Kress had to negate the existence of a conspiracy to refuse service and

to arrest Adickes. This could have been done by filing an affidavit that no police officer was in the store at the relevant time. Because Kress did not meet this burden, Adickes was not required to respond and provide evidence that the officer was in the store.

Answer (B) is incorrect. Justice Harlan's opinion does not focus on Kress' attack on Adickes' evidence, but rather on Kress' own summary judgment evidence designed to show the lack of conspiracy. His opinion states, "[a]s the moving party, [Kress] had the burden of showing the absence of a genuine issue as to any material fact, and for these purposes the material lodged must be viewed in the light most favorable to the opposing party." Harlan goes on to examine Kress' support for its motion: the store manager's deposition; the officers' affidavits. He also noted that Kress did not submit any affidavits from the food counter supervisor or from the waitress who actually refused to serve Adickes. He therefore concludes that Kress "failed to fulfill its initial burden of demonstrating what is a critical element in this aspect of the case — that there was no policeman in the store. . . . Because [Kress] did not meet its initial burden . . . [Adickes] was not required to come forward with suitable opposing affidavits."

Answer (C) is incorrect. The opinion does not discuss whether there had been adequate time for discovery.

Answer (D) is incorrect. Justice Harlan's opinion recognizes that once the movant has properly made and supported a motion for summary judgment, the non-movant must do more than simply rely on the contrary allegation in her complaint. The purpose of the 1963 amendment to FRCP 56(e) was to overcome case law to the contrary.

88.   **Answer (B) is correct.** *Celotex* rejects an approach under which a summary judgment movant must assume a burden he would not shoulder at trial. Thus, a defendant moving for summary judgment based on the weakness of the plaintiff's case does *not* need to negate some element of the cause of action. Instead, Justice Rehnquist's opinion allows the movant to "point out" the absence of evidence in the pretrial record.

Answer (A) is incorrect. See above.

Answer (C) is incorrect. Producing evidence showing that there is a material fact issue demonstrates that summary judgment would be improper.

Answer (D) is incorrect. While Justice Rehnquist did note that the plaintiff had had two years to do discovery, he did not list this as a prerequisite to the motion. Rule 56(a) provides that a defending party may move for summary judgment "at any time."

89.   **Answer (A) is correct.** Justice White's separate opinion emphasized that a naked motion with a conclusory statement that the plaintiff has no evidence would not meet the movant's burden.

Answer (B) is incorrect. Justice White's opinion does not require the moving party to negate anything.

Answer (C) is incorrect. Justice White specifically notes that a party need not depose witnesses to create a summary judgment record.

Answer (D) is incorrect. As noted above, simply moving for summary judgment does not require the non-movant to respond.

90. **Answer (D) is correct.** Once a motion for summary judgment has been properly made and supported, the non-movant must convince the court that it has some evidence to support its case, enough so a reasonable jury could find in its favor. This can be done by pointing to material in the record that the movant has ignored. It can also be done by filing affidavits in proper form supplying the necessary evidence, or by some combination of the two. The summary judgment proof does not have to be in admissible form, but it does have to be evidence that can be put in admissible form. This is because evidence that will not be admissible will not be available to help the non-movant meet its burden of production at trial. The summary judgment proof does not need to be direct evidence, but it does have to support at least a reasonable inference in the non-movant's favor.

Answer (A) is incorrect. The evidence need not be in admissible form.

Answer (B) is incorrect. Pointing to allegations in pleadings, even if they are sworn to, is not sufficient to demonstrate the existence of a fact issue. Rule 56(e) provides: "When a motion for summary judgment is made and supported as provided in this rule, an adverse party may not rest upon the mere allegations or denials of the adverse party's pleading, but the adverse party's response, by affidavits or as otherwise provided by this rule, must set forth specific facts showing that there is a genuine issue for trial."

Answer (C) is only partly correct. The non-movant may point to evidence already in the record, but it is not limited to such a response. It can also create new summary judgment evidence, such as affidavits, or provide the court with documents not yet in the record, to demonstrate that a fact issue exists.

91. **Answer (B) is correct.** The court ruling on a motion for summary judgment must look at the evidence in the light most favorable to the non-movant. The court is not supposed to weigh evidence, or to decide which of competing inferences is the more probable.

Answer (A) is incorrect. It is the non-movant, not the movant, in whose favor inferences are to be drawn if reasonable.

Answer (C) is incorrect. The court is not supposed to weigh evidence, but only to decide whether there is some legally sufficient evidence in the non-movant's favor.

Answer (D) is incorrect. At one time some courts used the "any doubt" test: summary judgment was improper if there was any doubt. This approach is no longer used in federal courts. Just as plaintiffs must show the existence of more than a "scintilla" of evidence to avoid judgment as a matter of law, a plaintiff opposing summary judgment must show that an inference on its behalf would be a reasonable one.

92. The Supreme Court has made it easier for parties without the burden of proof at trial to achieve summary judgment in their favor, and has encouraged trial courts to grant summary judgment. Without having to make a significant showing of its own, and without producing any of its own evidence, a defendant can move for summary judgment. Even if the motion is not granted, the defendant will get the benefit of a preview of the plaintiff's case and will force the plaintiff to spend time and money putting its evidence in proper summary judgment form. Systemically, it shifts power from juries to judges. The benefit of this approach is that it allows the court to dispose of non-meritorious claims more expeditiously, protecting defendants from the expense of litigation. The cost is that it creates a procedural disadvantage for plaintiffs, diminishes the role of the civil jury, and runs the risk that meritorious cases will be improperly eliminated.

93.   **Answer (B) is correct.** It is not entirely clear whether this motion meets the requirements of Rule 56 and Supreme Court cases. The motion was filed very early in the lawsuit, and it is fairly conclusory in nature. Pre-discovery summary judgment motions should be the exception rather than the rule. However, the motion does "point out" the plaintiffs' lack of evidentiary support by pointing to Estella's deposition testimony. It is likely that they could also point to the lack of support in the plaintiffs' automatic initial disclosures. [See Topic 13.] This is very similar to the *Celotex* case, in which defendant Celotex pointed to the plaintiff's interrogatory answer to demonstrate the plaintiff's lack of evidence. *Celotex Corp. v. Catrett*, 477 U.S. 317 (1986). It would therefore be strategically dangerous for the plaintiffs to ignore this motion and risk the chance of losing their chance to respond. Because they have no evidence at this time, their best bet is to ask the court for more time to respond under Rule 56(f). This will require the plaintiffs to present affidavits explaining why they cannot at this time present facts sufficient to oppose the motion. The court may well require the plaintiffs to describe the discovery they intend to seek, explain how that discovery would preclude the entry of summary judgment, and explain why that discovery could not have been done earlier. Having to reveal this is in itself a strategic disadvantage, but that damage may be outweighed by the danger that the court will consider and grant the motion for summary judgment.

      Answer (A) is incorrect. While it is probably true that the plaintiffs have not had enough time for discovery, ignoring the motion is a dangerous choice, as discussed above, especially given Estella's deposition testimony.

      Answer (C) is incorrect. The problem states that the plaintiffs have no evidence. If they have some, it would be wise to consider whether they could put it in a form to present to the court. The answer is incorrect, however, in stating that the evidence must be in admissible form. In *Celotex*, for example, the Court was willing to consider a letter written by the decedent's former employer which, although itself inadmissible as hearsay, demonstrated that the letter writer could be called as a witness to testify to relevant information within his personal knowledge.

      Answer (D) is incorrect. WYWTS does not need to disprove the plaintiffs' claim in order to be entitled to summary judgment.

94.   **Answer (C) is correct.** The parties' disagreement about the effect of the release centers on legal rather than factual issues. They agree that the release exists and that the plaintiffs signed it. They disagree about the legal effect of the release. WYWTS argues that the release is enforceable and covers the plaintiffs' claims. The plaintiffs argue that the release is unenforceable as applied to claims of the defendant's own negligence, and their legal argument is correct (for purposes of this question, anyway). Therefore, the court should deny the motion for summary judgment based on enforcement of the release. This denial is not based on the existence of a fact issue. Because the release is unenforceable even if signed, the question of whether or not the plaintiffs signed it is not a "material" fact.

Answers (A) and (D) are incorrect. Because the release is not enforceable as a matter of substantive law, it does not matter if the plaintiffs signed it, so they have no need to try to demonstrate that they did not.

Answer (B) is incorrect. Neither Rule 56 nor case law implementing it prohibit successive summary judgment motions. Recall that in *Celotex* itself the Court was considering a second motion for summary judgment. Successive motions might annoy the trial court, but they are not improper.

95. **Answer (C) is correct.** With this motion, WYWTS is assuming a heavier burden than that required by the rules: it is attempting to disprove an element of the plaintiffs' claim. While not required, this would certainly suffice to show that the plaintiffs cannot succeed. The affidavit testimony of the expert witness appears to cover the relevant issues and to be within the appropriate area of expertise. The plaintiffs could have responded in a way to defeat summary judgment, as by questioning the factual basis of the expert's opinion or by countering with an expert of their own, but given the plaintiffs' failure to respond, the court could properly grant summary judgment to the defendant.

Answer (A) is incorrect. Canvassing the discovery record and pointing out the lack of evidence to support the plaintiff is one way to show entitlement to summary judgment, but it is not the only way.

Answer (B) is incorrect. Expert testimony can form the basis of a motion for summary judgment. In certain cases, trial courts have the authority under *Daubert v. Merrell Dow Pharm. Inc.*, 509 U.S. 579 (1993), to exclude expert testimony as unreliable. In such a case, the expert's affidavit could be used neither to secure summary judgment nor to oppose it. Absent such a situation, however, expert deposition testimony or affidavits can be considered in summary judgment proceedings when they would be proper at trial.

Answer (D) is incorrect. The non-movant's failure to respond may create a situation in which the court may grant summary judgment, but this is not inevitable. If the movant has failed to meet its initial burden, summary judgment would be improper despite the lack of a response. Even if the movant has made a strong argument that there is no genuine issue of material fact, the trial court has some discretion to deny summary judgment and allow further factual development of the case.

96. **Answer (D) is correct.** While the defendant's affidavit in isolation might have justified summary judgment (see the previous question), the situation here is different. There are now two expert witnesses, each having examined the available evidence, who have reached different conclusions about the cause of the ceiling fan accident. In the absence of a *Daubert* problem with one of the experts, this merely demonstrates the existence of a genuine issue of material fact. That fact issue makes summary judgment improper. The judge is not to compare the testimony of the two experts and decide which one he finds more convincing; that is the jury's job.

Answers (A) and (B) are incorrect. As noted above, the judge's role in considering a motion for summary judgment is not to weigh or compare evidence, but merely to decide the threshold issue of whether there is a genuine issue of material fact to go to the jury.

Answer (C) is incorrect. The defendant's motion on its own was adequately supported (see the preceding question). The plaintiff's motion on its own might at least have justified a partial summary judgment (it would not be sufficient to prove the plaintiffs' damages as a matter of law). It is the conflict demonstrated by the two expert affidavits that leads to the need to deny the motion rather than the defects in either motion standing alone.

97. The court should deny the defendant's motion for summary judgment. The motion was properly made and supported because the plaintiffs were given an adequate time for discovery, and the motion seems to meet the requirements of the combined Rehnquist/ White opinions in *Celotex* of pointing out the lack of evidence. The motion would have been stronger if it also went through all of the existing discovery products (e.g., deposition testimony, documents produced, other interrogatories) and further demonstrated the lack of evidence of the defendant's fault and causation. The courts, after *Celotex*, however, have not tended to put a heavy burden on the moving party. *See* RICHARD L. MARCUS, MARTIN H. REDISH & EDWARD F. SHERMAN, CIVIL PROCEDURE: A MODERN APPROACH at 425 (3d ed. 2000) ("The majority of post-*Celotex* lower courts have read that decision not to impose a significant triggering burden on a movant who lacks the burden of production at trial. Indeed, many lower court decisions following *Celotex* have either reduced the burden dramatically or ignored it completely.")

The plaintiffs' response was sufficient to avoid summary judgment. The letter from the insurance adjuster is not itself admissible. Even if properly authenticated, it would constitute hearsay. If the insurance adjuster were to testify at trial, however, and his opinion were based on his observations and expertise, that would constitute some evidence of breach and causation. The plaintiffs would improve their response by making clear that they intend to call the adjuster as a witness at trial. The deposition of Mrs. Havisham will not be as helpful. It was taken in another proceeding in which WYWTS was not a party, and the former testimony exception to the hearsay rule will not make this deposition testimony admissible. Because Mrs. Havisham is dead, she cannot be called as a witness in this case. Further, the plaintiffs have pointed to crucial evidence that has been unavailable to them (they should explain the efforts they have made to show that they have been diligent and the reason they think the carpenter's testimony will help them), and by coming up with a plausible plan to get access to the carpenter's testimony they could ask the court to delay its ruling until this evidence is available.

98.   **Answer (D) is correct.** The Supreme Court's decisions in *Beacon Theatres, Inc. v. Westover*, 359 U.S. 500 (1959), and *Dairy Queen, Inc. v. Wood*, 369 U.S. 469 (1962), hold that where both legal claims and equitable claims are presented in a single case, the right to a jury trial exists for factual questions, regardless of whether the case would previously have been categorized as basically equitable or basically legal. Hence, because the money damages claim presents legal issues, all factual questions involving those issues (i.e., the elements of the trespass claim, including damages) must be tried to a jury, assuming a timely and proper demand is made for a jury trial.

Answer (A) is probably incorrect. If the issues are entirely equitable, there is no right to a jury trial. It is possible that one or more of the issues in Fred's trespass case for injunctive relief could be classified as legal under the Court's celebrated footnote in *Ross v. Bernhard*, 396 U.S. 531, 538 n.10 (1970) — "As our cases indicate, the 'legal' nature of an issue is determined by considering, first, the pre-merger custom with reference to such questions, the remedy sought, and third, the practical abilities and limitations of juries." But based on the factors identified, that classification is unlikely.

Answer (B) is incorrect. This action for damages is entirely legal.

Answer (C) is incorrect. The incidental character of the money damages claim does not matter. The equitable "clean up" doctrine has been eliminated by *Beacon Theaters* and *Dairy Queen*.

99.   **Answer (C) is correct.** The Supreme Court has held that the constitutional guarantee of a jury trial is applicable to antitrust damage suits, whether or not equitable (non-jury) claims are joined with the legal claim. *Beacon Theaters, Inc. v. Westover*, 359 U.S. 500 (1959).

Answer (A) is not correct. The "gist" or principal thrust of the action does not matter. That is not the test.

Answer (B) is not correct. Although the Sherman and Robinson Patman Acts are federal statutes enacted after 1791, the Seventh Amendment is not confined to causes of action recognized by English common law in 1791. The Seventh Amendment guarantee applies to actions for damages, particularly if there is an analogous common law cause of action that was triable to an English jury in 1791.

Answer (D) is not correct for the same reason that answer (C) is correct.

100.   Although the Third Circuit has recognized a complex case exception grounded on the Due Process clause of the Fifth Amendment for antitrust suits that are so complicated that a jury is unable to decide in a rational manner (*see In re Japanese Elec. Prods. Antitrust Litigation*, 631 F.2d 1069), there is probably no complex case exception. *See In re U.S. Fin. Sec. Litig.*, 609 F.2d 411 (9th Cir. 1979). Similarly, the celebrated footnote in *Ross v. Bernhard*, 396 U.S. 531, 538 n. 10, cannot be stretched to make complex cases equitable.

TOPIC 24:
BURDENS OF PROOF AT TRIAL; MOTIONS FOR JUDGMENT AS A MATTER OF LAW

ANSWERS

101. The court should grant the motion because although the Seventh Amendment affords Bunker the right to a trial by jury on all factual issues, expert testimony was necessary on the professional standard of care applicable to Dr. Kildare and on the cause of Bunker's injuries. The right to a jury trial of factual issues (i.e., the right to have a jury determine factual questions concerning the elements of legal claims) depends on the production of legally probative evidence concerning the factual issues. Because the substantive law requires expert testimony in medical negligence cases to set the professional standard of care and, in most cases, to provide evidence of the cause-in-fact of the claimant's injuries, Bunker presented no legally sufficient evidence for a reasonable jury to find in his favor on the issues of negligence and causation.

102. **Answer (A) is correct.** Ordinarily, the plaintiff has the burden both of production and persuasion on all of the elements of each cause of action. The burden of production can shift during trial (if, for example, Kate introduced such convincing evidence during her case in chief that no reasonable jury could fail to find for her, the burden of production would shift to Dave), but normally the burden of production for the plaintiff's own case is on the plaintiff, and the burden of persuasion stays with the plaintiff to prove her cause of action by a "preponderance of the evidence."

Answer (B) is incorrect. The burden of production only shifts to Dave if Kate introduces evidence that is so overwhelming that, in the absence of a rebuttal, it proves her claim as a matter of law. If Kate merely introduces enough evidence to meet her burden of production (i.e., to raise questions of fact for the jury on the elements of her claim), no burden of production shifts to Dave to introduce evidence to contest Kate's case-in-chief. Dave will have the opportunity to introduce rebuttal evidence, but he does not have the technical burden to do so. This answer is correct in that the burden of persuasion remains on Kate.

Answer (C) is incorrect. As noted above, the burden of production would only shift to Dave under limited circumstances, and the burden of persuasion would not shift to him.

Answer (D) is incorrect. Dave has the burden of production and persuasion on his affirmative defense of contributory negligence (i.e., that Kate was negligent and that her negligence was the cause of the occurrence in question), but that does not give him either burden with regard to Kate's claim that Dave was negligent.

103. **Answer (B) is correct.** If Kate fails to produce evidence on which a reasonable jury could find for her, she has failed to meet her burden of production. This would entitle

219

Dave to move for judgment as a matter of law and the judge could properly grant the motion rather than sending the case to the jury.

Answer (A) is incorrect. If Kate meets her burden of production, producing enough evidence that a reasonable jury could find in her favor, it is the jury and not the judge who decides whether Kate has met her burden of persuasion. It would therefore be improper for the judge to take the case from the jury.

Answer (C) is incorrect. While the Seventh Amendment does provide an important right to jury trial in civil cases, if there is no fact issue to decide there is no constitutional right to have a jury decide the case. Therefore, if Kate fails to meet her burden of production, the judge can properly take the case from the jury.

Answer (D) is incorrect. As the plaintiff, Kate will go first in presenting her evidence. At the end of this phase of the trial, when Kate rests, Dave has had the opportunity to cross examine Kate's witnesses but has not yet had the opportunity to put on evidence of his own. Although her case might appear very strong in isolation, Dave might be able to show its weaknesses with his own evidence. It is not at all irrelevant what evidence he might have. Only if the evidence for Kate remains conclusive after *both* Kate and Dave have rested and closed their cases may the judge grant judgment as a matter of law for Kate without sending the case to the jury.

104. **Answer (A) is correct.** The defendants have the burden of production and persuasion on almost all affirmative defenses; they must plead them, they must provide evidence to support them, and they must prove them by a preponderance of the evidence. The burden of persuasion on this issue will not shift but will stay on Dave throughout the case.

Answer (B) is incorrect. Dave has both the burden of persuasion and the burden of production on all the elements of his affirmative defense.

Answer (C) is incorrect. It would not be enough for Dave to carry the burdens on one element of contributory negligence. Unless there is enough evidence on *all* elements that a reasonable jury could find for Dave, evidence on one element will not be enough. Similarly, Dave must prove all the elements by a preponderance of the evidence.

Answer (D) is incorrect. As noted above, Dave has both burdens.

105. **Answer (B) is probably correct.** One of the most important aspects of the right to jury trial under the Seventh Amendment to the Constitution is the jury's ability to draw inferences from circumstantial evidence. Because juries typically decide mixed questions of law and fact and because most cases do not involve clashes between direct evidence presented by eyeball (percipient) witnesses, the power to choose between opposing reasonable inferences is extremely significant. Neither the trial judge nor a reviewing court is at liberty to substitute its view for the jury's decision, as long as the inference drawn by the jury is reasonable. If reasonable minds can differ, the fact finder's choice

is sustainable in the sense that it is supported by a legally sufficient evidentiary basis. Although News Ltd.'s evidence is probably sufficient to support the reasonable inference of Maurice's *de facto* membership in Creedlove, based on the totality of the evidence, reasonable minds could differ. Hence, News Ltd. is not entitled to judgment as a matter of law. The same would be true for Maurice.

Answer (A) is incorrect. Maurice's testimony may be unconvincing, but it is not incredible and lacking any probative value, such as if he had testified contrary to the laws of physics.

Answer (C) is probably incorrect. Maurice's so-called direct evidence about Creedlove does not negate the evidentiary value of any reasonable inference that could be drawn from the circumstantial evidence.

Answer (D) is incorrect. It is for the jury to decide the credibility of witnesses.

106.   The trial court may grant the motion if the trial judge concludes that Maurice's testimony is unconvincing. In contrast to a jury trial, in a bench trial Rule 52(c) authorizes a trial judge to render judgment against a claimant on a claim or defense if the claimant "has been fully heard on an issue" and the court "finds against the party on that issue." This means that the trial judge can render judgment against a claimant after the claimant rests, if the judge does not credit the claimant's evidence and finds that Maurice was a member of Creedlove.

107.   Whether it is regarded as a policy reason or simply an expedient, Rule 50(b) treats a postverdict motion as a renewed motion for a delayed directed verdict to avoid a direct clash with the Reexamination Clause of the Seventh Amendment, which states that "no fact tried by a jury, shall be otherwise re-examined in any Court of the United States, than according to the rules of the common law." Although the Supreme Court long ago determined that certain common law practices, somewhat different in form from directed verdict motions, were analogous to directed verdict motions such that the use of a directed verdict motion did not offend the Reexamination Clause, no common law analogs exist for postverdict motions for judgment contrary to the verdict. Accordingly, to comply with the Seventh Amendment, the post-verdict motion, which actually is filed after judgment, must be characterized as a renewed motion leading to a delayed, but constitutionally valid, directed verdict. State constitutions (which govern trial practice in state courts) that do not contain Reexamination Clauses do not require renewed motions.

108.   **Answer (D) is the best answer.** In 2006, the Supreme Court resolved a split of authority between the circuits by holding that an appellant must renew a pre-verdict 50(a) motion as specified in Rule 50(b) in order to make a sufficiency of the evidence challenge in the court of appeals. *Unitherm Food Systems, Inc. v. Swift-Eckrich, Inc.*, 546 U.S. 394 (2006); *see also Johnson v. New York, N.H. & H.R. Co.*, 344 U.S. 48 (1952). In other words, a denial of a pre-verdict Rule 50(a) motion is not reviewable on appeal unless

a Rule 50(b) motion renews the Rule 50(a) motion after judgment. The Rule 50(a) motion is a prerequisite to a Rule 50(b) motion, but is not sufficient to preserve a legal insufficiency complaint. Accordingly, **Answer (A) is clearly correct. Answer (C) is also correct**. The *Unitherm* opinion also explains that the denial of a post-judgment motion for new trial can be a basis for appellate complaint concerning the sufficiency of the evidence. In this situation, the movant/appellant is entitled only to a new trial, not to a judgment in its favor. In *Unitherm*, the appellant did not request a new trial under Rule 59.

Answer (B) is incorrect for the same reasons.

109. No, denial of a summary judgment motion is not reviewable after full trial on the merits. A district court's judgment on the verdict after a trial on the merits supersedes prior summary judgment proceedings. *Black v. J. I. Case Co.*, 22 F.3d 568, 569-70 (5th Cir. 1994) (circuit court will not review denial of pretrial summary judgment when, after full trial on merits, judgment is rendered adverse to movant).

110. **Answer (D) is correct.** Motions for new trial may be made and granted "for any reason for which a new trial has heretofore been granted in an action at law in federal court." [Restyled Rule 59(a).] This includes a lot of territory, including any error that occurred during the pretrial phase of the litigation or that occurred during trial. Significantly, however, the motion also may be used to challenge the verdict or a particular jury finding that is not supported by factually sufficient evidence, i.e., a verdict that is supported by some legally sufficient evidence but that is manifestly against the weight of the evidence.

Answer (A) is incorrect. Judge-made findings are generally inappropriate in a case tried to a jury.

Answer (B) is incorrect. Because the erroneous instructions actually favored Sunderland and Sunderland still lost, the problem lies elsewhere. However, it may be the case that the assessment of the sufficiency of the evidence would be affected by the erroneous charge.

Answer (C) is probably incorrect because the admission of improper evidence in a civil case normally does not entitle a complaining party to a new trial unless the entire case turned on the inadmissible evidence.

111. It is now clear that complaints concerning both the legal and the factual sufficiency of the evidence must be made in the trial court in order to challenge the sufficiency of the evidence on appeal. Legal sufficiency complaints are preserved by Rule 50(a) motions "renewed" as Rule 50(b) motions after judgments. Factual sufficiency complaints are preserved by Rule 59 motions for new trial. *Unitherm Food Systems, Inc. v. Swift-Eckrich, Inc.*, 546 U.S. 394 (2006).

112. **Answer (C) is correct.** Rule 50(b) provides expressly for alternative motions for new trial coupled with renewed motions for judgment.

Answer (A) is incorrect. Clark can move for judgment as a matter of law even if he had the burden of proof on the whole case, assuming compliance with Rule 50(b).

Answer (B) is incorrect. If the verdict is against the weight of the evidence, the remedy is a new trial, not a judgment contrary to the verdict.

Answer (D) is incorrect for the reasons stated above.

113. If the trial judge concludes that the jury's damage award is excessive as against the manifest weight of the evidence, the trial judge may grant a new trial. It is conceivable that the new trial could be granted on the issue of damages alone. A partial new trial is possible on an issue or issues that are separable without unfairness to the parties. Additionally, in cases of excessive verdicts, the trial judge can suggest a remittitur of the excess and condition the denial of a new trial on the acceptance by the plaintiff of the trial court's suggestion. On appeal, an abuse of discretion standard will be applied to the appellate issue of the factual sufficiency of the evidence to support the finding.

114. **Answer (D) is correct.** Duke has ten days after entry of judgment to move for a new trial on legal or equitable grounds. However, Rule 60(b) provides additional time. A Rule 60(b) motion based on "mistake, inadvertence, surprise or excusable neglect" may be made not more than one year after the entry of the judgment. Rule 60(c)(1).

Answer (A) is correct because the clerk is not authorized to enter a default judgment for unliquidated damages under Rule 55(b).

Answer (B) is correct for the reasons stated above.

Answer (C) is not correct. Judgments based on false testimony are not void, although they are subject to attack under Rule 60(b).

115. Duke can attack the judgment if Ace's affidavit was false or fraudulent. A Rule 60(b) motion based on fraud (whether previously called intrinsic or extrinsic), misrepresentation, or misconduct by an opposing party may be made "within a reasonable time" and no more than one year after the entry of the judgment. Rule 60(c)(1).

116. Rule 60(d) provides that an independent action may be brought to relieve a party from a judgment obtained by the commission of a "fraud upon the court."

117. **Answer (D) is correct.** The statute creating jurisdiction in cases involving citizens of different states (28 U.S.C. § 1332) has been interpreted to require complete diversity. In other words, no plaintiff can be a citizen of the same state as any defendant. In this case, the plaintiff is a citizen of Texas. One defendant, Mark, is a citizen of Mississippi, creating minimal diversity. However, defendant Acme is a corporation, and corporations are citizens both of their state of incorporation and of their principal place of business. Acme is therefore a citizen both of Delaware and of Texas. Therefore, both Tom and Acme are Texas citizens, destroying complete diversity.

Answer (A) is incorrect. Diversity does exist between Tom and Mark, but this is not sufficient for federal court jurisdiction.

Answer (B) is incorrect. It is the citizenship of plaintiffs vs. defendants that matters for purposes of diversity jurisdiction, not the citizenship of co-defendants. In fact, if the plaintiff were from Texas and both defendants were from Mississippi, diversity jurisdiction would exist.

Answer (C) is incorrect. As explained above, Tom and Acme are citizens of the same state because of the way corporate citizenship is determined.

118. Yes. Multiple parties on the same side of the lawsuit may be citizens of the same state, as long as all plaintiffs are diverse in citizenship from all defendants. Therefore, the fact that Clara and Carl are both from California, and that Ida and Irene are both from Illinois, does not destroy diversity.

119. **Answer (D) is correct.** A person when born acquires a domicile of origin (the parents' domicile). In order to change to a new domicile (a domicile of choice) one must intend to make the new place home for an indefinite period of time and must be physically present there at least briefly. Here, Pam has changed her domicile to Texas because she is a resident there and intends to make it her home. The fact that she has not yet secured a permanent job does not prevent Texas from being her domicile.

Answer (A) is incorrect. Pennsylvania is her domicile of origin. It is also true that students, especially undergraduates, often have not changed domicile by going off to school. They tend to lack the necessary intent to make the location of the school a permanent home. Pam's return during the summers to her parents' home reinforces this belief here. But it is not true that students can never acquire a new domicile of choice.

Answer (B) is incorrect. Under different circumstances, Pam might have changed her domicile to Massachusetts. She was physically present there. But her practice of returning home to Pennsylvania during the summers, her continuing financial dependence on her parents, and her apparent intention to leave Massachusetts upon graduation are indications that she did not change her domicile.

Answer (C) is incorrect. It is not clear whether Pam's domicile changed briefly to Virginia. If she considered it to be home, and had no intention of leaving at a fixed time, that might be true. It seems more likely, though, that Pam had already planned to leave Virginia to move to Texas to attend law school. In either case, her subsequent move to Texas with intent to stay there means that Virginia is not her domicile at this time.

120.   **Answer (A) is correct.** The statement that Karen has always lived in Kansas indicates that Kansas is her domicile of origin. She has the required intent to make New York her home. However, she lacks the second requirement for acquiring a domicile of choice: presence at the new domicile. A person keeps her old domicile until she acquires a new one, and because she did not yet reach New York, she is still domiciled in Kansas.

Answer (B) is incorrect. Karen is present in Ohio, but she lacks the necessary intent to make it her home. If a person intends to leave at some fixed point in time, for example graduation from school or, as here, recovery from her injuries, she does not have the intent required to acquire a domicile of choice.

Answer (C) is incorrect. As explained above, intent alone is not enough for a change of domicile.

Answer (D) is incorrect. Everyone has a domicile at all times (it's just a rule — while there may be a "man without a country" there is no such thing as a "man without a domicile"). Traditionally, people had a single domicile for all purposes, although the more modern approach might recognize different domiciles for different purposes.

121.   **Answer (B) is correct.** This question focuses on the timing of the domicile issue for purposes of diversity jurisdiction. At the time Mike's cause of action accrued, he was domiciled in (and hence a citizen of) Maine. However, he successfully changed his domicile to New Hampshire by moving there with the correct intent. It is his domicile at the time he files the lawsuit that determines his citizenship for purposes of diversity jurisdiction. While there is a statute forbidding improper or collusive joinder of parties to achieve diversity jurisdiction (28 U.S.C. § 1359), it does not apply to a bona fide change of domicile by a party to the suit.

Answer (A) is incorrect. It is his domicile at the time of commencement of the action, not at the time the cause of action arose, that counts.

Answer (C) is incorrect. Mike's change of citizenship does affect the existence of diversity jurisdiction.

Answer (D) is incorrect. The ownership of property is a factor that courts may consider in determining a person's domicile, but it is not determinative. For example, a person domiciled in New Jersey might own a summer home on Cape Cod and go there for a few weeks each summer, but the person's domicile would remain in New Jersey.

122. **Answer (C) is correct.** This claim could properly be brought in federal court based on diversity jurisdiction, because the parties are from different states and the amount in controversy is sufficient. Diversity jurisdiction, however, is just an option for the parties. The federal courts have concurrent jurisdiction with the state courts in diversity cases, and so these lawsuits can also be filed in state court. [Under certain circumstances, a defendant sued in state court may choose to "remove" the case to federal court. See Topic 31.]

    Answer (A) is incorrect. There is complete diversity between Greg and Frank and the amount in controversy requirement is satisfied, but federal jurisdiction is not exclusive.

    Answer (B) is incorrect. Although the purpose of diversity jurisdiction includes the protection of out-of-state defendants from local prejudice, that makes diversity jurisdiction available, not mandatory. And the facts of this question do not tell us whether Frank is being sued in Georgia or at home in Florida.

    Answer (D) is incorrect. Neither diversity jurisdiction nor generic federal question jurisdiction is exclusive in the federal courts. There are a few federal statutes requiring certain kinds of federal claims to be brought in federal rather than state court, but this is the exception rather than the rule. In general, both diversity and federal question jurisdiction are concurrent with the state courts.

123. **Answer (D) is correct.** The Supreme Court has held that an unincorporated association is a citizen of the states of each member. *See, e.g., United Steelworkers of America v. R.H. Bouligny, Inc.*, 382 U.S. 145 (1965). Therefore, the Brotherhood of Bison is a citizen of Wisconsin, Illinois, and all the other states in which members are domiciled, including Minnesota. Because Marilyn, the plaintiff, is from Minnesota, this case lacks complete diversity and cannot be brought in federal court on that basis.

    Answer (A) is incorrect. Although the principal place of business is significant in determining the citizenship of a corporation, the same is not true for an unincorporated association.

    Answer (B) is incorrect. The domicile of a majority of members is not the only citizenship of an unincorporated association.

    Answer (C) is incorrect. It can be difficult to get diversity jurisdiction when a party is an unincorporated association, because it may be a citizen of so many states. But it is not true that its citizenship can never form the basis of diversity jurisdiction.

124. **Answer (A) is correct.** For purposes of diversity jurisdiction, a class takes the citizenship of its named plaintiff(s). Here the only named plaintiff is Terry, a citizen

of Tennessee. There are class members from every state, but their domiciles are not considered for purposes of diversity jurisdiction. Because defendant Cheap Computers is a citizen of Montana, the diversity requirement is satisfied.

Answer (B) is incorrect. It is true that some members of the class will be citizens of Montana, but their citizenship does not count unless they become named plaintiffs.

Answer (C) is incorrect. The diversity of citizenship requirement does indeed apply to class actions.

Answer (D) is incorrect. Because the citizenship of class members is not counted, Terry need not exclude citizens of Montana from the class in order to achieve complete diversity.

125. **Answer (C) is correct.** Although under traditional principles of diversity jurisdiction this case could not be maintained in federal court, the new Multiparty, Multiforum Jurisdiction Act, 28 U.S.C. § 1369 creates jurisdiction for cases such as this. Because at least some of the plaintiffs are not citizens of either Utah or Delaware, there is minimal diversity. More than 75 people died in the accident, and UA resides in places in addition to Idaho, where a substantial part of the accident took place. Note that under § 1369(c)(2), a corporation resides in "any State in which it is incorporated or licensed to do business or is doing business."

Answer (A) is incorrect because complete diversity is not required under § 1369.

Answer (B) is incorrect because UA is a citizen of both Delaware and Utah.

Answer (D) is incorrect because "substantial parts of the accident" taking place in multiple states is only one of the possible situations under which § 1369 creates jurisdiction.

126. **Answer (C) is correct.** In order for diversity jurisdiction to be proper, the amount in controversy must exceed $75,000, exclusive of interest and costs (28 U.S.C. § 1332). There are various rules regarding the circumstances under which multiple claims can be aggregated (added together) to reach the $75,000 threshold. All claims asserted by one plaintiff against the same defendant may be aggregated (although the same damages may not be counted twice). Here, Nick can add the two distinct claims to reach a total of $80,000.

   Answers (A) and (B) are incorrect. The claims will be added, as noted above.

   Answer (D) is incorrect. Even if Nick is due interest on this breach of contract claim, interest is not counted in computing the amount in controversy.

127. No. You cannot aggregate the claims of multiple plaintiffs even against a single defendant. This question is governed by a different aggregation rule. Claims asserted by multiple plaintiffs against the same defendant, or claims asserted by the same plaintiff against multiple defendants, cannot be aggregated. There is a small exception to this rule for a historical category of "common and undivided interest," but that exception would not apply here.

128. **Answer (A) is correct.** Although the general rule is that the claims of multiple plaintiffs cannot be aggregated, there is an exception for claims that are jointly held by multiple claimants. The exception is based on the concept that joint claims are brought by the joint claimants collectively.

   Answers (B), (C), and (D) are incorrect. There is only one claim made under the circumstances of the problem, so the amount is $100,000.

129. **Answer (B) is the correct answer.** Because the defendants are not jointly and severally liable for the entire amount owed to Alice under the two separate contracts, there is no aggregation.

   Answer (A) is incorrect for the same reason that (B) is correct.

   Answer (C) is incorrect because diversity is complete between Alice and each defendant. Co-defendants may be citizens of the same state without destroying diversity of citizenship.

   Answer (D) is incorrect because (C) is incorrect.

130. **Answer (B) is correct.** Under traditional principles of tort law, joint tortfeasors are each liable for the entire loss under circumstances making the injury indivisible. Although modern tort reform legislation has frequently modified this approach, if joint and several liability is a possible outcome under the law and the evidence, the claims can be aggregated.

Answer (A) is incorrect for the same reason, i.e., joint and several liability is an exception to the normal nonaggregation rule.

Answer (C) is incorrect for the reasons stated in (B), i.e., either defendant could be liable for the entire loss.

Answer (D) is incorrect. Jurisdiction cannot depend on what is established at trial.

131. **Answer (B) is correct.** This question requires you to think about the difficulties in computing amount in controversy when the plaintiff seeks injunctive relief rather than money damages. The controversy must be quantified in some way. Case law is not entirely consistent in this area, but many courts measure the amount in controversy by the value of the claim to the plaintiff. One influential treatise advocates upholding jurisdiction if the amount exceeds the jurisdictional minimum from either plaintiff's or defendant's viewpoint. *See* 14B WRIGHT, MILLER & COOPER, FEDERAL PRACTICE AND PROCEDURE § 3703 (1998 & Supp. 2003). Here, that means that the value of the claim is the difference in value of Susan's property with and without the shack. So although the cost to Nate of complying with the injunction would be only $300, it is most likely that the amount in controversy is $100,000.

Answer (A) is incorrect. Susan's land is not worthless even with the shack, and so the full value of the land is not the best measure of the amount in controversy.

Answer (C) is incorrect. Most courts will not measure the amount in controversy by the cost to the defendant. A minority of courts might do so. Some academics have advocated using the smaller number, on the theory that the parties could bargain for a resolution at that amount, but this is not the majority view.

Answer (D) is incorrect. Even though the plaintiff is not seeking monetary relief, an amount in controversy must be calculated if jurisdiction is based on diversity of citizenship.

132. **Answer (A) is correct.** Although the courts are not entirely consistent on this issue, the majority ignores the value of the counterclaim when computing the amount in controversy. *See* 14B WRIGHT, MILLER & COOPER, FEDERAL PRACTICE AND PROCEDURE § 3706 (1998). The plaintiff must establish a basis for jurisdiction without adding the counterclaim to reach $75,000.

Answer (B) is incorrect. Counterclaims are not aggregated with the primary claim even when they are compulsory.

Answer (C) is incorrect. Counterclaims are also not compared with the plaintiff's claim to determine how much money might ultimately change hands.

Answer (D) is incorrect. As noted above, counterclaims are not aggregated with the plaintiff's claim to compute the amount in controversy.

133.   **Answer (A) is correct.** The court generally looks at the face of the plaintiff's complaint to determine the amount in controversy. However, if the plaintiff has requested damages that are legally unavailable, they will not be counted because they cannot be recovered whatever the facts of the case might turn out to be. Here, under the applicable law, the punitive damages are unavailable, so they may not be counted in computing the amount in controversy. The only remaining claim is for $15,000, well short of the required $75,000.

Answer (B) is incorrect. Courts will not try to predict whether the plaintiffs will really recover as much money as they have prayed for in computing the amount in controversy. Unless it appears to a legal certainty that the amount requested cannot be recovered, the plaintiff's complaint will determine the amount. This answer is therefore wrong because it indicates that it is the jury's probable reaction rather than the legal unavailability of the punitive damage claim that would defeat jurisdiction.

Answer (C) is incorrect. It is true that damages based on contract and tort theories can be aggregated (if they are different damages). That does not rescue the punitive damages in this case.

Answer (D) is incorrect. The problem is not whether Naomi's two types of damages can be added together, but that the $100,000 claim is legally invalid.

134.   **Answer (D) is correct.** Even cases that otherwise meet the requirements for diversity jurisdiction based on their citizenship and the amount in controversy may fall outside of federal jurisdiction if they fall within an exception created by the courts. One such exception, applicable here, is the domestic relations exception. This exception was carved out by the Supreme Court long ago, based on a belief that such cases are better left to the state courts. See *Ankenbrandt v. Richards*, 504 U.S. 689 (1992), for a discussion of the doctrine. The other such exception is for probate proceedings.

Answer (A) is incorrect. Romeo has apparently changed his domicile to Rhode Island. But this still does not confer diversity jurisdiction over a divorce case.

Answers (B) and (C) are incorrect. The size of the marital estate is immaterial.

135.   The court should deny the motion to dismiss. Plaintiffs, in their complaints, must plead the basis for federal jurisdiction. In diversity cases, this includes an allegation that the amount in controversy exceeds $75,000. If the existence of subject matter jurisdiction were to depend on the amount a plaintiff ultimately recovers, a number of cases could go through lengthy discovery and trial only to end up being thrown out of court when

the plaintiff recovered less than the jurisdictional minimum. This inefficient result is avoided by the "legal certainty" rule. Only if the defendant can prove to a legal certainty that the plaintiff cannot recover the amount requested should it dismiss the case for insufficiency of the amount in controversy. The measure of damages is determined by the applicable substantive law. In a breach of contract case such as this, Heather may be entitled to recover lost profits if they were contemplated by the parties at the time of contracting. It is more difficult for new businesses to prove lost profits, because damages must be supported by evidence and cannot be completely speculative. It may be difficult for Heather, as a business without a track record, to prove lost profits, but you cannot say to a legal certainty that her damages would be less than $75,000.

136. **Answer (D) is correct.** Tony's claim that excessive force used during his arrest violated his constitutional rights states a claim for relief under a cause of action created by federal law. It, therefore, can form the basis for federal question jurisdiction under 28 U.S.C. § 1331. Where federal question jurisdiction exists, the parties' citizenship and the amount in controversy are not relevant. *See also* 42 U.S.C. § 1983.

   Answers (A), (B), and (C) are incorrect. When a federal question exists, there is no minimum amount in controversy requirement, nor do the parties need to be from different states.

137. **Answer (C) is correct.** In most cases, the state and federal courts have concurrent jurisdiction over federal question cases. In a few situations, federal statutes make federal jurisdiction exclusive over particular claims. In most situations, including a civil rights claim such as this one, the plaintiff can choose to file the case either in state or federal court. [Under certain circumstances, the defendant may choose to remove a case filed in state court to federal court. See Topic 31.]

   Answers (A) and (B) are incorrect. Federal jurisdiction is not exclusive over federal questions generally or federal questions based on constitutional rights.

   Answer (D) is incorrect. Tony need not have a state law based claim to authorize state court jurisdiction.

138. **Answer (C) is probably correct.** In a case called *Louisville & Nashville R.R. v. Mottley*, 211 U.S. 149 (1908), the Supreme Court established the "well-pleaded complaint rule." Under this principle, the federal issue must constitute part of the plaintiff's claim and appear on the face of the complaint. The existence of a federal defense, even if that defense will be the primary issue litigated, does not confer federal question jurisdiction. Therefore, the existence of a First Amendment defense to this libel claim does not create federal question jurisdiction; it is still just a state law tort claim. An argument can be made that malice has become a federal "ingredient" of the common law defamation claim, turning the plaintiff's claim into one arising under the Constitution. This argument is not likely to be successful because it would turn too many common law defamation claims into federal question claims.

   Answer (A) is incorrect. The federal courts' interest in consistent interpretation of the Constitution would make a strong policy argument that federal defenses *should* confer federal question jurisdiction. Nevertheless, they do not.

Answer (B) is incorrect. An issue of federal law is highly likely to be determined in the case. It is nevertheless a defense and not a basis for federal question jurisdiction under *Mottley*.

Answer (D) is incorrect. Plaintiffs cannot get around this rule by anticipating the federal defense in the complaint. Nor can it be avoided by filing a declaratory judgment action for what would otherwise be a federal defense.

139.   **Answer (A) is the correct answer.** In *Merrell Dow Pharm., Inc. v. Thompson*, 478 U.S. 804 (1986), the Supreme Court ruled that in cases like this one the claim does not arise under federal law because no private federal cause of action exists for FDCA violations. The Court reasoned that "the mere presence of a federal issue in a state cause of action does not automatically confer federal question jurisdiction," thereby casting the "ingredient" theory of federal question jurisdiction in doubt. In a recent case, *Grable & Sons Metal Prods., Inc. v. Darue Eng'g & Mfg.*, 545 U.S. 308 (2005), the "ingredient" theory has made a substantial comeback. *Grable* rejected the claim that a private right of action under federal law is essential to federal question jurisdiction, but re-affirmed the result in *Merrell Dow* based on a balancing of state and federal interests.

Answer (B) is incorrect for the same reasons that answer (A) is correct.

Answer (C) is incorrect because it is sufficient but not always necessary for the federal law to create the claim.

Answer (D) is incorrect. Even though an issue may be the most important one in the case, the issue needs to be part of the plaintiff's case under the "well pleaded complaint" rule.

140.   **Answer (C) is correct.** As a general rule, the ultimate outcome of a case on the merits is not the determining factor in whether federal question jurisdiction exists. As with questions of amount in controversy, it would be extremely wasteful if losing a case resulted in the court losing jurisdiction. There is, however, a small exception to this rule. The Supreme Court has indicated that if the federal claim is "wholly insubstantial and frivolous" it cannot provide the basis for federal question jurisdiction. The line between a weak case and a frivolous one is not always easy to draw. Hamlet's claim for a constitutional right to an A, however appealing, is so totally unsupported that it would likely be considered frivolous.

Answer (A) is incorrect. In most cases, if the plaintiff pleads a federal claim, it will support federal jurisdiction. This one, however, crosses the line and could not support federal question jurisdiction. [It might also subject Hamlet to Rule 11 sanctions. See Topic 2.]

Answer (B) is incorrect. Normally, decisions about subject matter jurisdiction are not based on the ultimate merits of the federal claim. This is the exception.

Answer (D) is incorrect. This case can be dismissed from the outset. Losing a facially valid federal claim on the merits, however, does not demonstrate lack of subject matter jurisdiction.

TOPIC 29:
SUBJECT MATTER JURISDICTION: SUPPLEMENTAL JURISDICTION

ANSWERS

141.   **Answer (D) is correct.** When dealing with the addition of claims and parties, we tend to jump immediately to thinking about supplemental jurisdiction. But these added claims sometimes have their own independent bases for federal jurisdiction, making use of the supplemental jurisdiction statute unnecessary. Here, Dorothy's claim against the Clinic provides the initial basis for the case to be in federal court. She is a citizen of Texas, and the Clinic is a citizen of Minnesota, providing diversity. Her claim exceeds the $75,000 minimum. The Clinic has used Rule 14 to add Dr. Houston as a third party defendant. Dr. Houston is a citizen of Texas. As between the Clinic and Dr. Houston, the requirements of diversity of citizenship are also met. Because the Clinic seeks indemnification for the entire $5 million claim, the third-party claim also satisfies the amount in controversy test.

   Answer (A) is incorrect. The answer correctly notes jurisdiction over Dorothy's claim against the Clinic. However, because this third-party claim is (at this point) solely between the Clinic and Houston, and they are diverse, the fact that Dorothy and Houston are both Texans does not destroy diversity.

   Answer (B) is incorrect. The answer correctly notes jurisdiction over Dorothy's claim against the Clinic. It is also correct that the third-party claim arises out of a common nucleus of operative fact with Dorothy's claim against the Clinic. If supplemental jurisdiction were needed, this would be a crucial determination. However, because there is independent federal jurisdiction over the third-party claim, supplemental jurisdiction is unnecessary and this is not the determining issue.

   Answer (C) is incorrect. The specific claims involved are supported by diversity jurisdiction. (And even if they were not, e.g., if the Clinic and Houston were from the same state, supplemental jurisdiction would, in fact, allow a claim by a defendant/third party plaintiff against a third party defendant that arose out the same constitutional case as the original claim.)

142.   **Answer (C) is probably the best answer. Answer (D) also could be argued to be correct.** This question involves a counterclaim by the clinic against Dorothy. We know that their citizenship is diverse. But this claim is only for $50,000, and, therefore, taken alone it could not be brought in federal court. We therefore need to examine whether supplemental jurisdiction will allow the claim. The answer can be found by working through 28 U.S.C. § 1367. First, in order for there to be constitutional and statutory power to hear this counterclaim, it needs to be part of the same constitutional case as the claim that originally justified federal jurisdiction (here, Dorothy's claim against the

237

Clinic). The test here comes from a Supreme Court case called *United Mine Workers v. Gibbs*, 383 U.S. 715 (1966): we must look to see whether the claims share a "common nucleus of operative fact." Imagine that the claims went to trial. Would there be a significant overlap of facts necessary to support both claims? Dorothy's claim is for malpractice. It will require the court to look at the nature of the medical care provided to her and whether that care meets the applicable standard of care. The Clinic's counterclaim is for an alleged libel, based on statements that were made after Dorothy was no longer its patient. In order to prevail, the Clinic would have to prove that Dorothy made or was otherwise responsible for the statements, and that they were untrue. Some of Dorothy's statements had to do with her own experience. It, therefore, appears that the Clinic's defamation claim will also include examination of the nature and quality of Dorothy's medical treatment. This will provide some overlap in the claims. Is this enough to make it the same constitutional case? Probably. If it is, then answer (D) is incorrect. The § 1367 analysis proceeds to section (b), which prohibits certain kinds of claims that are inconsistent with the requirements of the diversity statute. The Clinic, although it is the party seeking to bring a claim for affirmative relief, is not a "plaintiff" within the meaning of § 1367(b). Therefore, the statute allows supplemental jurisdiction over the counterclaim. This makes answer (C) the best one. If, instead, you believe that the claims are not sufficiently related to form the same constitutional case, then answer (D) is correct. This would make answer (C) incorrect, because if it is not the same "case" then it does not matter that the Clinic is not a "plaintiff" — supplemental jurisdiction would still be improper.

Answer (A) is incorrect. Permissive counterclaims, which do not arise out of the same transaction or occurrence as the plaintiff's claim, would not satisfy the same constitutional case requirement of § 1367(a) and, therefore, the counterclaims would not be granted supplemental jurisdiction.

Answer (B) is incorrect. The insufficiency of the amount in controversy is what set us on our quest for supplemental jurisdiction. A claim over $75,000 would have an independent basis for federal jurisdiction. The smaller claim does not preclude supplemental jurisdiction, it just makes it necessary.

143.   **Answer (A) is correct.** Based on the "common nucleus of operative fact" test in *Gibbs v. United Mine Workers*, § 1367(a) is satisfied and none of the exceptions in 1367(b) applies.

Answer (B) is not correct because Cyrus appears clearly to fit within the exception to supplemental jurisdiction precluding persons from intervening as plaintiffs under Rule 24. *See* 28 U.S.C. § 1367(b).

Answer (C) is incorrect because answer (A) is correct and because a coplaintiff making his own distinct claim in a tort case is not a Rule 19 person needed for just adjudication.

Answer (D) is incorrect because answer (A) is correct.

144. If Cyrus had established a new domicile in Minnesota, he obviously would not be of diverse citizenship from National Clinic or Dr. Heart. So the first question would be whether § 1367(a) would allow his claim either as an original plaintiff or as an intervenor. It does not. As explained in *Exxon Mobil Corp. v. Allapattah Servs. Inc.*, 545 U.S. 546 (2005), "[I]n order for a federal court to invoke supplemental jurisdiction under *Gibbs*, it must first have original jurisdiction over at least one claim in the action. Incomplete diversity destroys original jurisdiction with respect to all claims, so there is nothing to which supplemental jurisdiction can adhere." Even if this logic cannot be applied easily if Cyrus intervenes (see last sentence of § 1367(a)), § 1367(b)'s hostility to intervention in diversity cases also slams the door on Cyrus.

145. **Answer (C) is the correct answer.** An indemnity claim is surely part of the same case as the main claim against the indemnitee because it arises from the same facts. In addition, although the exceptions in § 1367(b) are hard to understand, the best reading of the first exception in § 1367(b) does not prohibit third party claims by defendants (third party plaintiffs) against third party defendants in diversity cases. Defendants are not plaintiffs, even when they are third party plaintiffs under Rule 14, so indemnity claims are not "claims by plaintiffs against persons made parties under Rule 14."

Answer (A) is not correct for the same reason that answer (C) is correct.

Answer (B) is not correct for the same reason. An indemnity claim is part of the same case or controversy under Article III.

Answer (D) is not correct because the main case (*Woodman v. National Clinic*) provides a basis for federal jurisdiction and the "contamination" theory does not apply to cross-claims.

146. **Answer (D) is probably the best answer. Answer (C) could be argued to be correct.** Again the outcome turns on the relationship between the desired supplemental claim and the claim that provided the federal court with jurisdiction. The claim creating diversity jurisdiction was Dorothy's malpractice claim against the Clinic. The Clinic's third-party claim against Houston also has a basis for federal jurisdiction. The claim in question here is brought by a third-party defendant (Houston) against the original plaintiff (Dorothy). It must be proper under the joinder rules and must have some basis for federal jurisdiction. This claim does not have an independent basis for federal jurisdiction, because it is based on state contract law and the parties are from the same state. Rule 14 allows such claims if they arise out of the same transaction or occurrence as the original plaintiff's claim (Dorothy's claim) against the defendant/third-party plaintiff (Clinic). The supplemental jurisdiction statute supports jurisdiction if the new claim and the original claim share a common nucleus of operative fact. (These tests tend to be very similar in application.) Is the relationship sufficient? Dorothy's claim will involve evidence about her treatment by the Clinic and the relevant standard of care. The Clinic's third-party claim will involve disputes about whether Houston's treatment of Dorothy was negligent, and about what caused Dorothy's post-operative complications. Houston's proposed claim will involve evidence of her treatment of Dorothy and the proper charges for this treatment. Is that enough overlap for either Rule 14 or for § 1367(a)? If not, answer (D) is correct. Although answer (C) is correct, it would be irrelevant. On the other hand, if the overlap is sufficient to meet both tests, so that the claim is procedurally and constitutionally proper, then § 1367(b) would not bar supplemental jurisdiction. Houston's claim is one brought by a person made a party under Rule 14, not a claim by a plaintiff. Answer (C) would be the correct answer.

Answer (A) is not the best answer. Rule 14 does sometimes allow third-party defendants to bring claims against plaintiffs. It does not always do so. And it does not provide federal jurisdiction over those claims.

Answer (B) is incorrect. The parties' common citizenship and the size of the claim do create the need for supplemental jurisdiction. It does not, however, mean that those tests cannot be met.

147. This question deals with an unsettled issue in applying § 1367(b). This question assumes that the following claims are in the case: (1) Dorothy vs. Clinic; (2) Clinic vs. Houston; (3) Houston vs. Dorothy for fees. The issue is whether Dorothy can add a claim against Houston for malpractice. There is no independent basis for such a claim — both Dorothy and Houston are Texans, so diversity is lacking. It seems likely that the same constitutional case requirement of § 1367(a) is met. Dorothy's claim against Houston will overlap substantially with her claim against the Clinic and the Clinic's claim against Houston.

The problem is § 1367(b). Dorothy's claim against Houston is inconsistent with the requirements of the diversity statute. And Houston is a person made a party under Rule 14. Thus, supplemental jurisdiction will be improper if Dorothy is a "plaintiff." This is where the disagreement comes in. Some argue that Dorothy is of course a plaintiff. She brought this lawsuit and is making affirmative claims for relief. She chose a federal forum and should not be allowed an end run around the complete diversity requirement by waiting for the Clinic to implead Houston. Others argue that in this context Dorothy is not a "plaintiff." She is responding with a counterclaim, probably what would generally be a compulsory counterclaim, to a claim that Houston made against her. From the standpoint of judicial efficiency, these authorities argue, it would be far better to hear all of these claims in a single forum rather than to force a separate trial of Dorothy's malpractice claim against Houston. The Supreme Court has not yet had occasion to tell us which argument is correct.

148.   **Answer (A) is correct.** There is complete diversity between Sleep Hotels/Alice on the one side and Mall Mart on the other. Sleep Hotels' claim exceeds $75,000. The supplemental jurisdiction statute, 28 U.S.C. § 1367, provides jurisdiction over Alice's claim. It meets the requirements of § 1367(a) because the claims of Alice and Sleep Hotels share a common nucleus of operative fact — both will revolve around evidence of the method for calculating thread count and the failure of the sheets to truthfully represent the count (although evidence of damages and the specific sheets involved will differ). Since this is a diversity case and Alice is a plaintiff, we must also look to § 1367(b) to see if the claim is excluded. As the *Exxon/Ortega* case held, § 1367(b) does not exclude claims brought by plaintiffs joined under Rule 20. *See Exxon Mobil Corp. v. Allapattah Servs. Inc.*, 545 U.S. 546 (2005).

   Answers (B) and (C) are incorrect for the reasons stated above.

   Answer (D) is incorrect because the claims of multiple plaintiffs are not aggregated to determine the amount in controversy.

149.   **Answer (B) is correct.** Barbara's claim destroys jurisdiction. Like Alice's, it is part of the same case or controversy, but *Exxon* also noted that when the parties are not completely diverse, jurisdiction is destroyed and so there is no 'good' claim on which supplemental jurisdiction can be based. The presence of the non-diverse plaintiff 'contaminates' the entire case, leaving no proper basis for federal jurisdiction. There is no need to go on to § 1367(b).

   Answer (A) is incorrect for the reasons stated above.

   Answer (C) is incorrect because § 1367(b) is not the problem. As noted above, Barbara's citizenship means that the case structured this way does not even meet the requirements of § 1367(a), so § 1367(b) is irrelevant.

   Answer (D) is incorrect. While Article III can be satisfied, under some circumstances, by minimal diversity, jurisdiction also requires statutory authorization, and the general diversity of citizenship statute has consistently been interpreted to require complete diversity. Since § 1367 does not provide for supplemental jurisdiction under these facts, Article III's broader possible scope for jurisdiction does not create jurisdiction.

150.   No. The Court in *Exxon* found that § 1367(b), as drafted, does not prohibit supplemental jurisdiction over a claim by a plaintiff made a party under Rule 20 — and that's what

Sleep Hotels and Alice are. However, § 1367(b) *does* prohibit supplemental jurisdiction over claims *against persons made parties under Rule 20*. In this version of the case, Mall Mart and SheetSheet, as co-defendants, were made parties under Rule 20. Therefore, § 1367(b) does withdraw jurisdiction here. Sleep Hotels and Alice might try bringing separate lawsuits (SH & A vs. MM; SH & A vs. SS) in the same district and hope for consolidation, but filed as one suit there is no subject matter jurisdiction.

151.   **Answer (D) is correct.** Claire's claim, if filed alone, would be sufficient for jurisdiction. She is of diverse citizenship from defendant BBB and her claim exceeds $75,000. In class actions, it is only the citizenship of the named plaintiff that counts, and so it doesn't matter that some class members are citizens of the same state as the defendant. Their claims are too small to have supported jurisdiction if filed separately, but under *Exxon* the federal court has supplemental jurisdiction over those claims. They arise out of the same "case or controversy" as Claire's claims, they satisfy § 1367(a), and § 1367(b) does not prohibit supplemental jurisdiction over the claims of persons made parties under Rule 23.

Answer (A) is incorrect for the reason explained above — it doesn't matter that the class members' claims are too small.

Answer (B) is incorrect. In class actions, it is only the named plaintiff(s) who must be diverse from the defendants.

Answer (C) is incorrect. The Class Action Fairness Act would not provide jurisdiction over this case, because the aggregate class claims do not exceed $5 million.

152.   **Answer (D) is correct.** At first it appears that the Class Action Fairness Act would provide jurisdiction over this case. There is at least minimal diversity between a class member and the defendant. The class claims exceed $5 million (100,000 × $55). There are more than 100 class members. However, this case falls into the category in which the federal court "shall" decline jurisdiction: more than 2/3 of class members are from the forum state, as are all primary defendants (even if non-Connecticut defendants were added, the damage occurred in Connecticut, where the sheets were purchased, and Connecticut law will probably apply).

Answer (A) is incorrect. Under CAFA, the minimal diversity can be between a class member and the defendant — unlike under the normal rule, the citizenship of the named plaintiff is not the only relevant question.

Answer (B) is incorrect because the case is concentrated in one state and the statute contemplates trying such disputes in the relevant state court.

Answer (C) is incorrect. This class action would not be proper under supplemental jurisdiction. Dana does not satisfy the requirements for diversity jurisdiction (her claim is too small), and so there is no independently adequate claim for the others to supplement.

153. **Answer (C) is correct.** The removal statute (28 U.S.C. § 1446) provides that the notice of removal shall be filed "within thirty days after the receipt by the defendant, through service or otherwise, of a copy of the initial pleading . . . or within thirty days after the service of summons upon the defendant if such initial pleading has then been filed in court and is not required to be served on the defendant, whichever period is shorter." For a while, some courts interpreted this statute so that the receipt of a courtesy copy of a complaint, even if before the lawsuit was filed, started the running of the thirty days. The Supreme Court has recently held that this interpretation is incorrect. *Murphy Bros., Inc. v. Michetti Pipe Stringing, Inc.*, 526 U.S. 344 (1999). The time limit is started by formal service of process, or by unofficial service after commencement of the action. Applying this rule, it is service on Blue Hat on July 15 that starts the clock running. Thirty days from this date is August 14.

    Answer (A) is incorrect. The deadline does not run from the drafting of the complaint.

    Answer (B) is incorrect. As explained above, the pre-filing courtesy copy does not start the running of the thirty days.

    Answer (D) is incorrect. There is indeed a deadline for removal.

154. **Answer (D) is correct.** This case meets the requirement for diversity jurisdiction. Martin is a citizen of Michigan, and Blue Hat is a citizen of Delaware and Oregon. The amount in controversy is sufficient. Martin could have filed his suit in federal court. However, under these facts (filing in state court in Oregon), Blue Hat may not remove. The removal statute [28 U.S.C. § 1441(b)] does not allow a defendant sued in its home state to remove a case based on diversity jurisdiction. The fear of local court prejudice against a non-resident defendant does not apply when the defendant is a citizen of the forum state. Blue Hat is a citizen of Oregon and the case was filed there.

    Answers (A) and (C) are incorrect. It is not true that cases can be removed at any time, and timing aside, this one cannot be removed at all.

    Answer (B) is incorrect. Although Martin could have filed the case in federal court, because he chose state court, Blue Hat cannot remove it.

155. **Answer (C) is correct.** This time Martin has added a claim created by a federal statute, clearly meeting the requirements for federal question jurisdiction. This makes it removable despite the lack of diverse citizenship and despite the fact that Blue Hat is a citizen of the forum state.

Answer (A) is incorrect. The prohibition on removal by resident defendants applies only to cases in which jurisdiction is based on diversity.

Answer (B) is incorrect. Federal question jurisdiction does not require diversity of citizenship.

Answer (D) is incorrect. If this were a situation in which the defendant's citizenship mattered (and it is not), § 1441(b) prohibits removal if any of the "parties in interest properly joined and served as defendants is a citizen of the State in which such action is brought." A corporation is a "citizen" of both its state of incorporation and its principal place of business.

156.   **Answer (A) is correct.** The removal statute [28 U.S.C. § 1441(a)] provides that cases are removed "to the district court of the United States for the district and division embracing the place where such action is pending." In this case, that means that removal will be to the Eastern District of Michigan.

Answer (B) is incorrect. When a state has more than one federal judicial district, the case must be removed to the district in which the state court sits. The Western District of Michigan would be incorrect.

Answers (C) and (D) are incorrect. The defendant does not get to choose some other federal court, even if the plaintiff could properly have filed the lawsuit there originally.

157.   **Answer (C) is correct.** As discussed above, the defendant normally has only thirty days from being initially served with process to remove a case to federal court. There are special rules, however, for cases that were not originally removable but which become removable later. One such situation involves the addition for the first time of a federal claim that would create federal question jurisdiction. That is what has happened here. The removal statute [28 U.S.C. § 1446(b)] provides:

> "If the case stated by the initial pleading is not removable, a notice of removal may be filed within thirty days after receipt by the defendant, through service or otherwise, of a copy of an amended pleading, motion, order, or other paper from which it may first be ascertained that the case is one which is or has become removable. . . ."

In this case, when Blue Hat received a copy of the amended complaint containing the ADEA claim, it had thirty days to remove the case, despite the fact that more than thirty days had passed since it was served with the original complaint.

Answers (A) and (B) are incorrect for reasons set forth above.

Answer (D) is incorrect. The one-year limit applies to diversity cases, not federal questions.

158. **Answer (D) is correct.** This situation calls into play the exception to the rule in the previous question. In most cases, when an amendment makes a case removable for the first time, the defendant may still remove the case. This is not true in diversity cases. The remainder of § 1446(b) creates an exception: "a case may not be removed on the basis of jurisdiction conferred by § 1332 of this title [diversity jurisdiction] more than 1 year after the commencement of the action." Because Martin's case has been pending for eighteen months, dropping the non-diverse in-state defendant at this time does not allow removal.

Answer (A) is incorrect. Had Martin been dropped in time for Blue Hat to remove less than a year after the action was filed, this answer would be correct. After eighteen months, it is incorrect.

Answer (B) is incorrect. As discussed above, it is too late.

Answer (C) is incorrect. Subsequent changes to the lawsuit can create the potential for removal, but again, it is too late.

159. **Answer (A) is correct.** A party who believes that a case was improperly removed to federal court can file a "motion to remand." A motion to remand based on any defect other than lack of subject matter jurisdiction must be made within 30 days after the filing of the notice of removal [28 U.S.C. § 1447(c)]. Here, Martin's motion to remand is based on technical errors in the removal papers, and so he must make it within this deadline.

Answer (B) is incorrect. The deadline runs from the filing of the notice of removal, not from when the plaintiff receives it.

Answer (C) is incorrect. This motion to remand is not based on a lack of subject matter jurisdiction.

Answer (D) is incorrect. Cases may be remanded based on procedural defects in the removal process.

160. Martin is trying to add a non-diverse defendant in order to destroy complete diversity. When this happens after removal, the judge has a choice. She can deny joinder and allow the case to proceed in federal court without the new defendant. She can also permit joinder and remand the action to the state court. *See* 28 U.S.C. § 1447(e).

161. **Answer (B) is correct.** When a court has personal jurisdiction over a defendant, it is empowered to enter a judgment that fully adjudicates the dispute between the parties. The judgment makes all of the defendant's non-exempt assets available to satisfy the judgment, and a judgment awarding an injunction can be enforced through the court's contempt power.

    Answer (A) is incorrect. While the presence of property belonging to a defendant in the forum state might be relevant to the constitutionality of jurisdiction, it is neither necessary nor sufficient in all cases.

    Answer (C) is incorrect. Under proper circumstances, a defendant outside the forum state can be served with process and compelled to defend.

    Answer (D) is incorrect. When the court has *in personam* jurisdiction, its power is over the defendant, not just over some property in the state. The judgment is, therefore, not limited to some piece of property over which the court has jurisdiction.

162. **Answer (A) is correct.** A court acquires *in rem* jurisdiction by getting power over some thing, often real property, within its borders. Technically and formally the action is against the thing rather than against particular persons. And jurisdiction of this kind can result in a judgment affecting the interests of *all* persons in the thing (in Latin, the *"res"*).

    Answer (B) is incorrect. *In rem* jurisdiction gives the court power only over the disputed property, and not jurisdiction to adjudicate the plaintiff's rights generally.

    Answer (C) is incorrect. As noted above, *in rem* jurisdiction allows the court to enter a judgment that is not limited to parties before the court.

    Answer (D) is incorrect. When jurisdiction is *in rem*, it is the presence of the disputed thing rather than power over people that gives the court the authority to act.

163. **Answer (D) is the best answer.** (This means that **Answers (A) and (B) are also correct**, but not the best answer because each omits the other.) One type of *quasi in rem* jurisdiction involves a plaintiff seeking to apply the defendant's property to the satisfaction of a claim against the defendant that is unrelated to that property. It is, again, the court's power over the thing within its borders that allows it to act. However, the Supreme Court held in 1977 in *Shaffer v. Heitner* that *quasi in rem* jurisdiction must also satisfy the requirements of due process. *Shaffer v. Heitner*, 433 U.S. 186 (1977). This requirement removed a lot of the special appeal of *quasi in rem* jurisdiction, and

it is now used most often to enforce a judgment already rendered for the plaintiff in another state.

Answer (C) is incorrect. Where still proper, *quasi in rem* jurisdiction gives the court the power to adjudicate the rights of named parties in the property before the court, not the right to adjudicate the interests of anyone anywhere who might have some interest in the property.

TOPIC 33:
CONSENT, STATUS, DOMICILE & TRANSIENT JURISDICTION

ANSWERS

164. **Answer (C) is correct.** Defendants can consent to a court's personal jurisdiction before suit. If in a valid and enforceable contract a party agrees that suit may be filed in a given court, that contractual provision will be enforced. Sometimes the court will declare the provision to be unenforceable under applicable contract law, but absent such a finding the federal courts have tended to enforce such clauses, even when they purport to bar litigation in any other courts, and even when they are part of a contract of adhesion. For examples, see *Nat'l Equip. Rental v. Szukhent*, 375 U.S. 311 (1964) (Michigan defendants agreed to be sued in New York), and *Carnival Cruise Lines, Inc. v. Shute*, 499 U.S. 585 (1991) (enforcing choice of forum clause found on back of the plaintiffs' cruise tickets).

    Answer (A) is incorrect. Defendants can be sued in states other than their domiciles if the requirements of due process are otherwise met.

    Answer (B) is incorrect. The cases that allow suit to determine a person's status, even in the absence of personal jurisdiction over the defendant, concern issues such as the termination of a family relationship. The "status" exception does not permit the court to establish parties' rights under a contract under the guise of adjudicating their status under the contract. The status exception is extremely limited. For example, in a divorce case the court could assume jurisdiction to grant the divorce itself but could not divide marital property or order support payments in the absence of personal jurisdiction over the defendant.

    Answer (D) is incorrect. Even assuming Goneril and Regan lack sufficient purposeful contacts with the state of New York, the contractual clause consenting to jurisdiction allows the New York courts to assert jurisdiction over them.

165. **Answer (A) is correct.** This is a correct use of the status exception, unlike the misuse in answer (B) in the previous question. Goneril would not be able to get an enforceable order for spousal support, but because all she wants is the divorce itself the court will have the power to give her one even without jurisdiction over Albany.

    Answer (B) is incorrect. The state that was once a person's home does not permanently retain sufficient contacts to provide a basis for personal jurisdiction.

    Answer (C) is incorrect. It may be true that after five years Albany's contacts with Michigan are too attenuated to satisfy the minimum contacts test. But in this case that is immaterial. The fact that Goneril seeks only a declaration of divorce means that the court does not need to have personal jurisdiction over Albany.

Answer (D) is incorrect because it misconceives the issue involved. The issue of whether Michigan has jurisdiction to issue a divorce is not a question of whether Albany has consented, and so his lack of consent is irrelevant.

166.   **Answer (D) is correct.** Courts of a defendant's home state traditionally have personal jurisdiction over her whether or not the claim is otherwise tied to that state. The Supreme Court has long held that "domicile in the state is alone sufficient to bring an absent defendant within the reach of the state's jurisdiction." *Milliken v. Meyer*, 311 U.S. 457 (1940). The benefits of citizenship are said to justify reciprocal duties. As a practical matter, it is efficient for plaintiffs to know there is one place where a defendant is certainly amenable to jurisdiction, and those defendants will not usually be inconvenienced by being sued at home.

Answer (A) is incorrect. Service of process out of state (generally permitted by virtue of a state "long-arm statute") is constitutional if the defendant has the required contacts with the forum state.

Answer (B) is incorrect. When a human defendant is sued in her domicile, the cause of action need not have arisen out of contacts with the forum state.

Answer (C) is incorrect. Although Cordelia does have enough contacts with Iowa to justify specific personal jurisdiction over some claims, that is not the reason that jurisdiction would be correct in this case. That lower level of contacts, if that were all that existed, would not justify jurisdiction over Cordelia in Iowa with regard to a cause of action that arose in Delaware.

167.   **Answer (B) is correct.** This question highlights what is known as "transient jurisdiction" or "tag" jurisdiction. Dating back to the time when a court's jurisdiction was based on asserting power over a person within the state's boundaries, transient jurisdiction is based on service of process on the defendant within the state. Serving Kent with process in Colorado, even though Colorado is not his home, meets the requirements of transient jurisdiction. In *Burnham v. Superior Court*, 495 U.S. 604 (1990), the Supreme Court upheld transient jurisdiction in a very split opinion. Some Justices believe that transient jurisdiction, because it was traditionally accepted, is *per se* constitutional. Others believe that it must be subjected to a due process test, but nevertheless approved the service in *Burnham* based on service on a defendant who was in California on business and to visit his children. This opinion, joined by Justices Brennan, Marshall, Blackmun, and O'Connor found no due process problem when the defendant served in the state had even briefly taken advantage of "significant benefits provided by the State." It left open the possibility of a different result when the defendant's presence in the state is "involuntary or unknowing." Kent's regular visits to Colorado and the service of process on him there should meet the requirements for transient jurisdiction.

Answer (A) is incorrect. While coming to Colorado every summer, coupled with service in Colorado, met the requirements for transient jurisdiction, coming to Colorado every summer is not sufficient alone. The cause of action asserted by the plaintiff in this case is not related to Kent's activities in Colorado, and so for this cause of action the repeated summer contacts are insufficient. The result would be different if the cause of action arose out of a tort Kent committed while in Colorado that injured Colorado residents.

Answer (C) is incorrect. Transient jurisdiction includes jurisdiction over claims unrelated to the reasons the defendant was present in the state when served.

Answer (D) is incorrect. Transient jurisdiction, under most circumstances, remains constitutional, as noted above. In the international arena, however, a judgment based only on transient jurisdiction is generally considered to be improper. It could be difficult to enforce such a judgment abroad if the defendant does not have non-exempt assets in the U.S.

TOPIC 34:
IN PERSONAM JURISDICTION: OVERVIEW

ANSWERS

168. **Answer (C) is correct.** In cases such as *Pennoyer v. Neff*, 95 U.S. 714 (1877), the Supreme Court explained the traditional requirement for territorial jurisdiction. For *in personam* jurisdiction, the court needed power over a defendant, demonstrated by the presence of the defendant within the state's borders. For *in rem* jurisdiction, the court needed power over the disputed *res*, demonstrated by its presence within the state's borders.

Answer (A) is incorrect. Defendant's citizenship in the state was not always required, as in the transient jurisdiction cases discussed above.

Answer (B) is incorrect. Defendants who did not own property could still be subject to personal jurisdiction. It was presence rather than property ownership that was the key.

Answer (D) is incorrect. Defendants could be subject to personal jurisdiction even if they had insufficient assets in the state to satisfy the judgment. In fact, a judgment that satisfies the requirements of due process can be taken to a sister state and generally must be enforced there under the Full Faith and Credit Clause of the U.S. Constitution.

169. **Answer (D) is the best answer.** The reasons will be discussed for each of the correct options below. **Answers (A) through (C) are all correct, but incomplete** as the others are correct as well.

Answer (A) is correct. Because a corporation is not an actual physical entity but a collection of assets and employees, a legal fiction, it was more difficult to determine when a corporation was "present" in a state under the old formulation. Courts made this decision based on an analysis of the company's level of activity in the forum state, and the results were somewhat arbitrary and unpredictable. Were regular purchases from the state enough? Regular sales? Low level employees? In making these decisions about "presence," the courts were also considering whether the level of activity was sufficient for it to be "fair" for the company to be required to defend in the forum. The "presence" or "transacting business" approach came to be extremely unsatisfactory.

Answer (B) is correct. States wanted to be allowed to regulate conduct within their borders. Within the framework of traditional personal jurisdiction analysis, they began to legislate consent-based exceptions to the "presence" requirement. For example, states would require out-of-state corporations to register for a license to do business in the state, and that license would be said to include an actual or implied consent to service in the state. Similarly, states passed statutes providing that if a person did certain kinds of harm in the state (for example, caused an automobile accident), that person consented to be served in the state. These statutes either require the designation of a registered agent for service of process, or appoint some state official such as the secretary of state to accept service on the defendant's behalf. Either resulted in service of process on the defendant within the state, and personal jurisdiction. This created a kind of jurisprudential doublethink, with some defendants unreachable under *Pennoyer* and some subject to jurisdiction based on this type of legal fiction. Most states still have statutes requiring businesses who engage in a high level of intrastate business to get a license to do business, and such statutes may provide that the business consents to the jurisdiction of the state's courts.

Answer (C) is correct. The increasing mobility of the population (accelerated by the proliferation of the automobile), and the increasing likelihood that companies would engage in business in a number of states, meant that these issues of personal jurisdiction were arising more and more often. The unworkable old rule finally had to go.

170.   **Answer (A) is correct.** In specific jurisdiction cases, there must be some kind of relationship between the defendant's contacts with the forum and the plaintiff's cause of action. Courts often describe this by saying that the cause of action "arises out of" the contacts. For example, assume the defendant comes to the forum state and drives negligently, causing harm to the resident plaintiff. The contacts are coming to the forum and driving. The cause of action arises directly from those contacts. Sometimes the required relationship is described as requiring that the cause of action "relate to" the contacts. The meaning of this test is a little fuzzier. What is clear, though, is that this lower level of contacts does not provide the basis for jurisdiction over the defendant when the claim is unrelated to its contacts with the forum.

Answer (B) is incorrect. While "general jurisdiction" allows the assertion of claims against the defendant that did not arise out of its contacts with the forum state, specific jurisdiction does not.

Answer (C) is incorrect. While the similarity of names might be confusing ("specific jurisdiction" and pleading with "specificity"), the concepts are unrelated. The distinction between specific and general jurisdiction turns on the relationship between the forum and the cause of action, not on the level of detail in the complaint.

Answer (D) is incorrect. The existence of proper jurisdiction over the defendant on one claim does not confer proper jurisdiction over the defendant on all claims. When the defendant's contacts with the forum are only sufficient for claims arising out of those contacts (specific jurisdiction), those contacts do not also authorize the court to take jurisdiction over additional claims that do *not* arise out of the defendant's contacts with the forum (general jurisdiction).

171.   **Answer (B) is correct.** The Supreme Court has interpreted the Due Process Clause of the Fourteenth Amendment to require that before a state may exercise jurisdiction over a defendant, that defendant must have sufficient contacts, undertaken purposefully by

the defendant, with the forum state, and it must be fair to subject the defendant to suit there. This standard has been applied in a long line of cases beginning with *Int'l Shoe v. Washington*, 326 U.S. 310 (1945). It is often described as a two-step test. The first step involves showing a sufficient level of purposeful contacts with the forum. The second step involves analyzing whether the exercise of jurisdiction would be fair, taking into consideration a list of factors. You should also be aware, however, that the two steps may interact. Justice Brennan's opinion in *Burger King* indicates that the fairness factors may bolster a comparatively weak showing of purposeful contacts. *Burger King v. Rudzewicz*, 471 U.S. 462 (1985). It can also work the other way: even a defendant who has enough contacts to meet the contact requirements of step one may not be subject to jurisdiction, because such jurisdiction would be unfair under step two. An example of the latter situation is found in *Asahi Metal Indus. Co. v. Superior Court*, 480 U.S. 102 (1987).

Answer (A) is incorrect. States are permitted to exercise jurisdiction over non-residents if the requirements of due process are met.

Answer (C) is incorrect. When a defendant's contacts with the forum are so extensive that they can be labeled "continuous and systematic," that defendant is subject to general jurisdiction. This is a higher level of contacts than is required for specific jurisdiction.

Answer (D) is incorrect. "Presence" was the test before the Court's decision in *International Shoe*. It is no longer required, however. All states have "long-arm statutes" that allow service on persons outside the state as long as certain statutory requirements are met. The application of the long-arm statutes to the defendant must also satisfy the constitutional requirements of due process.

172. **Answer (C) is correct.** In order to be subjected to general jurisdiction, a defendant's contacts with the forum must be so extensive that it is fair to compel it to defend a claim that arose elsewhere. The term of art that the Supreme Court has used to describe this level of activity is "continuous and systematic." It comes from the old pre-*Shoe* cases trying to decide whether a defendant was "present" in the forum. There is not much Supreme Court case law to flesh out the meaning of "continuous and systematic" — there is one case in which the company's activities were found to be sufficient, and one in which they were not. *Compare Perkins v. Benguet Consol. Mining Co.*, 342 U.S. 437 (1952) *with Helicopteros Nacionales de Colombia, S.A. v. Hall*, 466 U.S. 408 (1984). These authorities suggest that the defendant's contacts with the forum must be substantial. Some commentators argue that thinking of a clear dichotomy between specific and general jurisdiction is not helpful, with the reality being a kind of sliding scale involving the comparative level of contacts and the comparative relatedness of the contacts and the cause of action. The Court, however, has to date discussed it as two types of personal jurisdiction.

Answer (A) is incorrect. The fact that a defendant conducts some business in the forum will not subject it to general jurisdiction. The level of business activity needs to be substantial and of the right kind. For example, in *Helicopteros*, the Court ruled that purchases of goods and services were not sufficient for general jurisdiction. In contrast, the operation of a principal place of business in a particular forum would be sufficient.

Answer (B) is incorrect. This is the test for specific jurisdiction. This level of contacts may not be sufficient to support general jurisdiction.

Answer (D) is incorrect. The *plaintiff's* residence is not relevant to the existence of general jurisdiction over the defendant. It is the defendant's contacts with the forum that determine whether the court has jurisdiction.

173.   **Answer (B) is correct.** Once a defendant is found to have continuous and systematic contacts with the forum state, a plaintiff may sue it there for claims that did not arise out of those contacts. A defendant with such a high level of contacts with the state is thought to have benefited significantly from its presence there. Such a defendant is also not generally placed at a disadvantage to defend itself there.

Answer (A) is incorrect. General jurisdiction does allow adjudication of claims that arise out of the defendant's contacts with the forum, but it is not limited to such claims.

Answer (C) is incorrect. The *Perkins* case, the only case in which the Supreme Court has found sufficient contacts for general jurisdiction, involved a situation such as this. *Perkins v. Benguet Consol. Mining*, 343 U.S. 917 (1952). But the Court has not discussed the category as limited to these facts.

Answer (D) is incorrect. Jurisdiction must be established over each defendant. Jurisdiction over one defendant, whether specific or general, does not by itself confer jurisdiction over co-defendants.

174.   **Answer (C) is correct.** The Texas store may have wronged Carton, but it did so at its home in Texas. It does not have sufficient contacts with Virginia to be sued there. Nor did the store take any purposeful act aimed at Virginia or seek to serve the Virginia market. The fact that a Virginian was allowed to enter the store does not provide the kind of contact with Virginia that the courts look for to establish personal jurisdiction. The facts do not even indicate that the store was aware that Carton was from Virginia during its encounter with him.

      Answer (A) is incorrect. The tort of wrongful imprisonment is an intentional one. But it was not committed in Virginia or directed toward injuring a Virginia citizen in Virginia. The intentional nature of the tort does not change the result under these facts.

      Answer (B) is incorrect. While it will often be true that plaintiffs can sue at home, that is not invariably true. The jurisdictional analysis is based on the defendant's relationship with the forum, not the plaintiff's relationship with it.

      Answer (D) is incorrect. The defendant did not initiate its contacts with Carton; Carton came to it. The constitutional test requires that the defendant take some purposeful act directed at the forum state, and selling a small item to a customer who has come to the defendant's home base is not sufficient to provide jurisdiction in the customer's home state over the customer's wrongful imprisonment claim.

175.   **Answer (C) is correct.** The store's contacts with Virginia are still insufficient. These facts have raised the volume of contacts slightly from the previous question. But Virginia's claim to personal jurisdiction is still weak. First, this is still a fairly low level of activity, and it was initiated by the Virginians. Second, the sale of knives is unrelated to Carton's cause of action and therefore cannot be used to support jurisdiction over the store on his wrongful imprisonment claim.

      Answer (A) is incorrect. As was true in the previous question, the fact that the cause of action is an intentional tort does not improve the jurisdictional claim when neither the tortious act nor its consequences took place in the forum state.

      Answer (B) is incorrect. As noted above, these contacts are still fairly minimal — they certainly would not justify the exercise of general jurisdiction. Therefore, because they are not related to Carton's cause of action, they do not "count" when assessing the store's amenability to Carton's cause of action. Some commentators argue that courts should be allowed to consider both related and unrelated contacts in determining the appropriateness of jurisdiction in a kind of "hybrid" jurisdictional analysis, but it is not clear whether the Supreme Court would adopt such an analysis.

Answer (D) is incorrect. The mere existence of some amount of profits generated by sales to residents of the forum state does not guarantee the existence of personal jurisdiction, particularly when the cause of action is unrelated to those profits.

176. **Answer (A) is probably correct.** This situation has the kind of contacts that Carton's case lacked. Here DeFarge regularly and purposefully made a large volume of direct sales to the forum state. Lucie's claim arises out of DeFarge's contacts with California: it sold knitting needles there, and her claim is that one of those needles was defective and injured her. This defendant has benefited from the California market, and it is fair to require it to defend itself in a California court in a suit involving the products voluntarily sold there.

Answer (B) is incorrect. DeFarge has done a sufficient volume of voluntary business with California to provide sufficient contacts for the state to constitutionally assert jurisdiction over it. That does not, however, mean that it has actually consented to jurisdiction.

Answer (C) is incorrect. Continuous and systematic contacts are not required for specific jurisdiction, and Lucie's cause of action (defective knitting needle) arises out of DeFarge's contacts with California (selling knitting needles).

Answer (D) is probably incorrect. An isolated sale of goods initiated by a consumer might not be sufficient to justify jurisdiction. However, a large volume of voluntary sales over some period of time will be sufficient for jurisdiction, even if the contracts are structured so that the "offers" come from the customers. Be aware, however, that some courts defer to defendants' attempts to structure their businesses to avoid jurisdiction, and so if all of DeFarge's contacts with California were initiated by the customers, some courts might find that California lacked jurisdiction over DeFarge on Lucie's claim.

177. **Answer (D) is probably correct.** DeFarge has deliberately marketed its product in the state of Maine. This was done partly through a national publication that is available in Maine. It was also done by sending a representative to Maine to sell the Super Chopper. Further, this is a large, expensive machine, so that a single sale is more significant than the sale of a single pair of knitting needles. That same machine is now said to have injured the plaintiff in Maine. That combination of facts should be sufficient to support a conclusion that DeFarge has sought to serve the Maine market, and that its contacts are sufficient to support personal jurisdiction. Although there is only a single sale, it was purposeful, and it is precisely this contact that is alleged to have caused damage to the plaintiff.

Answer (A) is probably incorrect, but it might be held to be correct by some courts. Some state courts and lower federal courts confuse stream of commerce cases with cases involving purposeful direct sales to the forum and hold that a single transaction can never meet the minimum contacts requirement. They apply this reasoning to cases in which the defendant has a single transaction with the forum, even if it is that transaction that gives rise to the cause of action, and even if the out-of-state defendant initiated the transaction. This is probably an erroneous reading of the stream of commerce cases, which involve situations in which the defendant did not make a sale directly into the forum state (e.g., component part manufacturers; sales through distributors; consumers bringing products to the forum). But you should be aware that these cases exist. (Compare question 182, which is a more typical stream of commerce situation.)

Answer (B) is incorrect because it is incomplete. If DeFarge's only contact with Maine had been one ad in a nationally-circulated publication, that would not be a sufficient level of contact to support jurisdiction. A similar situation exists when a defendant advertises on a web site that is available in the forum. These contacts can be considered along with others, but they do not alone constitute the kind of targeted contacts that the courts require.

Answer (C) is incorrect. There may be substantive tort law issues concerning when a person who did not purchase a defective product may sue for injuries caused by the defect. There may also be substantive state law issues concerning suits by workers based on workplace injuries. But from a personal jurisdiction standpoint, DeFarge has still purposefully created sufficient contacts with Maine by marketing and selling the machine there. A contractual relationship with Lorry is not required.

178. **Answer (C) is correct.** Catherine was the consumer of the ladder and saw, and she purchased both in Kentucky from a local business. There is no indication that Hindley's attempted to market its products in Tennessee. When Hindley's sold the ladder, Catherine was a Kentucky resident. When Hindley's sold Catherine the saw, the salesman was aware that Catherine lived in Tennessee, but that awareness will not be sufficient to support an argument that Hindley's sought to serve the Tennessee market. The potentially defective products were brought into Tennessee by the consumer, not by the seller. They are not even inherently mobile products like the car in *World-Wide Volkswagen Corp. v. Woodson*, 444 U.S. 286 (1980), and the Supreme Court rejected a claim of jurisdiction there. At the risk of being repetitious, it is the defendant's voluntary acts directed at the forum, and not the plaintiff's ties to the forum, that provide the basis for jurisdiction over the defendant. The plaintiff's "unilateral acts" cannot fill in the gap.

Answer (A) is incorrect. Foreseeability, in the sense that Hindley's could imagine that its products might end up in Tennessee, is not the proper inquiry for personal jurisdiction. Instead, the Court has looked for situations in which the defendant could "reasonably anticipate being haled into court" there.

Answer (B) is incorrect. Hindley's knowledge that its customer was from Tennessee is not sufficient to say that it sought to serve the Tennessee market. Hindley's wanted to sell the saw, and was probably indifferent regarding where Catherine would use it.

Answer (D) is incorrect. The problem with jurisdiction here is not that it involved inexpensive, low-profit products. The problem is that it was the consumer rather than Hindley's who took the products to Tennessee.

179. In this question, the subject of an allegedly libelous story wants to sue the reporter who wrote it. This is very similar to *Calder v. Jones*, 465 U.S. 783 (1984), in which Shirley Jones was allowed to sue not only The National Enquirer but also the writer of a story about her, even though the story was written and printed in Florida, and even though the reporter did not control the distribution of the newspaper. The Supreme Court noted that the defendants aimed their tortious actions at California: they knew that the article would have an impact on Jones and that the impact would be felt in California. In *Calder* the story concerned a California resident, was drawn from California sources, was about an alleged California incident, and most of the injury Jones suffered would be felt in California where she lived and worked. The National Enquirer also had its largest circulation in California. In Catherine's case some but not all of those facts are present: the publication had more limited circulation in Tennessee; Nelly knew that the article would have an impact on Catherine that she would feel at her home in Tennessee; some of the sources were likely from Tennessee, although more were probably from Kentucky; and Nelly sent a photographer to Tennessee to try to get a photo to accompany the story. It is likely, but not inevitable, that in this situation a court would find jurisdiction over Nelly in Tennessee. The level of sales of the Journal (12/issue) in Tennessee are probably not sufficient to justify jurisdiction under *Keeton v. Hustler Magazine*, 465 U.S. 770 (1984). In that case, the Court relied on sales of 10,000 to 15,000 copies of the magazine in the forum state to find sufficient contacts to justify personal jurisdiction over Hustler.

180. The issue of interstate defamation has now spread to the internet. Here there are no physical sales of the publication to bolster the finding of jurisdiction. Instead, there is a web site which produces images that can be viewed anywhere in the world, but those images are not physically distributed in Tennessee in the same way that the Journal was in the previous question. The law in this area is still developing, but there is an argument for jurisdiction over TheDirt.com just as there was jurisdiction over Nelly. Courts seem to be looking to see whether the publication "targeted" the forum state. One factor relevant to the existence of targeting is the publication's knowledge that the plaintiff lives in the forum. However, more indications that the publication aimed its story at the forum may be required. Here, TheDirt.com knew that Catherine lived in Tennessee and that its story would affect her there. It did not do the original research, but it did add some items with ties to Tennessee. The tort alleged is once again intentional rather than negligent. It is quite likely that internet journals and their reporters may find themselves the subject of lawsuits in the domiciles of the persons about whom they write; whether personal jurisdiction will be upheld is still unpredictable at this time. This is an even more difficult issue when the setting becomes international and non-U.S. plaintiffs, who live in countries whose laws do not provide the same kind of free speech protections as the U.S. Constitution to media defendants, want to sue the U.S. publication in their home countries.

181. **Answer (B) is probably correct.** Jurisdiction arising out of internet-based contractual relationships is also still evolving. At the present time, courts trying to evaluate virtual contacts look at the nature of the web page on a kind of sliding scale. *Zippo Co. v. Zippo Dot Com*, 952 F. Supp. 1119 (W.D. Pa. 1997), is often cited as the source of this test. A purely passive web page (just pictures and text, with little or no interactivity and no way to purchase a product online) will not provide the contacts needed for personal jurisdiction. The customer generally will be regarded as having come to the website, rather than the website being regarded as having sought to sell to the forum residents. At the other end of the scale, a very interactive website through which the merchant conducts business over the internet with forum residents will often support jurisdiction. Nile.com may fall into this category, particularly if it has a high volume of sales to forum residents. While online merchants whose products are delivered through cyberspace sometimes claim not to know where their customers are located, technology is developing that can identify the location of the customers in many cases. Web sites with an intermediate level of interactivity are judged on a case-by-case basis. The *Zippo* sliding scale is increasingly unsatisfactory as a way to make jurisdictional decisions about web-based contacts. You can expect that during your practice lifetimes this area of the law will continue to develop; you can hope that it will become more predictable.

Answer (A) is incorrect. A purely passive website will not alone support jurisdiction.

Answer (C) is incorrect. Even though in a technical sense a website is perpetually available, in another sense it is not located anywhere at all in physical space. Courts have rejected the argument that the always-on quality of the internet results in continuous and systematic contacts of the kind required for general jurisdiction.

Answer (D) is incorrect. Internet contacts, whether contractual as in this question, or tort-based as in the previous question, can sometimes provide the basis for personal jurisdiction. Some internet contacts solicit business, some provide the means of contract formation, and some (as in defamation cases) communicate the allegedly wrongful message. Because website and e-mail based transactions interact with and predictably affect real world people and entities, they will continue to be part of a jurisdictional analysis, even as the technology enabling the contacts and the courts' method for analyzing these contacts become more sophisticated.

182. **Answer (B) is probably correct.** This case involves a component part manufacturer's amenability to suit when the "stream of commerce" takes the finished product to a state in which the parts manufacturer does not reside. The Supreme Court case law on this subject is inconclusive (and aging fast). In *Asahi Metal Indus. Co. v. Superior Court*, 480 U.S. 102 (1987), Justice O'Connor's plurality opinion argued that the component part manufacturer's knowledge that the finished product (containing its part) would end up in the forum, and its profits from those sales, were not enough to support jurisdiction. The O'Connor group (which also included the Chief Justice and Justices Powell and Scalia) wanted to see more evidence that the defendant was seeking to serve the forum state. It noted possible ways a company might do that: advertise; appoint a sales agent in the state; create a consumer advice mechanism; customize the product for the forum state (all actions that seem fairly unlikely for most component part manufacturers). Although this opinion was supported by only four votes, it seems to be the one that many lower courts are following. Justice Brennan (joined by Justices White, Marshall, and Blackmun) would have found the defendant's knowledge of, and profits from, a large sales volume over time to be sufficient. The *Asahi* case was decided in 1987, and given the personnel changes on the court since that time and the unusual party structure in the case, it would be fair to say that the law in this area remains unclear.

Answer (A) is incorrect. The knowledge of a large volume of sales (and profits) over a long number of years would satisfy those Justices who agreed with Justice Brennan, but it would not be enough under Justice O'Connor's opinion.

Answer (C) is incorrect. The relevance of *Asahi* as precedent is clouded by the fact that it involved only non-U.S. parties (a Taiwanese tire manufacturer and a Japanese tire valve manufacturer). The original U.S. plaintiff, who was injured in a motorcycle accident, had sued the Taiwanese company, which had impleaded the Japanese company. All of the plaintiff's claims settled, leaving only the indemnity claim between the two component part manufacturers. All of this makes it difficult to directly apply *Asahi*, particularly its analysis of the fairness of subjecting the component part manufacturer to jurisdiction. Nevertheless, it is *not* true that the case is irrelevant to cases involving U.S. defendants.

Answer (D) is incorrect. Even Justice O'Connor's more demanding minimum contacts analysis does not say that component parts manufacturers must control the chain of distribution before they are subject to jurisdiction. While it does envision some kind of purposeful contact with the forum, that contact does not have to take the form of control over the finished product's destination.

183.   **Answer (D) is correct.** When analyzing specific jurisdiction, the question of the nature and sufficiency of the defendant's contacts with the forum is only the first step. In *Burger King v. Rudzewicz*, 471 U.S. 462 (1985), the Court articulated a two-step analysis. The question of minimum contacts/purposeful availment is step one. Step two considers fairness. Remember the old *International Shoe* formulation: "certain minimum contacts . . . such that the maintenance of the suit does not offend 'traditional notions of fair play and substantial justice.'" Step two is where the fair play and substantial justice come in. The Court has listed factors that should be considered: (1) the burden on the defendant; (2) the forum state's interest in adjudicating the dispute; (3) the plaintiff's interest in obtaining convenient and effective relief; (4) the interstate judicial system's interest in obtaining the most efficient resolution of controversies; and (5) the shared interest of the several states in furthering fundamental substantive social policies. Answer (D) corresponds with the second factor. *Int'l Shoe v. Washington*, 326 U.S. 310 (1945).

Answer (A) is incorrect. The details of the forum's procedural rules (which could be the FRCP, or state rules very similar to the FRCP, or state rules that are not as similar) are not one of the issues that the court is to consider. Note, though, that in considering the burden on the defendant in *Asahi*, the Court did point out that the geographic inconvenience was heightened by the foreign nature of the legal system (California's) to the defendant, who would have been more familiar with the Japanese system.

Answer (B) is incorrect. The trial judge (who would be ruling initially on a motion to dismiss for lack of personal jurisdiction) does not consider whether he considers himself to be a good judge, nor do the appellate courts consider this issue as part of the fairness analysis.

Answer (C) is incorrect. The plaintiff's interest in obtaining convenient and effective relief *is* a factor. This could include considerations such as whether the plaintiff is a resident of the forum and whether the forum allows jurisdiction over all necessary parties. It does not, however, measure the fervency with which the plaintiff prays to keep the case in the forum state.

184. **Answer (B) is correct.** The facts of this problem are similar to those of *Perkins v. Benguet Consol. Mining Co.*, 343 U.S. 917 (1952), the only case in which the Supreme Court has upheld jurisdiction based on contacts unrelated to the forum. Benguet was a Philippine corporation whose operations there were disrupted by World War II. During that time period, the company's president moved its operations to his home in Ohio. The court noted that the president kept office files in Ohio, carried on correspondence from Ohio, drew and distributed salary checks drawn on an Ohio bank, and maintained two active bank accounts carrying substantial balances of company funds. He generally supervised the company's rehabilitation efforts back in the Philippines from the Ohio office. In addition, several directors' meetings were held in Ohio. The Supreme Court found that these contacts permitted Ohio to exert jurisdiction over Benguet even though the plaintiff's claim "arose from activities entirely distinct from" the activities in Ohio. MC's activities in Vermont are very similar and should similarly support jurisdiction.

Answer (A) is incorrect. Because Mrs. Morgan's claim does not arise out of MC's Vermont activities, a level of contacts that would suffice for specific jurisdiction would not be sufficient to support jurisdiction.

Answers (C) and (D) are incorrect. Because MC's level of involvement in Vermont is continuous and systematic, it can be sued there on causes of action arising elsewhere, whether they involve mining or not. Commentators disagree about the extent to which the Court's opinion in *Perkins* can be extended beyond its facts. The situation described in this question, however, would meet even the stricter interpretation of *Perkins*.

185. **Answer (C) is correct.** Dave's claim against Coaster Country is unrelated to its contacts with Texas, so his suit would depend on the existence of general jurisdiction. Coaster Country does have a longstanding relationship with Texas, and that would be the basis of a claim that it has "continuous and systematic" contacts with the state, justifying such general jurisdiction. However, these kinds of contacts, although of some substance and of long duration, will not suffice. In *Helicopteros Nacionales de Columbia v. Hall*, 466 U.S. 408 (1984), the Supreme Court's only general jurisdiction case since *Perkins*, the Court stated that "mere purchases, even if occurring at regular intervals, are not enough to warrant a State's assertion of *in personam* jurisdiction over a nonresident corporation in a cause of action not related to those purchase transactions." It thus rejected a claim of general jurisdiction in Texas over a company that had purchased 80% of its helicopter fleet, over a number of years, and at a cost of more than $4 million from a Texas company. Coaster Country's longstanding purchases of food from Texas will likewise fail to provide a source of general jurisdiction.

Answer (A) is incorrect for the reasons set forth above.

Answer (B) is incorrect. Dave's claim about the flaws in the roller coaster operation and design are not related to the purchase of food.

Answer (D) is probably incorrect. Dave could certainly sue in North Dakota. The park is located there, its allegedly wrongful acts occurred there, and that is where he was injured. It is unlikely, however, that he could sue the park in New Mexico. Although he is from New Mexico, he chose to go to the park's home in North Dakota and his contacts with Coaster Country occurred there. Unless the park aggressively advertised for New Mexico residents to come (which is possible, but not included in the question), it is unlikely that it has sufficient contacts with New Mexico to be sued there.

186.   **Answer (C) is correct.** This question involves a suit against a corporation in the state of its main office when that suit involves a cause of action that arose elsewhere. In this case, RBE has its principal place of business in Illinois, but Little's claim arose in California. There is considerable controversy about the level of activity necessary for general jurisdiction over corporations. This, however, is a clearer case. The defendant corporation is sued at the location of its principal place of business (comparable to suing a human in his home state), and the cause of action is similar to one which could have arisen from its Illinois business (all involve fast food sales). The more difficult corporate general jurisdiction cases involve national businesses that regularly conduct some business in the forum, but which are not headquartered there. For example, should a person who fell in a Wal-Mart store in California be able to sue Wal-Mart in Texas because Wal-Mart has a large number of stores there? Courts and commentators are split on this issue.

Answer (A) is incorrect. It is true that the contacts and cause of action are not directly related, but if general jurisdiction exists that is not important. In addition, the case for jurisdiction here is strengthened by the similarity between the contacts that are the basis for Little's claim and RBE's contacts with Illinois.

Answer (B) is incorrect. While the level of activity required is not clear, it is likely that there is some type of general jurisdiction over corporations, even if it is not as extensive as some lower court cases have held it to be. In *Helicopteros*, the Court recognized the existence of the concept, while finding it inapplicable to the facts before it. *Helicopteros Nacionales de Columbia v. Hall*, 466 U.S. 408 (1984).

Answer (D) is incorrect. Even the most expansive notion of general jurisdiction does not contend that a "huge" corporation (whatever that would mean) can be sued anywhere, regardless of the extent of its contacts with that forum.

187. **Answer (B) is correct.** Dan has properly raised the issue of personal jurisdiction under Rule 12, and if the court agrees that it lacks jurisdiction over him it should dismiss the case. Such a dismissal does not adjudicate the merits, however, so Peter may refile it in a jurisdiction that does have jurisdiction over Dan.

Answer (A) is incorrect. The correct remedy for a case lacking personal jurisdiction over the defendant is dismissal. In some cases, when a defendant moves for change of venue within the federal system in addition to attacking personal jurisdiction, the court is allowed to transfer the case to a district in which venue (and personal jurisdiction) are proper instead of dismissing the case. Even under these circumstances, however, the plaintiff, who has filed in the wrong place, has lost the right to absolute choice among proper fora.

Answer (C) is incorrect. A dismissal for lack of personal jurisdiction should not be a dismissal with prejudice. The court has held that the defendant may not be sued there, not that the plaintiff has no claim on the merits.

Answer (D) is incorrect. Rule 12 allows the defendant to ask the court to dismiss the case for lack of personal jurisdiction without generally appearing, if it raises the issue at the proper time under Rule 12(g) and (h).

188. **Answer (D) is correct.** Unlike the previous question, in which the defendant raised the issue of personal jurisdiction before answering, Dick has filed an answer first, and that answer did not raise the defense of lack of personal jurisdiction. It is now too late to amend this answer as a matter of course under Rule 15(a). Dick has waived his right to raise the issue of personal jurisdiction. Even if Dick has no contacts with the forum, this appearance means that the court may not grant his late-filed motion and (absent some other reason for dismissal or transfer) the case will stay in Wyoming.

Answer (A) is incorrect. The case will not be transferred, as noted above.

Answer (B) is incorrect. Dick has waived his objection to the court's lack of jurisdiction over his person.

Answer (C) is incorrect. The court should not dismiss the case at all.

189. **Answer (B) is correct.** Because she did not participate in the Wisconsin case, Donna retains the right to raise the issue of personal jurisdiction as a defense to enforcement of the judgment against her. If she is correct, and the Wisconsin court lacked personal jurisdiction over her, then the judgment is not enforceable. Had she appeared in

Wisconsin and challenged personal jurisdiction, she would not be allowed to re-raise this issue when enforcement was sought in Pennsylvania.

Answer (A) is incorrect. Donna has not yet litigated the issue of personal jurisdiction, and the lack of personal jurisdiction is a defense to the enforcement of a sister state judgment.

Answer (C) is incorrect. It is correct that Donna may complain about the Wisconsin court's lack of jurisdiction over her. However, if she is wrong about that (the court did have jurisdiction), then she has lost the ability to defend on the merits. This makes the route that Donna has chosen (ignoring the case rather than fighting jurisdiction in Wisconsin) a risky one. If she has guessed wrong about the personal jurisdiction issue, she has lost any defenses that she might have had to the case.

Answer (D) is incorrect. (In fact, it is exactly backward.) See the explanations above.

190. **Answer (D) is correct.** Woolf's suit against Austen could only be in federal court based on diversity jurisdiction, so for venue purposes it would be covered by 28 U.S.C. § 1391(a). This section provides that venue is proper in a judicial district in which any defendant resides, if all defendants reside in the same state. As there is only one defendant, the judicial district of her residence, W.D. La., is proper. Section 1391(a) also provides that venue is proper in a judicial district in which a substantial part of the events or omissions giving rise to the claim occurred. In this case, the negligence and its consequences occurred in E.D. Okla., making venue proper there as well. Because both Sections 1 and 2 make U.S. venue available, Section 3 does not apply.

Answer (A) is incorrect. The plaintiff's residence is not for that reason a district of proper venue.

Answers (B) and (C) are incorrect because they are incomplete. The various venue options listed in § 1391 are all available, and the plaintiff may choose among the districts in which venue is proper.

191. **Answer (D) is correct.** This time Woolf's suit against Austen is in federal court based on federal question jurisdiction, so for venue purposes it would be covered by 28 U.S.C. § 1391(b), but the applicable language is the same. Venue is proper in a judicial district in which any defendant resides, if all defendants reside in the same state. Here both defendants reside in Louisiana, so both E.D. La. and W.D. La. would be proper. Venue is also proper in a judicial district in which a substantial part of the events or omissions giving rise to the claim occurred, making E.D. Okla. proper as well. Because both Sections 1 and 2 make U.S. venue available, Section 3 does not apply.

Answer (A) is incorrect. When multiple defendants reside in the same state, any of their districts of residence provide proper venue, but other districts in the state do not. The Middle District of Louisiana is therefore improper.

Answer (B) is incorrect because it is incomplete. It omits the districts in which the defendants reside, as both reside in Louisiana.

Answer (C) is incorrect, as it includes a district in which no defendant resides and in which no part of the events or omissions giving rise to the claim occurred.

192. **Answer (D) is correct.** This question examines the problem of what constitutes a "substantial part" of the events or omissions giving rise to the claim. The legislative history makes clear that more than one district can qualify — the statute does not require the identification of a single district that has the most events or omissions. In this case,

it is likely that a district in which trade secrets were stolen and a district in which they were wrongfully used would both qualify as places where a "substantial part" of the events or omissions occurred. Again, Section 3 is not applicable.

Answers (A) and (B) are incorrect because they omit districts in which venue would be correct for the reasons set forth above.

Answer (C) is incorrect. The statute does not make the district of the plaintiff's residence a place of proper venue.

193.   **Answer (D) is correct.** This case would be governed by § 1391(a), as it is a diversity case. The defendants do not live in the same state, making Section 1 unavailable. That leaves Section 2, a district in which a substantial part of the acts or omissions occurred. Here the trespass alleged occurred in D. Mass., making it a district where venue is proper. Because Section 2 produced a district in which venue is available, Section 3 is not applicable.

Answers (A), (B), and (C) are incorrect. Because the defendants do not reside in the same state, none of their districts of residence can form the basis of proper venue.

194.   **Answer (D) is the best answer.** Absent enough contacts for general jurisdiction in some other district, the only district in which Fast Ride has sufficient contacts to subject it to personal jurisdiction *in this case* is the Central District of California.

Answer (A) is incorrect because California has more than one district and Fast Ride is not subject to personal jurisdiction in all of them. Section 1391(c) requires a district by district analysis.

Answer (B) is incorrect because Lance's residence is immaterial under current law.

Answer (C) is incorrect for the same reason that answer (D) is correct. Fast Ride's contacts with California are not sufficient to subject it to general jurisdiction.

195.   The question of venue in *Dawson v. Wow Chemicals* will be determined under § 1391(a) because this is a diversity case. Starting with Section 1, one option will be a district in which the defendant resides. This time the defendant is a corporation rather than a human, so the question of where it "resides" is governed by § 1391(c). It provides that "a defendant that is a corporation shall be deemed to reside in any judicial district in which it is subject to personal jurisdiction at the time the action is commenced." In states having one judicial district, then, the defendant "resides" in a state if it is subject to personal jurisdiction there. In states having more than one judicial district, if the defendant is subject to personal jurisdiction in the state, it "resides" in "any district in that State within which its contacts would be sufficient to subject it to personal jurisdiction if that district were a separate state. In this case, it appears that Wow "resides" in the Southern and Northern Districts of Texas, but not in the Eastern or Western Districts. Section 1391(a)(2) also applies, making venue proper in the Northern

District where a substantial part of the events or omissions giving rise to Jack's claim occurred.

If Wow Chemicals obtained a certificate of authority to transact business in Texas, it could be argued that the certificate would be sufficient to subject Wow Chemicals to personal jurisdiction and venue throughout Texas. Although this argument has some surface appeal, the obtaining of such a certificate and the concomitant appointment of a registered agent for service at a particular office should not be sufficient to allow suit to be brought anywhere in Texas under venue principles. In other words, Dawson should not be able to sue Wow Chemicals in Austin or, even worse, El Paso (W.D. Texas), unless the corporation's registered office and registered agent are located in one of those cities, both of which are located in the Western District of Texas.

196. **Answer (C) is correct.** This question illustrates the unusual case in which the fallback venue provisions found in Section 3 of 1391(a) and (b) come into play. This lawsuit would be in federal court based on diversity jurisdiction, and so § 1391(a) applies. Section 1 will not result in a district of proper venue, because the defendants reside in different states. Section 2 will not result in a district of proper venue, because the events giving rise to the claim occurred wholly outside the United States. Section 3 permits venue in a judicial district "in which any defendant is subject to personal jurisdiction at the time the action is commenced." By serving the defendants with process at the airport in New York, Kathy is trying to subject them to personal jurisdiction through the doctrine of transient jurisdiction. Under these facts that might or might not be constitutional. Even if it were, it will not provide a proper basis for venue here. Kathy's action will have been "commenced" before service on Otis and Nancy. At this time, neither was subject to personal jurisdiction in New York. Transient jurisdiction will not, therefore, provide a basis for venue under § 1391(a)(3). Section 3 would permit venue in either N.D. Okla. or D. Neb., but Kathy would also have to get personal jurisdiction over the non-resident defendant and that might not be possible.

Answer (A) is incorrect. Neither defendant's residence could form the basis of a venue claim under § 1391(a)(1) because they reside in different states. However, as noted above, § 1391(a)(3) makes venue proper in a district in which *any* defendant is subject to personal jurisdiction at the time the action is commenced. This makes venue correct in *both* N.D. Okla. *and* D. Neb. Answer (A) is incorrect because it omits D. Neb. as an option.

Answer (B) is incorrect. If Kathy's claim were based on a federal question, § 1391(b)(3) would allow venue in a judicial district "in which any defendant may be found," which might allow for transient jurisdiction to form the basis for venue (although that is not entirely clear). That section, however, is inapplicable to a diversity case.

Answer (D) is incorrect for reasons explained above.

197. Bloomer has filed her suit in a district in which venue is improper. This diversity case could have been filed in D. Utah (Pankhurst's residence) or D. Colo. (where the "omission" of delivery of the widgets occurred), but no provision of § 1391(a) makes venue proper in Wyoming. Pankhurst can file a motion to dismiss, or, in the alternative, transfer the case for improper venue under 28 U.S.C. § 1406(a). (She must be careful to file this Rule 12 defense at the proper time or it will be waived. See Topic 2.) The court may either dismiss the action, or transfer it to any district or division in which it could have been brought. The trial court in D. Wyoming will most likely transfer the case either to D. Utah or D. Colorado.

198. Wendy has filed her suit in a district of proper venue. Iowa, where the plane crashed and Peter was killed, would be a district of proper venue under § 1391(a)(1) (where Pepper, which is subject to personal jurisdiction there, "resides") and under § 1391(a)(2). Pepper may nevertheless file a motion to transfer venue under 28 U.S.C. § 1404. This statute permits transfers for "the convenience of parties and witnesses, in the interest of justice." The case could be transferred to any district or division where it might have been brought, which would include the Eastern District of Missouri. In ruling on a motion under § 1404, the court will consider whether party and forum convenience override the plaintiff's choice of forum, which is given considerable weight. Party considerations include relative ease of access to witnesses and evidence, the cost of obtaining the attendance of witnesses, the ability to compel the attendance of key witnesses and, where applicable, the jury's ability to view the scene of the accident. Forum considerations include the effect on the courts' dockets, the burden of jury duty on the possible fora, local interest in the case, and the substantive law that will apply to the issues in the case.

199. **Answer (C) is correct.** A court, even though it has jurisdiction over the case and the defendant, may choose to dismiss a lawsuit under certain circumstances under the doctrine of forum non conveniens. The leading case is *Gulf Oil Corp. v. Gilbert*, 330 U.S. 501 (1947). A party moving for a transfer under the doctrine must show that considerations of party and forum convenience override the plaintiff's choice of forum and justify dismissal. Party considerations (sometimes called "private considerations") include things like comparative ease of access to proof, the ability to compel the attendance of witnesses, and, where applicable, the jury's ability to view the scene of the accident. Sometimes, especially when the plaintiff resides in the forum state, this will act as a strong private factor in favor of keeping the case in the forum; the plaintiff's choice of forum is given great weight. Considerations of forum convenience (sometimes called "public factors") include a comparison of the burdens and benefits of locating the litigation in the two fora. Courts may consider the case backlog of the two systems, local interest in the dispute, and the burden that jury service would impose. Public factors also include considerations of choice of law — litigation is thought to be simpler in the forum whose substantive law will govern the case.

Answer (A) is incorrect. The defendant's residence in the forum is not (at least formally) a factor in forum non conveniens analysis. A defendant may do business in the forum and nevertheless succeed in urging dismissal, as, for example, when all the events relevant to the suit and all the evidence related to the dispute are located elsewhere.

Answer (B) is incorrect. The location where the cause of action accrued is also not formally a part of forum non conveniens analysis. It may be that the location where a claim arose is also the place where the bulk of the witnesses and other evidence are located, in which case a motion to dismiss based on forum non conveniens would be unlikely to succeed. It may also be true that the law of a place where a cause of action accrued will govern the dispute. However, it is these convenience-based factors, rather than a search for the birth of the cause of action, that are relevant to the forum non conveniens analysis.

Answer (D) is incorrect. A party seeking dismissal must show that an adequate alternative forum is available. This does not require, however, that the alternative forum be procedurally identical to the American forum, or even that the relief available in the alternative forum would be the same as that available under U.S. law.

200. Most (but not all) judges in cases parallel to the problem case have dismissed them. Although some evidence (in the form of Wow Chemical documents and employees) will be available in the Southern District of Texas, the plaintiffs themselves, the plaintiffs' employers, and the evidence regarding the application of the chemicals and the plaintiffs' damages are located in Costa Rica. The plaintiffs' lack of a tie to the forum is also generally seen as weakening the deference ordinarily due to the plaintiffs' choice of forum. Product liability claims such as these can be time consuming to the courts, and so the public factors are often seen to militate in favor of the Costa Rican forum — the citizens of Texas are seen as having little stake in whether the Costa Rican plaintiffs were wronged or whether they will be compensated. It is also possible that Costa Rican rather than Texas law would be applied to the case, making it more convenient for the Costa Rican court system than for the Texas court system. The smaller number of judges that have retained these cases have emphasized the plaintiffs' willingness to make themselves available for discovery and trial, the defendant's access to evidence about its chemical, and the forum state's interest in the behavior of its corporate citizens, even when that behavior is alleged to have caused injury outside of the United States.

201. **Answer (B) is correct.** The federal "full faith and credit" statute requires that the judicial proceedings of "any State, Territory or Possession of the United States" "shall have the same full faith and credit in every court within the United States . . . as they have by law or usage in the courts of such State." 28 U.S.C. § 1738. Hence, the key question is what test does Texas use in its own courts to determine the analytical contours of a cause of action for claim preclusion purposes. Texas has adopted the "transactional" approach in preference to the "individualized" or "same rights" or "same evidence" approaches. Under the "transactional" test, a breach of an express contract claim and a *quantum meruit* claim involving the same project are considered to be the same "cause of action" even though the elements of the two claims differ.

   Answer (A) is incorrect. Federal courts sitting in Texas also use the transactional approach to claim preclusion in assessing the preclusive effect of federal question cases in federal court. But that does not matter because the "full faith and credit" statute requires a federal court to follow Texas preclusion law for a Texas judgment.

   Answer (C) is incorrect for the same reasons.

   Answer (D) is incorrect for the same reasons.

202. **Answer (C) is correct.** The preclusive effect of the first judgment entered by the Texas district court again is controlled by the Texas law of judgments under the "full faith and credit" statute. Because Texas procedural law does have a compulsory counterclaim rule (Tex. R. Civ. P. 97(a)) patterned on Federal Rule 13(a), Marriott was required to file its counterclaim against Roadway in the Texas action. Marriott's failure to do so bars the counterclaim in federal court because that would be the result in a Texas court.

   Answer (A) is incorrect. Even though Marriott was the prevailing party in the Texas district court case, its compulsory counterclaim was lost because Marriott failed to assert it.

   Answer (B) is arguably correct as a recapitulation of answer (C) but it is not the best answer. Although the preclusive affect of a party's failure to prosecute a compulsory counterclaim is the same as under common law principles of claim preclusion, the procedural duty arises under the procedural rules, not (strictly speaking) under the common law of claim preclusion.

   Answer (D) is incorrect because it is at variance with basic preclusion doctrine.

203.   **Answer (B) is correct.** Under federal law in federal question cases, there is no mutuality requirement for the application of principles of issue preclusion (sometimes called collateral estoppel or estoppel by judgment). As long as the issue in question was actually litigated in the first action, was essential to the first judgment, and the losing party had a full and fair opportunity to litigate the issue in the first case, the losing party in the first case will be estopped from relitigating the issue. But in *Semtek Int'l Inc. v. Lockheed Martin Corp.*, 531 U.S. 497 (2001), a unanimous Supreme Court decided that in diversity cases the federal common law preclusion rule would generally adopt "the law that would be applied by the courts of the state in which the federal diversity court sits." The question here is what law New York would apply and whether that law contains a mutuality component or a law against offensive use. New York case law indicates that it uses nonmutual offensive collateral estoppel. *See Kaufman v. Eli Lilly & Co.*, 482 N.E. 2d 63 (N.Y. 1985).

      Answer (A) is incorrect. The former mutuality requirement under which neither party could use a prior judgment as an estoppel against the other, unless both parties were bound by the judgment, is no longer used by either federal or New York courts. *See Parklane Hosiery Co., Inc. v. Shore*, 439 U.S. 322 (1979). Not all American jurisdictions have abandoned the mutuality doctrine.

      Answer (C) is incorrect. There is no privity requirement. The existence of privity would satisfy the mutuality doctrine, which is no longer part of federal law.

      Answer (D) is incorrect for the reasons stated above.

204.   **Answer (C) is the best answer.** Wings-Are-Up's liability was actually litigated and the judgment in favor of Henrietta and Polly clearly rests on the findings of defect, unreasonable danger, and causation. Assuming the nonexistence of a mutuality requirement in the unspecified jurisdiction, the question becomes whether the findings can be used "offensively" by Larry's parents. This is a very controversial issue from jurisdiction to jurisdiction. Some jurisdictions disallow offensive use, while others (like the courts in the federal system) permit its use unless its use would be unfair because the first action involved a minor damages claim, the first action involved procedural disadvantages to the defendant, or for other similar reasons.

      Answer (A) could be correct, if, for example, the first action was litigated to judgment in a state that retained a mutuality requirement or that prohibited offensive use. But it is **not the best answer.**

Answer (B) is probably not correct because of the fairly widespread abolition of a mutuality requirement by American courts.

Answer (D) is incorrect. Larry's parents could not be bound or barred by the first judgment because neither Larry nor his parents were parties to the first action.

TOPIC 43:
PERSONS BOUND BY PRIOR ADJUDICATION

ANSWERS

205. **Answer (C) is correct.** Persons who are bound include parties to the first action or persons in privity with them. Although there is no all-inclusive and procedurally satisfying definition of the privity concept for preclusion purposes, most (if not all) courts would agree that nonparties who derived no rights (as, for example, successors in interest) and who had no say in the conduct of the prior action, are not considered to be in privity with any party. Under this approach, an employee is not in privity with his employer despite the existence of a contractual agency relationship between them.

Answers (A) and (D) are not correct for the reasons stated above.

Answer (B) is partially correct but not the best answer. Jones' administratrix is in privity with Jones, but Jones is not in privity with Classic Cars. That is the key.

206.   **Answer (C) is correct.** The law of the case doctrine is not inexorable. It is typically regarded as a discretionary doctrine that gives way if a change in the law or the facts requires reconsideration of the earlier decision.

Answer (A) is not correct for the reasons stated above.

Answer (B) is incorrect because the law of the case doctrine does have vitality as a preclusion doctrine, despite its discretionary character. A *de novo* standard would ignore the effect of the earlier order.

Answer (D) is not correct. It is a classic red herring. The rejected intervenors are likely to lose their appeal on the merits, but an argument does not lose jurisdiction because it is weak.

207.   **Answer (B) is correct.** One of the peculiarities of the American federal republic is that both the common and statutory laws of the states differ in a wide variety of significant details. These variations include the law that the states use to choose what state's law or laws will be applied by the forum state. These choice of law rules, based largely on the First and the Second Restatements of the Conflict of Laws, depending on the state in question, govern the choice. For example, Virginia (the forum state) will apply its choice of law rules applicable to tort actions to decide whether Virginia or Pennsylvania law should be applied. Virginia will likely apply Pennsylvania law because it is the place of the "wrong," generally the place the plaintiff was injured. This is because Virginia follows the traditional choice of law rules of the First Restatement of the Conflict of Laws.

   Answer (A) is incorrect. The forum state will apply its own procedural law, but not necessarily its own substantive law.

   Answer (C) is incorrect. The Full Faith and Credit Clause of the Constitution puts only the smallest of limits on choice of law decisions. A state can choose what law to apply, as long as the state chosen "has a significant contact, or significant aggregation of contacts, creating state interests, such that choice of its law is neither arbitrary nor fundamentally unfair." *Allstate Ins. Co. v. Hague*, 450 U.S. 971 (1981).

   Answer (D) is incorrect. Although the application of complicated choice of law rules (particularly the type of analysis used by the Second Restatement of the Conflict of Laws) can be problematic, the judge is required to follow the methodology of the state in which she sits. She does not have discretion to choose any law she wants to.

208.   In most contexts, unless someone points out the existence of a conflict, the forum state will apply its own law to the dispute, typically under a cosmetic presumption that the law of the other state or states is identical to forum law. Choice of law rules are not applied automatically.

209. **Answer (B) is correct.** Virginia follows traditional First Restatement of the Conflict of Laws choice of law principles. Under the traditional view, the forum applies its own law to issues of procedure. General statutes of limitation are categorized as procedural, and so the forum applies its own law to limitations questions. This was true no matter what state's law was applied to the substantive issues in the case. This result, which was set forth in the First Restatement of the Conflict of Laws, was changed in the Second Restatement (see below).

Answer (A) is not likely to be correct, unless Virginia adopts amended § 142. As amended in 1988, § 142 of the Second Restatement provides that unless "exceptional circumstances" exist, the forum (1) will apply its own statute of limitations barring the claim and (2) will apply its own statute of limitations permitting the claim unless the limitation period of the state whose law will otherwise govern the merits bars the action. This approach has the result of applying, in most cases, the shorter statute of limitations.

Answer (C) is incorrect. Under modern systems of choice of law, each issue is analyzed separately. Even under a traditional approach, "procedural" issues were governed by the law of the forum, so it was not unusual for a forum to apply its own procedural law and the substantive law of a sister state. Virginia could apply its own statute of limitations even if it applied Pennsylvania law to the substantive issues.

Answer (D) is incorrect. Federal courts must apply the choice of law rules of the states in which they sit.

210. **Answer (B) is correct.** In 1938, the Supreme Court decided the celebrated case of *Erie RR Co. v. Tompkins*, 304 U.S. 64 (1938), which stands for the proposition that a federal court in a diversity case must apply the substantive law of the state in which the federal court is located. Thereafter, in *Klaxon Co. v. Stentor Elec. Mfg. Co.*, 313 U.S. 487 (1941), the Supreme Court extended the *Erie* doctrine to the field of conflict of laws by holding that a federal court must apply the law — including the choice of law principles — applied by the state in which the federal court sits.

Answer (A) is incorrect. Prior to the *Erie* decision in 1938, federal courts applied federal substantive common law principles, making the applicable law possibly depend on whether the case was litigated in a state or a federal court sitting in the same state. That is no longer true.

Answer (C) is incorrect. The federal court does apply the law of the state in which it sits, but as explained above this includes the state's choice of law principles. The federal court sitting in Virginia, therefore, would only apply Virginia law if a state judge in Virginia would do so.

Answer (D) is also incorrect. Although there are some constitutional limits on choice of law, they do not prohibit a forum from applying the law of the state in which the plaintiff was injured. *See Phillips Petroleum Co. v. Shutts*, 472 U.S. 797 (1985) ("[F]or a state's substantive law to be selected in a constitutionally permissible manner, that State must have a significant contact or significant aggregation of contacts, creating state interests such that choice of law is neither arbitrary nor fundamentally unfair.").

211.   **Answer (D) is probably the best answer.** (This means that **Answers (B) and (C) are also correct.**) Under both the "outcome determinative" test developed in *Guaranty Trust Co. v. York*, 326 U.S. 806 (1945), as recast in *Hanna v. Plumer*, 380 U.S. 460 (1965) ("The 'outcome determinative' test . . . cannot be read without reference to the twin aims of the *Erie* rule: discouragement of forum-shopping and avoidance of inequitable administration of the laws"), and the interest balancing approach developed in *Byrd v. Blue Ridge Elec. Coop., Inc.*, 356 U.S. 525 (1958), the application of Kansas state law is required. This question is very similar to *Walker v. Armco Steel Corp.*, 446 U.S. 740 (1980), which concluded that Rule 3 was not meant to "affect states' statutes of limitation."

Answer (A) is incorrect because Rule 3 has been specifically held to be a procedural rule that "governs the date from which various timing requirements of the federal rules begin to run, . . . not [to] affect state statutes of limitation." *Walker v. Armco Steel Corp., supra*. If, however, Federal Rule 3 had been otherwise interpreted as broad enough to reach limitations questions, it probably would govern based on the presumed validity of the federal rules as provided in *Hanna v. Plumer*, 380 U.S. 460 (1965), but not necessarily. *See Gasperini v. Center for Humanities*, 518 U.S. 415 (1996).

212.   **Answer (D) is probably the best answer.** This means that **Answers (B) and (C) are also correct.**) Both authors of this book agree that this is the bottom line, but disagree somewhat as to how that result is reached. One argues that although *Hanna v. Plumer*, 380 U.S. 460 (1965), holds that a controlling federal rule or rules will override state law unless it can be said that the federal rule really does not regulate procedure, the twin aims of the *Erie* rule — discouragement of forum shopping and avoidance of the inequitable administration of the laws — still have to be considered and probably call for the Texas statute to be enforced in federal court. Unlike the situations in *Hanna*, it is abundantly clear that plaintiffs in medical malpractice cases would choose a federal forum if the statute did not apply in federal court. Thus, even a controlling federal rule must still pass the "outcome determinative" test. The other author believes that rather than face the possible situation in which a valid federal rule, though procedural, would "abridge, enlarge, or modify" substantive rights (assuming this refers to state-created rights), the federal court would interpret the federal rules narrowly ("with sensitivity to important state interests and regulatory policies") as in *Walker* and *Gasperini*. She thinks the court would for that reason proceed to analyze the case under the "outcome

determinative" side of *Hanna*, as in *Gasperini*. Both authors agree that 1) the difference between the state and federal procedures would encourage forum shopping, 2) that the federal interest in its notice pleading/discovery system would not be strong enough to outweigh the high degree of 'outcome determinativeness' and 3) that the court would in the end apply Texas law.

Answer (A) is probably incorrect for the same reason. Rules 8, 26, 37, and 56 are procedural rules that govern pleadings, discovery, and summary judgment, but they do not cover the issue of whether an expert report should be required in medical malpractice cases. These federal rules are not meant to establish federal standards for asserting and prosecuting medical malpractice claims in federal court that are inconsistent with the Texas statute's threshold expert report requirement. *See Chamberlain v. Giampapa*, 210 F.3d 154 (3d Cir. 2000) (federal rules not broad enough to cover; state law applies); *Cruz v. Chang*, 400 F. Supp. 2d 906 (W.D. Tex. 2005) (same result). *But see Poindexter v. Bonsukan*, 145 F. Supp. 2d 800 (E.D. Tex. 2001) (federal rules regarding expert reports and sanctions broad enough to cover; state law does not apply). *See generally* Dace A. Caldwell, Comment, *Medical Malpractice Gets Eerie: The Erie Implications of a Heightened Pleading Burden in Oklahoma*, 57 Okla. L. Rev. 977 (2004).

213.   **Answer (A) is the correct answer.** The dismissal of both health care claims with prejudice disposed of all issues and parties in the case and is a final judgment as provided in 28 U.S.C. § 1291.

        Answer (B) is incorrect. Rule 54(b)'s method of finalizing separate claims was not used or needed to dispose of any of the health care claims.

        Answer (C) is incorrect. The dismissal with prejudice is a merits dismissal because it precludes refiling even though it is grounded on the plaintiff's failure to file expert reports during the pretrial phase of the litigation.

        Answer (D) is incorrect. The collateral order doctrine is inapplicable. To come within the small class of cases covered by the doctrine the order must conclusively determine the disputed question, resolve an important issue completely separate from the merits and be effectively unreviewable on appeal from a final judgment. *Cohen v. Beneficial Indus. Loan Corp.*, 337 U.S. 541, 546 (1949); *Coopers & Lybrand v. Livesay,* 437, U.S. 463, 468 (1979). In this problem, the issues to be covered by the expert reports are not "completely separate" from the merits and the propriety of the dismissal order is reviewable on appeal.

214.   **Answer (B) is correct.** Rule 54(b) allows a trial judge to finalize an order that "adjudicates fewer than all the claims or the rights and liabilities of fewer than all the parties" involved in the case by including in the order "an express determination that there is no just reason for delay" and "an express direction for the entry of judgment." Fed. R. Civ. P. 54(b). Although Rule 54(b) is applicable to the facts presented in the problem, which involves an order that adjudicates the rights and liabilities of fewer than all of the parties, the dismissal order must be drafted in compliance with the requirements of Rule 54(b) to finalize the order dismissing HCH.

        Another somewhat disfavored method for finalizing the HCH order would be by a severance of Payne's claim against HCH from Payne's claim against Dr. Practer. *See* Fed. R. Civ. P. 21.

        Answer (A) is incorrect. Neither the dismissal order involving HCH nor the denial of Dr. Practer's motion disposes of the entire case. A final judgment "ends litigation on the merits." *See Catlin v. United States*, 324 U.S. 229, 253 (1945).

        Answer (C) is incorrect because the dismissal with prejudice is an adjudication of the merits of Payne's malpractice claim against HCH. The problem is that the order is not a final judgment because it does not end the case or comply with Rule 54(b).

Answer (D) is incorrect. To come within the small class of cases covered by the doctrine the order must conclusively determine the disputed question, resolve an important issue completely separate from the merits and be effectively unreviewable on appeal from a final judgment. *Cohen v. Beneficial Indus. Loan Corp.*, 337 U.S. 541, 546 (1949); *Coopers & Lybrand v. Livesay,* 437, U.S. 463, 468 (1979). The collateral order doctrine probably does not apply to a dismissal in this situation both because the order is not completely separate from the merits or unreviewable on appeal of the ultimate final judgment.

215.   **Answer D is the best answer.** (Thus, **Answer (B) or Answer (C) is correct**). Answer (B) is correct because the Supreme Court has ruled that a denial of a motion to dismiss on the basis of qualified immunity from suit is a collateral order if the denial of the officers' summary judgment rests on a question of law, rather than the existence of a disputed factual question. *See Mitchell v. Forsyth,* 472 U.S. 511, 528 (1985) ("The entitlement [to summary judgment] is an *immunity from suit* rather than a mere defense to liability; and like an absolute immunity, it is effectively lost if a case is erroneously permitted to go to trial."); *see also Behrens v. Pelletier,* 516 U.S. 299, 313 (1996) (case is appealable when it involves "a dispute concerning an 'abstract issu[e] of law' relating to qualified immunity", such as whether the law proscribed the actions the plaintiff claims the officer took). But if the collateral order doctrine does not apply under the circumstances of the case, Answer (C) is probably correct because a permissive appeal of an interlocutory order under 28 U.S.C. § 1292(b) can be sought if the district court certifies that (1) the order raises a controlling law question, (2) there is substantial ground for difference of opinion on the question and (3) an interlocutory appeal may materially advance the ultimate termination of the litigation. 28 U.S.C. § 1292(b). If such a certification is obtained, the appropriate court of appeals may permit an appeal to be taken from the order if application is made to the court of appeals within ten days after entry of the order. *See* 28 U.S.C. § 1292(b); *see also* Fed. R. App. P. 5.

Answer (A) is incorrect for the same reasons that answers (B) and (C) are correct. In addition, a collateral order is regarded as a final judgment.

216. **Answer (D) is the best answer.** The second dismissal order's entry in the civil docket disposed of the remaining issues in the case. But it did not satisfy the requirement of Rule 58 (or Appellate Rule 4) that a "separate document" must be used for entry of a final judgment. *See* Fed. R. Civ. P. 58. Rule 58 requires that there must be a self-contained document distinct from any opinion and any other orders that don't dispose of the entire case. *Bankers Trust Co. v. Mallis,* 435 U.S. 321, 385 (1978). So the order did not start the appellate clock contained in Appellate Rule 4. As provided in Rule 58 and Appellate Rule 4, the judgment was "entered" by law when 150 days ran from entry of the second dismissal order. Fed R. Civ. P. 58(b); Fed. R. App. P. 4(a)(7). As the following excerpt from the Supreme Court's *Mallis* opinion shows, the appellant may waive the separate document requirement over the objection of the appellee as long as the order in question clearly evidences the trial court's intent that the order is a "final decision" for the purposes of 28 U.S.C. § 1291.

> "The separate-document requirement was . . . intended to avoid the inequities that were inherent when a party appealed from a document or docket entry that appeared to be a final judgment of the district court only to have the appellate court announce later that an earlier document or entry had been the judgment and dismiss the appeal as untimely. The 1963 amendment to Rule 58 made clear that a party need not file a notice of appeal until a separate judgment has been filed and entered. *See United States v. Indrelunas,* 411 U.S. 216, 220-22 (1973). Certainty as to timeliness, however, is not advanced by holding that appellate jurisdiction does not exist absent a separate judgment. If, by error, a separate judgment is not filed before a party appeals, nothing but delay would flow from requiring the court of appeals to dismiss the appeal. Upon dismissal, the district court would simply file and enter the separate judgment, from which a timely appeal would then be taken. Wheels would spin for no practical purpose."

Bankers Trust Co. v. Mallis, 435 U.S. 381, 385 (1978). *See also* Fed R. App. P. 4(a)(7)(B) (codifying *Mallis*).

Answer (A), (B), and (C) are incorrect. Fed. R. App. P. 4 authorizes the filing of a premature notice of appeal. Fed. R. App. P. 4(a)(2). But neither of the two dismissal orders disposes of the entire case. Hence, another "separate document" is needed to finalize the case before expiration of 150 days.

217. **Answer (C) is correct.** If a motion for new trial is filed, the time for giving notice of appeal runs from the entry of the order denying a new trial. Fed. R. App. P. 4(b). Moreover, another "separate document" is (sensibly) not required. The entry of the order denying the last postjudgment motion finalizes things and starts the appellate clock. *See* Fed. R. Civ. P. 58(a)(1).

Answers (A) and (B) are incorrect for the same reason. The dates of the earlier orders don't matter.

Answer (D) is incorrect because only 30 days are allowed for the filing of notices of appeal unless the United States or its officer or agency is a party. Fed. R. App. P. 4(a).

218. **Answer (C) is the best answer.** Appellate Rule 4 allows for reopening the appeal for a period of 14 days after the date when the court's order to reopen is entered under the following conditions: (A) the moving party did not receive notice under Rule 77(d) of the entry of the order to be appealed within 21 days after entry; (B) the motion to reopen is filed within 180 days after the judgment or order is entered or within 7 days after the movant receives a Rule 77(d) notice, whichever is earlier; and (C) no party would be prejudiced. Fed. R. App. P. 4(a)(6).

Answer (A) is incorrect because Appellate Rule 4 does provide a safe harbor under the circumstances stated in (C). *See* Fed. R. App. P. 4(a).

Answer (B) is incorrect because a motion for extension must be filed within 30 days after entry of the order denying Payne a new trial.

Answer (D) is probably incorrect because the detailed requirements of Appellate Rule 4 probably preclude using Rule 60(b) to avoid them.

219. In addition to the notice of appeal, an appellant in a civil case may be required to file a cost bond (Fed. R. App. P. 7), will need to file the record (Fed. R. App. P. 10, 11) and file an appellant's brief and an appendix (Fed. R. App. P. 28, 30-32).

Unless another time is designated by the court, the attorney who filed the notice of appeal must, within 10 days after filing notice of appeal, file a statement with the circuit court clerk naming the parties the attorney represents on appeal. Fed. R. App. P. 12(b).

To obtain preparation of the record, the appellant must first order from the court reporter a transcript of the parts of the proceedings that the appellant needs to prosecute the appeal. The order must be made in writing within 10 days after filing the notice of appeal or entry of the order disposing of the last timely postjudgment motion specified in Rule 4(a)(4)(A), whichever is later. Within the same period, a copy of the order must be filed with the district clerk. Fed. R. App. P. 10(b)(1). At the time of ordering, the appellant must make satisfactory arrangements with the reporter for paying the cost of the transcript. Fed. R. App. P. 10(b)(4).

The appellant must do whatever else is necessary to enable the clerk to assemble and forward the record. *See* Fed. R. App. P. 11.

The appellant must serve and file a brief within 40 days after the record is filed. The appellee must serve and file a brief within 30 days after the appellant's brief is served. The appellant must serve and file a reply brief within 14 days after service of the appellee's brief, but at least 3 days before argument, unless the court allows a later filing. Fed. R. App. P. 31(a).

The circuit court clerk is required to advise all parties whether oral argument will be scheduled and, if so, the date, time, and place for it, and the time allowed for each side. Fed. R. App. P. 34(b).

PRACTICE FINAL EXAM: ANSWERS

220. One vehicle would be to file a counterclaim and to add Mark as an additional party. Rule 13(h) permits defendants to make "persons other than those made parties to the original action" parties to a counterclaim. The claim used to add the new party must meet the requirements of Rule 20. Another option is to use Rule 14 to bring a derivative claim against Mark. He could be alleging that if he is liable to plaintiff, Mark is liable to him. The Rule 14 process, also known as impleader, is often used to assert contribution and indemnity claims when those claims are authorized under the applicable state law.

221. **Answer (B) is correct.** Once a party has brought a claim for relief as an original claim, counterclaim, cross-claim, or third-party claim against another party that meets the requirements of the joinder rules, Rule 18 allows the addition of as many other claims as the party has against the opposing party. Here Donald has brought the contribution claim against Mark and can use Rule 18 to add the negligence claim. Incidentally, the negligence claim would also satisfy the requirements of Rule 20 as it arises out of the same transaction or occurrence as the contribution claim and raises common questions of law and fact.

Answer (A) is incorrect. Rule 13 governs counterclaims and cross-claims, and it does not address when a party can add claims against a third-party defendant (which is what Mark is here).

Answer (C) is incorrect. Donald was required to use a derivative claim to bring Mark into the lawsuit under Rule 14 — the contribution and indemnity claim is a derivative one. However, additional claims may be added that are not derivative in nature, as explained above.

Answer (D) is incorrect. Because Donald has a proper claim against Mark already (the contribution and indemnity claim), Rule 18 permits the addition of other claims even if they do not arise out of the same transaction or occurrence as the others. (Whether the federal court has jurisdiction over these claims is another issue, which questions 182-184 address.)

222. **Answer (B) is correct.** Rule 18 permits the addition of other claims whether or not they arise out of the same transaction or occurrence. The court is not required to try unrelated claims together. It may, for example, order separate trials under Rule 42. But the claims are not misjoined.

Answer (A) is incorrect. Rule 20 would require the claims to arise out of the same transaction, occurrence, or series of transactions or occurrences and to share a common question of law or fact. It is unlikely that the breach of contract claim and negligence claims meet this test. They did occur close together in time, and anger regarding the negotiations may have contributed to some party's negligence, but that is not apt to be a close enough logical tie or a sufficient overlap of evidence to be considered part of the same transaction or occurrence.

Answer (C) is incorrect. As explained above, the defendant/third-party plaintiff is allowed to add non-derivative claims to the claim that supports impleader under Rule 14.

Answer (D) is incorrect. Because Donald has a proper claim against Mark already (the contribution and indemnity claim), Rule 18 permits the addition of other claims even if they do not arise out of the same transaction or occurrence as the others.

223.   **Answer (D) is correct.** Rule 14(a) allows third-party defendants such as Mark to bring claims against the original plaintiff (Charley), but only if those claims arise out of the same transaction or occurrence that is the subject matter of the plaintiff's claim against the defendant/third-party plaintiff. This would allow Mark to bring a negligence claim against Charley, but not a contract claim on its own. Once a proper negligence claim is filed, however, Rule 18 would allow Mark to add the contract claim against Charley.

Answer (A) is incorrect because Rule 18 does not help Mark until after he has filed a proper Rule 14 claim against Charley.

Answer (B) is incorrect. The answer correctly states the requirements for the claims that Rule 14 allows, but it ignores the additional claims that Rule 18 makes possible.

Answer (C) is incorrect. Rule 14 does allow some claims by the third-party defendant against the plaintiff, but they must arise out of the same transaction or occurrence as the plaintiff's claim against the original defendant.

224.   **Answer (A) is correct.** As explained above, Rule 13(h) permits the addition of parties to a counterclaim, but the requirements of Rule 20 must be met. This means that Donald's claim against Mark would have to arise out of the same transaction or occurrence as Donald's claim against Charley. A claim for negligence would meet this requirement. Once that negligence claim has been brought, Rule 18 allows the addition of the unrelated contract claim. The contract claim alone, however, would not be proper.

Answer (B) is incorrect. Rule 13(h) allows the addition of new parties to counterclaims, but only if additional requirements are met as explained above.

Answer (C) is incorrect. Impleader under Rule 14 is one method (probably the most common one) by which defendants can add parties to the lawsuit. But it is not the only method, as Rule 13(h) allows the addition of parties to a counterclaim or cross-claim.

Answer (D) is incorrect. As long as Donald brings a related claim against Mark (here, the negligence claim), he can also add an unrelated claim (the contract claim).

225. **Answer (D) is correct.** Charley's claim against Donald provides a basis for federal jurisdiction: the parties are of diverse citizenship and the amount in controversy exceeds $75,000. The counterclaim, however, does not meet these requirements because it is too small. Donald must look to supplemental jurisdiction to justify the presence of his counterclaim in federal court. Under 28 U.S.C. § 1367(a), district courts have supplemental jurisdiction over claims "that are so related to claims in the action within such original jurisdiction that they form part of the same case or controversy under Article III of the United States Constitution." Donald's counterclaim for negligence, involving claims about the same accident, will meet this requirement. In addition, jurisdiction must not be negated by § 1367(b). This would be true if the case were in federal court based solely on diversity jurisdiction, and the claim in question were a claim by a plaintiff against a person made a party under Rule 14, 19, 20, or 24, and when exercising supplemental jurisdiction would be inconsistent with the requirements of the diversity statute. Here, although Donald is asserting a claim for relief, he is not a "plaintiff" within the meaning of the statute. Donald's counterclaim will be eligible for supplemental jurisdiction.

Answer (A) is incorrect. Although the parties are from different states, this is not sufficient to provide diversity jurisdiction when the amount in controversy does not exceed $75,000.

Answer (B) is incorrect. The amount in controversy is too low to provide an independent basis for federal jurisdiction, but supplemental jurisdiction is available as explained above.

Answer (C) is incorrect. Allowing jurisdiction over the Donald v. Charley claim, if it stood alone, would be inconsistent with the requirements of § 1332. However, because it is a counterclaim, it can be supported by supplemental jurisdiction. Because it is not a claim by a plaintiff, it is not booted out by § 1367(b)'s requirement that exercising jurisdiction not be inconsistent with § 1332.

226. **Answer (B) is correct.** The contribution and indemnity claim, which would request that Mark pay any sums that Donald is ordered to pay Charley, is large enough to have an independent basis for federal jurisdiction. The negligence claim by Donald against Mark is part of the same constitutional case and is not a claim by a plaintiff under § 1367(b), so the court would have supplemental jurisdiction over the negligence claim. The contract claim, however, is only for $50,000, and so it does not have an independent basis for federal jurisdiction. Nor is it related to Charley's negligence claim against Donald or Donald's indemnity claim against Mark. The court may not exercise supplemental jurisdiction over the contract claim under § 1367(a).

Answers (A) and (C) are incorrect, because the court has jurisdiction over two of the three claims, as set forth above.

Answer (D) is incorrect. The supplemental jurisdiction statute may provide jurisdiction over claims that are too small. In addition, the amount in controversy requirement is computed according to the plaintiff's good faith claim for relief, and not by the amount the plaintiff eventually recovers.

227.   **Answer (A) is correct.** Mark and Charley are from different states, and the amount in controversy exceeds $75,000. There is, therefore, no need to rely on the supplemental jurisdiction statute to allow this claim. (The joinder rules probably make it improper, depending on all the various claims by the parties, but this question asked only about subject matter jurisdiction.)

Answer (B) is incorrect. Since Mark's claim has an independent basis for federal jurisdiction, it does not matter whether it shares a common nucleus of operative fact with Charley's claim against Donald. If Mark's claim did not exceed $75,000, supplemental jurisdiction would be necessary, and "common nucleus of operative fact" is the test for whether the claims are part of the same constitutional case.

Answer (C) is incorrect. It is a claim by a person made a party under Rule 14. But this is not relevant to the issue of subject matter jurisdiction here.

Answer (D) is incorrect. It is true that Mark is not a plaintiff under § 1367(b) — but as supplemental jurisdiction is not required here, that fact is irrelevant.

228.   **Answer (C) is correct.** This question is governed by the rules of *res judicata*, or claim preclusion. The judgment in the original case was a final decision, on the merits, between the same parties (here, Donald and Mark), on the same cause of action. Under modern rules of preclusion, a person's claim for personal injuries is part of the same cause of action as that person's claim for property damage arising out of the same occurrence. Since Donald got a judgment against Mark in the original case, his claim for personal injuries is said to be "merged" into the original judgment. Had Donald lost the first case, his claims would be said to be "barred."

Answer (A) is incorrect. The fact that the personal injury claim was not actually litigated prevents it from being subject to collateral estoppel, or issue preclusion. However, claims that are part of the same cause of action cannot be the subject of a later suit even if they were not actually litigated the first time around.

Answer (B) is incorrect. As noted above, when a party has won a claim, and then seeks to recover additional damages from the same cause of action, the omitted damage claims are properly referred to as having been "merged" into the judgment, not barred by it.

Answer (D) is incorrect. The Second Restatement of Judgments § 24 uses a "transaction" test and defines the claim precluded by the judgment to include "all rights of the plaintiff to remedies against the defendant with respect to all or any part of the transaction, or series of connected transactions, out of which the [original] action arose." The test for "transaction, or series of . . . transactions":

> "is to be determined pragmatically, giving weight to such considerations as whether the facts are related in time, space, origin, or motivation, whether they form a convenient trial unit, and whether their treatment as a unit conforms to the parties' expectations or business understanding or usage."

While each state determines its own preclusion rules, the Second Restatement approach is the most common test today.

229. **Answer (A) is correct.** Donald did not actually bring a contract claim against Charley in the original suit, so issue preclusion will not bar it. Claim preclusion does not bar it either. Donald did bring a negligence claim against Charley, but the breach of contract claim is not part of that "transaction" and so not part of the same cause of action. Charley did not bring a breach of contract claim against Donald, and so it was not a compulsory counterclaim. Donald was free to wait and bring that claim later, subject only to the statute of limitations.

Answer (B) is incorrect. Charley only sued Donald for negligence. Any counterclaim, including the contract claim, arose out of a different transaction or occurrence and was permissive rather than compulsory.

Answer (C) is incorrect. Donald's claim against Mark does not involve the same parties as Donald's claim against Charley, and this is a requirement for claim preclusion.

Answer (D) is incorrect. State law varies as to when a judgment is "final" for preclusion purposes. One of the most common differences has to do with whether a judgment that is on appeal is "final" while the appeal is still pending. A final trial court judgment that has not been appealed, however, will be final for purposes of preclusion.

230. **Answer (D) is correct.** The issue of Donald's negligence was actually litigated in the original suit. However, preclusion does not operate against a person who was not a party (or in privity with a party) to that original case. This rule grows out of considerations of fairness: Ed has not yet had a chance to litigate this issue, and he should not be bound by the results of a case in which he was not involved. He will therefore be allowed to bring his case and to attempt to prove Donald's negligence. (Whether he would be better advised to sue Mark is a separate issue.)

Answer (A) is incorrect. The finding of Donald's lack of negligence was necessary to the first case. Had he been negligent to some degree, he might have been ineligible to recover damages from Mark, or his recovery might have been decreased, and he might have been liable to Charley. Even had it not been necessary, however, Ed would not have been estopped by the finding because he was not a party to the original case, as explained above.

Answer (B) is incorrect because Ed was not a party to the original case.

Answer (C) is incorrect. Even jurisdictions that allow non-mutual collateral estoppel apply estoppel principles *only against* a person who *was* a party to the first suit. The element that varies is whether a stranger to the first action may estop someone who was a party or whether identity of all parties is required.

231. This pleading is probably insufficiently specific. Claims for fraud are governed by a more exacting standard of pleading than claims generally. Rule 9(b) requires that "[i]n all averments of fraud . . . the circumstances constituting fraud . . . shall be stated with particularity. Malice, intent, knowledge, and other condition of mind of a person may be averred generally." Here, Steven's complaint has referred to the allegedly fraudulent statements only generally — "guaranteed law review membership." Most courts would require Steven to plead more precisely the statements that constituted the fraud and the facts that make the statement false. Some would even require more detail in the pleading of DTPA Press' knowledge of the falsehood, although that is not as common outside the area of securities fraud.

232. **Answer (C) is correct.** Interrogatories may only be sent to parties under Rule 33.

Answer (A) is incorrect. The question may, in fact, be one in which the burden of answering exceeds the likely materiality of the answer, but even if that were not true the interrogatory need not be answered. Steven has used the wrong device to try to get this information.

Answer (B) is incorrect. It is a correct statement about discovery relevance, and the names of the book's purchasers might indeed lead to the discovery of admissible evidence — the fates of others who bought and relied on The Ultimate Study Guide. However, that does not overcome the impropriety of sending interrogatories to non-parties.

Answer (D) is incorrect. Had the bookstore been a party to the case, the burden imposed by the question might lead the court to refuse to compel an answer, as in answer (A), or to reduce the scope of the question, as in answer (D). Again, however, an interrogatory will not work here at all.

233. **Answer (B) is probably correct.** Trade secrets are sometimes hard to define. In discussing trade secrets, the Restatement of Torts describes it as:

> "any formula, pattern, device or compilation of information which is used in one's business, and which gives him an opportunity to obtain an advantage over competitors who do not know or use it. It may be a formula for a chemical compound, a process of manufacturing, treating or preserving materials, a pattern for a machine or other device, or a list of customers. A trade secret is a process or device for continuous use in the operation of the business. Generally it relates to the production of goods as, for example, a machine or formula for the production of an article."

Restatement of Torts, § 757, comment b. DTPA Press would have to show that its research meets these requirements and that it was kept confidential. It seems unlikely to be the kind of information that constitutes a trade secret. Even if it did, however, trade secrets are entitled to only a conditional privilege. When the information is extremely important to the lawsuit, the information may be ordered produced, although it may be accompanied by a protective order requiring the discovering party to use the information only in the suit and to keep it confidential. Here, Steven must prove that DTPA Press' claims were false, and that it knew they were false. The information on which DTPA relied in making these claims is central to this determination, and it is probable that a court would order the documents produced.

Answer (A) is incorrect. The factual basis, if any, for the statements that The Ultimate Study Guide would guarantee law review status is relevant both to Steven's claim that the statement was false and to his claim that DTPA Press knew it was false.

Answer (C) is incorrect. Although this may vary by jurisdiction, the trade secret privilege is generally a conditional one, meaning that it can be overcome under the right circumstances. (The protection for ordinary work product, for example, is also conditional in that it can be overridden with a showing of substantial need and undue hardship.)

Answer (D) is incorrect. Trade secrets are generally protected, and more than ordinary relevance is required to overcome that protection.

234. **Answer (C) is correct.** Consulting experts (experts retained for litigation who will not testify) are generally protected from discovery. There is an exception if the discovering party can show exceptional circumstances. This might be true if the consulting expert had done destructive testing on some object in issue in the suit, or if the number of experts in the field were very small and all had been hired by the other party. In this case, there are likely to be a number of educational experts who can provide information and expertise about the benefits of student study aides, so Blackstone will be protected from deposition.

Answer (A) is incorrect. Blackstone's information undoubtedly is relevant, but relevant information is not discoverable if protected by a privilege.

Answer (B) is incorrect. While consulting experts can rarely be deposed, it is not true that it can never be allowed.

Answer (D) is incorrect. As explained above, exceptional circumstances are such that the consulting expert has information otherwise unavailable, or that no other expert is available. Just because a party has hired the best known expert to consult does not satisfy the requirement of exceptional circumstances.

235. **Answer (B) is correct.** This question is controlled by Rule 26(a)(2)(B). In the absence of agreement or court order, parties must identify testifying expert witnesses and provide

a report prepared and signed by the witness. Among other things, this report must include "a listing of any other cases in which the witness has testified as an expert at trial or by deposition within the preceding four years."

Answer (A) is incorrect. The rule is limited as to time and does not include cases in which the expert did not testify.

Answer (C) is incorrect. The report also needs to disclose cases in which the expert's only testimony was by deposition.

Answer (D) is incorrect. Information about the expert's testimony in other cases may be relevant in discerning the basis for the expert's opinion, and it may also be relevant for purposes of impeachment. Imagine, for example, that the witness has testified in a prior case in a way that is inconsistent with her testimony in this case.

236. **Answer (A) is correct.** Steven needs to prove that his failure to make law review was caused by the flaws in The Ultimate Study Guide. Defendants will want to challenge that assertion, and one way to do that is to explore other possible causes of Steven's law school grades. The way he spent his time, and his mental and physical health, may be relevant to the issue of causation. Since Steven is claiming damages based on mental anguish, his mental state may also be relevant to the issue of damages. The identity of his friends and health care providers is not itself admissible, but those identities may lead to the discovery of admissible evidence when DTPA follows up by deposing or interviewing these people. This kind of information is generally considered private, and some of it may be privileged. Nevertheless, by bringing a lawsuit that makes this information relevant, Steven will be held to have waived his rights to keep this information secret.

Answer (B) is incorrect for the reasons explained above.

Answer (C) is incorrect. The privacy rights of parties and others are often protected in discovery. This privacy interest, however, can be waived as noted above.

Answer (D) is incorrect. Lawsuits may make information about non-parties relevant and therefore generally discoverable. Absent a statute or rule providing otherwise, these non-parties are not entitled to advance notification before they are named or discussed during the discovery process.

237. **Answer (C) is correct.** The work product doctrine protects communications made in anticipation of litigation or for trial. The question here is whether casual conversations with friends are "in anticipation of litigation" just because the friends are law students. The answer is 'no'. The protection from discovery is intended to protect trial preparation materials, and to allow parties a zone of privacy in which to prepare their cases. It is not intended to protect all conversations a party might have about his case.

Answer (A) is incorrect. Conversations do not become work product merely because their subject is litigation.

Answer (B) is incorrect. Steven cannot convert non-privileged communications into privileged ones by repeating them to his attorney. However, the defendant would not be able to ask "What did you tell your attorney about what you told your friends?" The communication between attorney and client *is* privileged. But it does not prevent a question like "What did you tell your friends about your lawsuit?"

Answer (D) is incorrect. DTPA Press will not need to show substantial need/undue hardship because the communications are not protected. If they did need to make such a showing, this would not be sufficient. Because DTPA Press can do its own interviews or depose Steven's friends, the likelihood that the friends will be less cooperative than they were for Steven does not constitute substantial need.

238. **Answer (D) is correct.** Conversations between attorney and client are only privileged if they were made for the purpose of obtaining legal advice. Here, it appears that the President was asking for business rather than legal advice, and so the communication is not privileged just because one of the parties to it was the company lawyer.

Answer (A) is incorrect. The President would be the "client" under either test, but this is the wrong kind of conversation.

Answer (B) is incorrect. The President was asking for advice, but it was not legal advice.

Answer (C) is incorrect. The attorney-client privilege does not require that the communication be made in anticipation of litigation.

239. **Answer (C) is correct.** The requirement that the party opposing the class has acted or refused to act on grounds generally applicable to the class applies only to class actions certified under Rule 23(b)(2), not to all class actions. Steven's class action is for damages for fraud and breach of warranty, and it would be certified, if at all, under Rule 23(b)(3). All class actions must show that the class is so numerous that joinder is impracticable and that the named plaintiff's claim is typical of the claims of class members [Rule 23(a)]. And damages class actions under Rule 23(b)(3) must also be superior to other methods of adjudicating the controversy.

Answers (A), (B), and (D) are incorrect (i.e., Steven *must* demonstrate them in order to secure class certification) for the reasons explained above.

240. The judge probably should not certify this class. The requirements of Rule 23(a) are probably met. This class seems large enough that joining all purchasers in a single suit would not be practicable. There are questions of law and fact common to the class — what representations did DTPA Press make, were they false, do they constitute a breach of warranty, etc. Steven's claims are typical of those of the class members, and it appears that he and his lawyers will adequately represent the class. The bigger obstacles are the additional requirements of Rule 23(b)(3). The court would have to find that the common questions predominate over questions affecting only individual members. The

differences in the substantive law applicable to class members in various states will tend to work against a finding that common questions predominate, as will the need of each class member to individually prove reliance, and to prove his or her own damages. On the other hand, the alleged fraud seems to have been made as identical printed representations to book purchasers, and it is possible that the kinds and degrees of reliance will be very similar. Also, Steven has alleged that each class member (all of whom are law students or lawyers) has at least $75,000 in damages, a stake which may give the class members an interest in individually controlling their claims. Some courts might certify this case as a class action, but nationwide damage classes based on varying state law are unusual.

241.   **Answer (A) is probably correct.** Since its decision in *Hanna v. Plumer*, 380 U.S. 460 (1965), the Supreme Court has used different kinds of analysis in considering whether the federal court must apply state law. One track is followed when the normal federal rule comes from a Federal Rule adopted pursuant to the Rules Enabling Act, or a federal statute regulating procedure. In such cases, the court is supposed to begin the analysis by asking whether the federal rule involved is broad enough to cover the issue raised by the state law. This test is sometimes phrased as asking whether the two rules collide, or whether they are inconsistent with each other. In this case, Rule 11(a) states, "[e]xcept when otherwise specifically provided by rule or statute, pleadings need not be verified or accompanied by affidavit." The court would begin by deciding whether Rule 11 covers the issue of whether a complaint seeking punitive damages must be made under oath.

Answers (B) and (D) are incorrect. Only if Rule 11 does not cover the issue should the court apply the "outcome determinative test," and that test turns on a comparison of the state and federal rules rather than one rule alone.

Answer (C) is incorrect. The source of the state rule is not relevant.

242.   **Answer (A) is correct.** If Rule 11 does cover the issue, the court must ascertain whether the rule really regulates procedure and does not modify or abridge any substantive right. These requirements come from the Rules Enabling Act. Assuming these tests are met, the federal court should apply the federal rule.

Answer (B) is incorrect. The outcome determinative test does not apply when the rule adopted under the Rules Enabling Act covers the issue.

Answer (C) is incorrect. This option restates the outcome determinative test.

Answer (D) is probably incorrect. When the court is using the Rules Enabling Act analysis, a state interest does not come into play unless the Federal Rule of Civil Procedure in question goes so far as to modify or abridge a substantive right (in which case the Rule is invalid). Note, though, that in *Gasperini v. Center for Humanities, Inc.*, 518 U.S. 415 (1996), the Court noted the importance of "accommodating" state interests.

243. **Answer (D) is probably correct.** Even under the more lenient *Celotex* standard, the summary judgment movant needs to point out to the court the parts of the record that demonstrate that the non-movant will have no evidence to prove some element of its claim or defense. *Celotex Corp. v. Catrett*, 477 U.S. 317 (1986). Justice White's opinion, needed for the fifth vote in *Celotex*, notes that a naked motion is insufficient. Here, Alpha Omega has done nothing more than file a motion. The suit has only been pending for a month, there has been no discovery, and so there is nothing in the record except Rodriguez's complaint (and possibly Alpha Omega's answer) on which to base the motion. Unless the movant needs to do nothing more than file the motion, this one is insufficient.

Answer (A) is probably incorrect. As noted above, the *Celotex* plurality plus Justice White require more than a conclusory motion, and Rule 56 refers to a motion for summary judgment being "made and supported." Identifying the issue in question, without more, is probably insufficient.

Answer (B) is incorrect. Alpha Omega does not have to disprove an element of Rodriguez's claim in order to be entitled to summary judgment.

Answer (C) is incorrect. Although waiting until the parties have had an opportunity for discovery is preferable, Rule 56 allows a defendant to move for summary judgment "at any time."

244. **Answer (C) is correct.** Parties who "admit away" their cases at deposition are not always allowed to create a fact issue by contradicting those admissions in an affidavit. However, when there is a reasonable explanation for the change, as when the admission was equivocal or the questions were unclear, a witness may be permitted to clarify that testimony through an affidavit. Here, the affidavit is not directly contrary to the deposition testimony in any case — the deposition questions concerned the particular carts that injured Rodriguez. Her affidavit concerns the condition of carts generally at the Alpha Omega store where she fell. The fact that the questions were couched in legal jargon and that English is Rodriguez's second language also make the need for clarification understandable. Looking at the affidavit, Rodriguez has provided circumstantial evidence that grocery carts at this store are often bent and in bad condition. She has also described her fall, including a claim that the carts stuck together and pushed her over. In ruling on Alpha Omega's motion for summary judgment, the court must give credence only to evidence in Rodriguez's favor and consider reasonable inferences in her favor. While her evidence is circumstantial rather than direct, it is still some evidence of dangerous baskets and of Alpha Omega's knowledge, so the court should deny the motion for summary judgment.

Answer (A) is incorrect. First, Rodriguez admitted only that she lacked direct knowledge that any employee knew about the particular baskets that caused her fall. This may not be necessary. Second, given the nature of the questions and Rodriguez's statement that she had a hard time understanding those questions, the court may consider her affidavit.

Answer (B) is incorrect. Parties do not need direct evidence in order to prevail at trial or to avoid summary judgment. They do need circumstantial evidence from which a reasonable inference can be drawn.

Answer (D) is incorrect. A "mere scintilla" of evidence is not enough to avoid summary judgment. The party with the burden of proof must produce at least enough evidence to support a reasonable inference in its favor.

245.   **Answer (C) is correct.** In ruling on a motion for judgment as a matter of law, the court will first review the whole record in order to identify the direct and circumstantial evidence favoring the non-movant (Rodriguez). Based on the evidence and reasonable inferences favorable to the non-movant, the court tests the sufficiency of the evidence by "giving credence" only to the evidence that supports a finding in the non-movant's favor. (The court may also consider uncontradicted, unimpeached evidence in favor of the movant, but there is no indication in this hypothetical that there is any such evidence in the record.)

Answer (A) is incorrect. In moving for judgment as a matter of law at this point, Alpha Omega is arguing that Rodriguez has produced legally insufficient evidence on a crucial element of her cause of action. It is Rodriguez's evidence that is in issue and Rodriguez's evidence that the court should examine. The court is not acting as a finder of fact here, and it is generally not allowed to consider evidence in favor of the party who moved for judgment as a matter of law.

Answer (B) is incorrect. The motion is not premature. Rodriguez has rested her case. Rule 50 allows the motion to be filed once "a party has been fully heard on an issue."

Answer (D) is incorrect. The judge is not supposed to weigh the evidence in ruling on a motion for judgment as a matter of law. The question is not which evidence the judge finds most convincing, but whether the party with the burden of proof has produced sufficient evidence that a reasonable jury could find in her favor.

246.   Alpha Omega has re-urged its motion for judgment as a matter of law at the close of all the evidence. The judge must consider the evidence in favor of Rodriguez and the reasonable inferences in favor of Rodriguez. The judge may also consider evidence for Alpha Omega *if* that evidence is uncontradicted and unimpeached. Under these principles, the court may consider the testimony of Rodriguez and the witnesses in her favor. This testimony supports at least an inference that baskets at this Alpha Omega store are often bent and stick together, and that Alpha Omega is aware of this problem. It supports an inference that the baskets that injured Rodriguez were defective in this way. The cross-examination of Kay Rett supports Rodriguez's claim and so it, too, may be considered. It provides more circumstantial evidence that the baskets at the Alpha Omega store in question were in poor condition and that the company knew about the condition of the carts. The court should not consider the testimony of Hugh Cumber. It does not favor the non-movant (Rodriguez), nor is it the type of evidence that the

jury would be required to believe, as his testimony has been impeached by evidence of his recent promotion. Unless the substantive law requires proof that the defendant knew about these particular carts on the day that Rodriguez fell, the court will likely deny the motion.

247. **Answer (D) is correct.** The right to jury trial is protected by the Constitution, and the jury's function is central to our court system. It is the jury, and not the judge, that holds the power to decide disputed fact issues. The jury's decision is, therefore, entitled to great deference. In order to protect the jury's role, the judge who is ruling on a motion for new trial does not sit as a "thirteenth juror." The question is not whether the judge would have ruled the same way had this been a bench trial. The question is whether the jury's verdict is so far out of line with the evidence that the trial should be done over. In federal court, this is often expressed as a question of whether the verdict was "clearly erroneous" or "against the clear weight of the evidence." In making this decision, the judge is allowed to consider all of the evidence.

Answer (A) is incorrect. See above.

Answer (B) is incorrect. The question of whether a reasonable jury could have found for Rodriguez is relevant to the motion for judgment as a matter of law. If a reasonable jury could have found for Rodriguez, it was correct to submit the case to the jury for decision. A party can avoid a judgment as a matter of law, but the state of the evidence can still be such that a grant of a new trial would be proper.

Answer (C) is incorrect. The judge is not permitted to quiz the jurors about their reasoning process in order to decide whether to grant a new trial. In fact, the rules of evidence prohibit most inquiry into the jury's deliberations.

248. **Answer (A) is correct.** The long-arm statute allows service here, since Pilchard entered into a contract with Builder, an Ohio resident. However, long-arm statutes must also be constitutional before personal jurisdiction is proper. Here, Builder solicited the contract, it was to be performed wholly outside of Ohio, and Pilchard's only "contacts" consisted of Pilchard in Pennsylvania talking on the phone to Builder while he was in Ohio. This is not a strong case for personal jurisdiction over Pilchard in Ohio. In addition, venue is probably also improper. This is a diversity case, and under 28 U.S.C. § 1391(a) venue would be proper either where Pilchard resides (and if there is no personal jurisdiction over Pilchard in the relevant judicial district in Ohio it does not "reside" there for venue purposes under § 1391(c)) or where a substantial part of the events or omissions giving rise to the claim occurred. It is unlikely that the phone calls to Ohio negotiating the deal or the fact that a resident of Ohio suffered financial losses would be sufficient to meet this test. Although more than one location may be proper under this test, in this case it is more likely that West Virginia (where the materials were to be delivered) or Pennsylvania (where the contract was made and where the defendant was going to perform the contract in part) would be the places where the events or omissions were "substantial."

Answers (B), (C), and (D) are incorrect. See above.

249.   **Answer (B) is correct.** The court, after deciding that personal jurisdiction and venue were both improper, could dismiss the case. But such a dismissal would at least allow Builder to refile in West Virginia, his second choice for a forum. The court can instead choose to transfer the case to another federal court in which venue would be proper and where there would be personal jurisdiction over the defendant. Pennsylvania meets these requirements. And this type of transfer would result in the new forum's applying its own choice of law rules. This would leave Builder in a jurisdiction in which he would be entitled only to recover about $100,000 even if he prevailed on the merits. Even if he could convince the E.D. Pa. to again transfer the case, this time from Pennsylvania to N.D. W.Va. under 28 U.S.C. § 1404, the transfer would not bring a choice of law change, and the court would still apply Pennsylvania law. This would leave Builder unhappy indeed.

   Answer (A) is less correct. Dismissing the case would not make Builder happy, but it would be less disastrous than the transfer to Pennsylvania.

   Answer (C) is incorrect. Lack of personal jurisdiction and incorrect federal venue are not a basis for sending a case to state court. And as this case was originally filed in federal court and not removed to there, "remand" is not an option.

   Answer (D) is incorrect. The court could choose to transfer the case to West Virginia. While Builder's first choice of forum is Ohio, if Ohio is improper, West Virginia is actually his next best option.

250.   Yes, a federal court in Pennsylvania would have jurisdiction over Pilchard and proper venue in Builder's case. Pennsylvania may easily have general jurisdiction over Pilchard Supplies, which is headquartered there. Even if it does not, in this case Pilchard negotiated the contract from Pennsylvania, entered into the contract there, and probably would have performed its obligations there, at least in part. This would be sufficient for personal jurisdiction. (Nor would Pilchard be likely to object to being sued at home where the law is favorable, and it could waive an objection to personal jurisdiction if it had one.) Venue is also proper in the district of Pennsylvania in which Pilchard has its headquarters, as it "resides" there, and it is also likely to be a district in which a substantial part of the acts or omissions giving rise to Builder's claim occurred.

251.   **Answer (D) is correct.** That means that **Answers (B) and (C) are both correct.** Answer (B) is correct because "residence" of a corporation for venue purposes is determined according to whether the corporation is subject to personal jurisdiction. It is likely that Pilchard would be subject to personal jurisdiction here in the district of West Virginia (N.D. W.Va.) in which it had contracted to deliver materials to Builder's job site. This would make venue proper under § 1391(a)(1). Answer (C) is correct because Pilchard "omitted" to deliver the building materials to N.D. W.Va. as promised.

Answer (A) is incorrect for the reasons stated above. "Residence" for venue purposes is a different issue from where a corporation "resides" for purposes of diversity of citizenship.

252. Pilchard could choose to file in Ohio, hope that it can convince the judge that Ohio has personal jurisdiction, and go for the best of the available laws. However, unless there are facts strengthening the argument that Pilchard is subject to personal jurisdiction in Ohio that the problem does not mention, I would recommend that Builder file his lawsuit in West Virginia. Going for the long-shot Ohio forum creates a substantial risk that the case will end up in Pennsylvania and be governed by Pennsylvania law, and this would cost Builder $900,000.

253. **Answer (A) is correct.** Ohio does not have personal jurisdiction over Pilchard here, so the court must dismiss the case. A state court does not have the option of transferring a case to a court in another state — this option only exists in the federal court system. The dismissal would be without prejudice, so Builder could refile the case.

   Answer (B) is incorrect. A dismissal for lack of personal jurisdiction is not a dismissal on the merits, and so Builder will be allowed to refile it.

   Answer (C) is incorrect. An Ohio court does not have the power or mechanism to transfer a case to a state court in Pennsylvania (or any other state).

   Answer (D) is incorrect. Because it is unlikely that Ohio has personal jurisdiction over this claim against Pilchard, it should dismiss the case.

254. Yes, if Builder filed the case in state court in Ohio, Pilchard could properly remove it. There is complete diversity of citizenship (Builder/Ohio vs. Pilchard/Pa.) and the amount in controversy exceeds $75,000. This is a diversity case, and Pilchard is not a resident of the forum state (Ohio). The time for removal has not run out.

255. **Answer (C) is correct.** As discussed above, the Ohio court lacks personal jurisdiction over Builder's claim against Pilchard. Venue is correct, however, because cases are removed to the district "embracing the place where such action [the state case] is pending." 28 U.S.C. § 1441(a). Normal venue analysis does not apply in removed cases. *See* 17 Moore's Federal Practice § 110.08 (3d ed. 2000). The case would therefore be removed to the district in Ohio in which the state court sits, and this would be correct venue. The motion to transfer for the convenience of parties and witnesses and in the interests of justice under § 1404, however, would likely succeed. Although the plaintiff's choice of forum is given great weight, it seems probable that in this case most of the witnesses and evidence except the plaintiff himself will be in Pennsylvania. There could be facts beyond those in the problem that change this result, but from what we know at this point transfer seems likely. Since the Ohio forum lacks personal jurisdiction over Pilchard, this time the transfer would achieve a change in choice of law rules, and Pilchard would have secured both a transfer and a change to more favorable substantive

law. (The court could also choose to dismiss the case, but this was not one of the multiple choice options.)

Answer (A) is incorrect. Filing a removal petition does not waive the right to complain about personal jurisdiction and venue if the defendant raises them properly as soon as the case lands in federal court.

Answer (B) is incorrect. Venue is proper in this removed case as explained above.

Answer (D) is incorrect. While venue is correct, personal jurisdiction is not and so the court may not keep the case.

256.   Pilchard could argue that the case should be dismissed under the doctrine of forum non conveniens. Its argument would be that the case has very little connection with Ohio, because the contract was made in Pennsylvania, and was to be performed in Pennsylvania and West Virginia. It would have to convince the court that the private and public factors outweigh Builder's choice of an Ohio forum. This would include pointing out that other than Builder himself, all witnesses are in other states, and they might not be subject to compulsory process in Ohio. Also, Pilchard should point out whatever he can about the comparative dockets of the courts and the burden on Ohio juries of hearing a case with little connection to Ohio. Pilchard's argument will be weakened by the fact that Builder is an Ohio resident and that Ohio law would be applied by the Ohio court. But if Pilchard's argument succeeds, the court would dismiss the case because there is no mechanism for one state court to transfer to another.

257.   Pilchard would like the case to end up in Pennsylvania and with Pennsylvania law applying. While not a guaranteed result, removing the case to federal court and moving to transfer to Pennsylvania provides Pilchard's best chance at achieving this goal. If the case stays in state court it would merely be dismissed, and we can imagine that Builder would refile in West Virginia, where Pilchard might still be liable for $1 million. The federal court, however, might choose to transfer to Pennsylvania rather than dismissing the case, and so the removal/motion to transfer option provides Pilchard with more control over the destination of the case than does the state court dismissal motion.

258.   **Answer (C) is correct.** A ruling on personal jurisdiction is not a final judgment and is not on the merits, so claim preclusion is not applicable here. However, a decision that Pilchard had sufficient contacts with Ohio might lead to issue preclusion under some facts. This is not true here, as it is not the same issue. The earlier case decided that the contacts arising out of that plaintiff's cause of action were sufficient to justify specific personal jurisdiction. That is not the same issue as whether Pilchard has sufficient contacts with Ohio out of which Builder's claim arises. Pilchard is, therefore, not estopped from challenging the sufficiency of its contacts in this case.

Answer (A) is incorrect. Offensive non-mutual collateral estoppel is not recognized in every jurisdiction, but it is not considered improper everywhere.

Answer (B) is incorrect. Pilchard did litigate a personal jurisdiction issue, but it was not the same issue and so issue preclusion does not apply here.

Answer (D) is incorrect. The first case's decision about personal jurisdiction was necessary to its decision — absent personal jurisdiction it would not have been justified in keeping the case. However, as before, the issue litigated there was a different one from the issue in Builder's case.

259. There are several limits on the plaintiff's choice of forum. First, the plaintiff can only choose a federal rather than state court if there is either a federal question or diversity of citizenship. Second, the plaintiff's choice of a state rather than federal forum is subject to the defendant's right to remove the case where allowed by statute. In terms of geography, the plaintiff must choose a state with which the defendant has sufficient contacts to justify personal jurisdiction. The plaintiff must also choose a location in which venue is correct. In federal court this will mean a state tied either to defendants' residence or to the events leading to the cause of action. State court systems will have their own venue rules that must be satisfied.

260. **Answer (C) is correct.** The Class Action Fairness Act would provide jurisdiction over this case because there is minimal diversity between a class member and the defendant (*see* 28 U.S.C. § 1332(d)(2)(A)); the class claims exceed $5 million (60,000 × $100) (*see* 28 U.S.C. § 1332(d)(2)); there are more than 100 class members (28 U.S.C. § 1332(d)(5)(B)); and less than one-third of the class members are from California, where the action was filed. (28 U.S.C. § 1332(d)(3),(4)).

Answer (A) is incorrect. Under CAFA, the minimal diversity can be between one class member and the defendant. Whether there is diversity of citizenship between the class representative and the defendant is not the only relevant question. Prior to CAFA, federal jurisdiction of class action lawsuits required complete diversity of citizenship between the class representative and the defendant without regard to the citizenship of the class members. *See, e.g., Supreme Tribe of Ben-Hur v. Cauble*, 255 U.S. 356, 365-366 (1921).

Answer (B) is incorrect. This class action would not be proper under supplemental jurisdiction because Amy is a citizen of California and her claim is too small. Thus, Amy has no independently adequate claim for the others to supplement. *See Exxon Mobil Corp. v. Allapattah Servcs. Inc.*, 545 U.S. 546 (2005).

Answer (D) is incorrect. Although answer (C) is correct, answer (B) is incorrect.

261. **Answer (D) is the best answer.** Although Rule 34 allows the requesting party to specify its preferred format, and the producing party to suggest a format, neither is absolute. Rule 34(b) explains that absent agreement between the parties or court order specifying a format for the production of electronically stored information ("ESI"), documents shall be produced "as they are kept in the usual course of business or shall [be organized and labeled] to correspond with the categories in the request." Fed. R. Civ. P. 34(b)(i). Rule 34 also states that the information must be produced "in a form or forms in which

it is ordinarily maintained or in a form or forms that are reasonably usable" if the requesting party did not specify a form for production. Fed. R. Civ. P. 34(b)(ii).

Answer (A) is incorrect. A responding party may indicate the format it intends to use for production if it objects to the format specified by the requesting party or if the requesting party did not specify a format. Fed. R. Civ. P. 34(b). But the responding party does not have the right to choose the format in which it will produce the ESI.

Answer (B) is incorrect. Although the requesting party can specify a format that it prefers, the producing party may object to the requested format. Fed. R. Civ. P. 34(b).

Answer (C) is incorrect. According to Rule 34, a party is not required to produce the same ESI in multiple forms, unless the parties so agree or the court orders production of the information "in more than one form." Fed. R. Civ. P. 34(b)(iii).

262. **Answer (C) is probably correct.** In *Zubulake*, the court explained that "it would be wholly inappropriate to even consider cost-shifting" when the producing party "maintains the data in an accessible and usable format, and can respond to [the] request cheaply and quickly." *Zubulake v. UBS Warburg LLC*, 217 F.R.D. 309, 320 (S.D.N.Y. 2003). The *Zubulake* court, however, differentiated between the information stored in an easily accessible format and information stored on backup tapes, because the information stored on backup tapes is not easily accessible. Under Rule 26, the court can order discovery of information that is not reasonably accessible for good cause and with conditions, including cost-shifting. *See* Fed. R. Civ. P. 26(b)(2)(B),(C).

Answer (A) is incorrect. According to the Advisory Committee Note to Rule 26(b)(2), the rule requires that "reasonably accessible" ESI must be produced. *See* Fed. R. Civ. P. 26. *Zubulake* explains that the producing party should bear the cost of production for reasonably accessible ESI. *Zubulake v. UBS Warburg LLC*, 217 F.R.D. 309, 320 (S.D.N.Y. 2003). The e-mails currently stored on the company's computers are reasonably accessible; therefore, Hayden Corp. will bear the cost of producing those documents.

Answer (B) is probably incorrect because depending on the circumstances, a trial court can limit discovery of the e-mails that are difficult to retrieve, shift the cost of some or all of the expense to the requesting party, or deny discovery of those e-mails altogether. *See* Fed. R. Civ. P. 26(b)(2)(B),(C).

Answer (D) is incorrect because the court will weigh several factors in order to decide whether to limit discovery. Even if Hayden Corp. demonstrates that the ESI is not reasonably accessible, the court will likely order discovery if Smith "shows good cause," but the court may also limit discovery to make it less burdensome on Hayden Corp. Under Rule 26(b)(2)(B), the scope of discovery of ESI that is not reasonably accessible is in the court's discretion.

263. **Answer (D) is correct. Answer (B) is correct** because the summary judgment obtained by Anderson did not dispose of the entire case. A final judgment "ends litigation on

the merits." *See Catlin v. United States*, 324 U.S. 229, 253 (1945). **Answer (C) is also correct.** Rule 54(b) allows a trial judge to finalize an order that "adjudicates fewer than all the claims or the rights and liabilities of fewer than all the parties" involved in the case by including in the order "an express determination that there is no just reason for delay" and "an express direction for the entry of judgment." Fed. R. Civ. P. 54(b). Although Rule 54(b) is applicable to the facts presented in the problem, which involve an order that adjudicates the rights and liabilities of fewer than all of the claims made against the parties, the dismissal order must be drafted in compliance with the requirements of Rule 54(b) to finalize the summary judgment in favor of Anderson.

Answer (A) is incorrect. To come within the small class of cases covered by the doctrine, the order must conclusively determine the disputed question, resolve an important issue completely separate from the merits, and be effectively unreviewable on appeal from a final judgment. *Cohen v. Beneficial Indus. Loan Corp.*, 337 U.S. 541, 546 (1949); *Coopers & Lybrand v. Livesay*, 437, U.S. 463, 468 (1979). The collateral order doctrine does not apply to the problem both because the summary judgment is not separate from the merits or unreviewable on appeal of the ultimate final judgment.

264.   **Answer (C) is correct.** Entry of the second dismissal order in the civil docket disposed of the remaining issues in the case. However, Rule 58 (or Appellate Rule 4) states that a "separate document" must be used for entry of a final judgment. *See* Fed. R. Civ. P. 58. Rule 58 requires a self-contained document distinct from any other orders in the case. *Bankers Trust Co. v. Mallis,* 435 U.S. 381, 385 (1978). Thus, neither dismissal order started the appellate clock, as neither meets the "separate document" requirement. Therefore, as provided in Rule 58 and Appellate Rule 4, the judgment was "entered" by law when 150 days ran from entry of the second dismissal order. The Advisory Committee Notes to Rule 58 indicate that the 150 day rule was only "intended to apply to cases in which the court intended its order to be final," but due to mere oversight, the court fails to enter a separate document. *See Utah v. Norton*, 396 F.3d 1281, 1287 (10th Cir. 2005).

Answers (A), (B), and (D) are incorrect because neither the July 24 summary judgment order nor the July 26 summary judgment order is considered a final judgment.

265.   **Answer (D) is correct.** Appellate Rule 4 allows for reopening the appeal for a period of 14 days after the date when the court's order to reopen is entered under the following conditions: (A) the moving party did not receive notice under Rule 77(d) of the entry of the order to be appealed within 21 days after entry; (B) the motion to reopen is filed within 180 days after the judgment or order is entered or within 7 days after the movant receives a Rule 77(d) notice, whichever is earlier; and (C) no party would be prejudiced. Fed. R. App. P. 4(a)(6).

Answer (A) is incorrect because Appellate Rule 4 does allow for reopening the appeal under the circumstances explained above. *See* Fed. R. App. P. 4(a).

Answer (B) is incorrect because a motion for extension must be filed within 30 days after entry of the order denying Kent a new trial.

Answer (C) is incorrect because Appellate Rule 4 probably precludes the use of Rule 60(b) to vacate and reenter the order denying a new trial in order to restart the appellate clock.

266. **Answer (D) is correct.** Based on the Supreme Court's analysis and application of Rule 19(b) in *Provident Tadesmens Bank & Trust Co. v. Patterson*, 390 U.S. 102 (1968), Pickles' attempt to obtain a windfall escape from his defeat at trial is foreclosed.

Answer (A) is incorrect because Travis Bank should not be "regarded as indispensable" because the trial court could grant relief to the plaintiffs that protects Travis Bank's lien interest without its joinder as a party to the case.

Answer (B) is incorrect. Under modern Rule 19, the issue is procedural, not jurisdictional.

Answer (C) is incorrect. Even if Pickles' lien is inferior, that is not an issue that the court of appeals would resolve in deciding joinder issues.

267. **Answer (C) is correct.** Hybrid Cars can file a cross-claim for contribution, as the contribution claim need not be mature when the cross-claim is filed. *See* Fed. R. Civ. P. 13(g). It should not matter that contribution counterclaims must be mature. Otherwise, ASAP could cross-claim against Hybrid Cars and not be subject to a responsive claim.

Answers (A), (B), and (D) are incorrect for the same reason answer (C) is correct.

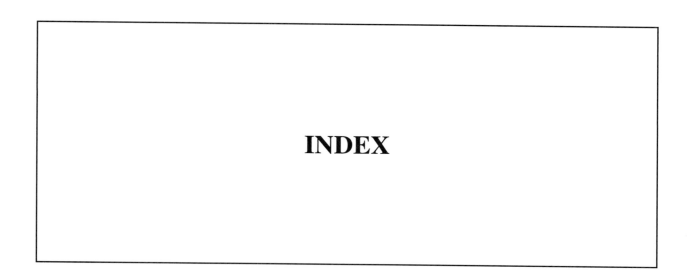

INDEX

INDEX